John L Ragle

DAY BEFORE
YESTERDAY

DAY BEFORE YESTERDAY

An Autobiography and History
of Michigan Schools

By
JOHN L. RIEGLE

Publishers
T. S. DENISON & COMPANY, INC.
Minneapolis

6484

T. S. DENISON & COMPANY, INC.

Copyright © 1971 by John L. Riegle

Library of Congress Card Number: 70-183714
Printed in the United States of America
by The Brings Press
Copyright © by John L. Riegle
Minneapolis, Minn. 55437

TO ELEANOR,
    my collaborator
    my critic
    my tranquilizer
    my joy
    my wife

Acknowledgments

I wish to express my appreciation to the many friends and relatives who by their help and encouragement have helped me to write this book. Several of them have been mentioned in the book. Others were Mr. Clarence Young of Flint, who loaned me the Report of the Superintendent of Public Instruction for 1853, and my old friend, Mr. John Dennis of Flint, who loaned me a similar Report for the year 1867. Mr. Young also loaned me a book about John D. Pierce, written by Professors Hoyt and Ford of Ypsilanti Normal School in 1905.

My nephew Clinton Riegle, his wife Erma, and daughter Ina Jean furnished the photographs of the Dodge School and the Riegle farmhouse.

I am indebted to Mr. Ezra Perry of Grand Blanc, Michigan, who was a member of the first Genesee County board of education, for the minutes of the initial meeting of the board.

Mrs. James Schweikert, M.A., of Hollywood, Florida, the wife of a cousin of mine, made helpful suggestions on the manuscript, and Mr. Christian Roosenraad of Lansing, Michigan, gave me information on the Lansing vocational educational program.

I also wish to thank publicly Mrs. Mary Ann Homer and Mrs. Jean Barons of the Flint Public Library, whose friendly assistance was a great help.

Mr. L. B. Avison, Jr., executive director of The Michigan Colleges Foundation, Inc., also helped me to obtain pertinent information on the private and denominational colleges of Michigan.

Most important of all, I am indebted to my amanuensis—my wife Eleanor—whose patience and skill in deciphering my handwriting and in typing the manuscipt have been of inestimable value to me.

JOHN L. RIEGLE

October 1, 1971

Contents

BOOK I

Foreword to Book I

For many years I have hoped that someday I would have the time to write an account of my life and times. Because the endeavors of my adult life that I have enjoyed the most have been closely connected with our Michigan schools, I have gone into some detail about my experiences in this field. Because our early schools were tied so intimately to pioneer life and developed as pioneer life changed, I thought it might be interesting to give a picture of this early life and its changes. Also, it might benefit those of the present generation to be made to realize the back-breaking labors of their grandfathers and great-grandfathers which have made it possible for them to live in our affluent society. In Plymouth, Massachusetts, on the monument to Governor Bradford, are carved these words, "What your fathers with so much difficulty secured, do not basely relinquish."

—JOHN L. RIEGLE

CHAPTER I

My Family History

The eighty-four years since I was born on June 8, 1887, have been the most eventful years since the dawn of civilization. When I was a child, Mr. Allen, who lived three miles north of us, drove a span of oxen, hitched to a wagon, past our house to Davison, a small village six miles southwest of our farm, to do his trading. Mrs. Allen rode in the wagon and Mr. Allen walked beside the oxen, guiding them and urging them on with commands of "Gee" and "Haw" if he wanted them to turn. In 1965, my wife, Eleanor, and I boarded a plane in Flint at 10:30 a.m., changed planes in Chicago and again in San Francisco and slept that night in Honolulu!

My father was John Riegle, born in 1840 on a farm near Clarence Center, Erie County, New York. His father, also named John, was born in Pennsylvania in 1808, the son of Jacob Riegle, born June 1, 1777, and Elizabeth Bacher. My father's mother was Nancy Blocher, the daughter of John Blocher (1774-1856) and Martha Frick Blocher (1776-1859). These families, of German descent, settled in Lancaster County, Pennsylvania, before the American Revolution. They emigrated from that state to western New York about 1820. My grandmother, Nancy Blocher Riegle, died about 1845 or 1846 of childbirth fever.

My mother's maiden name was Mary Bahnmiller. She was born in Germany in 1849, the daughter of Jacob and Mary Lutz Bahnmiller, who emigrated from Kirchentellensfurt Württemberg, Germany, about 1854, to a settlement near Ann Arbor, Michigan. Shortly afterwards, they settled on a farm in Argentine Township, Genesee County, Michigan.

Father's education was limited to that which he could get in a one-room school—the three R's, "reading, 'riting, and 'rithmatic," but he evidently had good training in these subjects. He was an avid reader of his newspaper and farm magazines. Mother could read newspapers and the Bible in both English and German and she wrote letters in both languages. Father could speak and understand German, but the only time they spoke it in our home was when they wanted to say something not intended for small ears.

In 1861, when Abraham Lincoln called for seventy-five thousand volunteers to enlist for three months to preserve the Union, Father was one of the first to enlist in the 21st New York Regiment. He went in as a fifer in the drum corps and served for two years. At the end of the two years, he came to Michigan to visit his older sister, Maria, who had married a man named Schweitzer, and who lived in Atlas Township. During the summer of 1863 Father worked at the Zimmerman brickyard in Flint, located near Asylum Street in the old Fourth Ward. Later, when we lived in Flint, he pointed out a brick building on Saginaw Street for which he had helped to make the bricks.

In the fall of 1863, he re-enlisted in the army, was made a corporal, and served until the end of the war. As corporal, he was drill master of the company. During his second enlistment, he contracted typhoid fever, an illness which nearly took his life. He was taken to the "dead house," a place for the sick and wounded thought to be too ill to recover. His younger brother, David, who was also in the army, got a furlough, took him out of the "dead house" and nursed him back to health. Uncle David then came down with typhoid himself and Father acted as his nurse. Because Father, after typhoid, was never strong enough for the battlefield, he served as a nurse until the end of the war.

When the war ended in April 1865, Father returned to Flint. In the meantime, his father and stepmother, Anna Catherine, had moved from Clarence Center, New York, to Michigan, settling on a farm on State Road (now M-15) about two miles south of Davison.

On February 27, 1869, Father married Mary Bahnmiller. Their union lasted fifty-nine years and produced seven children: William, born April 27, 1871; Sarah, born August 5, 1873; Andrew, born September

25, 1875; Frederick, born January 8, 1878; Addie May, born September 9, 1882; and John Louis, born June 8, 1887. In 1889, an infant son was born. This baby lived only six weeks before he died, unnamed, of cholera infantum.

In 1868, Father bought a farm, the SE ¼ of the SE ¼ of Section 14 of Richfield Township with the money saved from his army pay, which included a $500 bonus for re-enlistment. This farm, on the corner of the present Henderson and Coldwater roads, had ten acres that had been "chopped"; that is, the big trees covering the land had been chopped down but still lay on the ground. To earn money to buy lumber to build a house, Father worked in a sawmill in Otisville, owned by David Crawford, founder of a prominent Flint family.

THE PARENTAL HOME

My parents first lived in a small log cabin that had been built by the man from whom Father bought the farm. One of the first tasks was to clear enough of the ten "chopped" acres to plant a garden. The next step was the building of a new house.

First the cellar had to be dug. This digging had to be done by hand, after the size and shape of the cellar (the same size as the proposed building) had been marked out by driving stakes at the four corners and encircling the area to be dug by a string tied to each stake. The dirt to be removed was shoveled into a wheelbarrow, then wheeled a short distance and dumped where it would not be in the way. When the excavation was so deep that the dirt could not be shoveled into the wheelbarrow, an alleyway about four feet wide was dug on the north side with the ground slanted so the barrow could be wheeled out. Field stones were used to build the walls of the cellar and the alleyway, which then became the outside entrance to the cellar when provided with swinging hinged doors. There used to be an old song with the phrase, "Sliding down our cellar doors," inspired by a favorite pastime of farm children. All rural homes had to be equipped with such entrances because much of the food for winter was stored in barrels and bins kept in the cool cellar. The walls had to be laid by an experienced stonemason. Quicklime and sand were mixed to make the mortar that held the stones in place. The finished walls extended about eighteen inches above the ground.

The original house had a combination living room and kitchen, a parlor, one bedroom on the first floor and two bedrooms on the second. When the increase in the family made more room necessary, Father built an addition on the north side of the house. The new part was divided into three rooms: a combination kitchen-and-dining room, a bedroom, and a buttery or pantry. The old kitchen then became the "sitting room." Father said he patterned our house after the one in which he was born. The farm-house that Father built is now owned by his grandson, Clinton Riegle, where he and his family still live.

FIELD STONES

In those early days there were no such things as cement blocks. The walls under all houses and barns were made of the stones which could be found scattered over the ground in nearly every field in southern Michigan. When the country was new there were so many stones in the fields that they were a nuisance. They were of all shapes and sizes. Brought down from the north by glaciers during the ice ages, some lay on top of the ground; some were half or fully buried. The largest were several feet in circumference. When Father found stones too large to lift, he used a stone boat. He made this tool by cutting two pieces of a small tree trunk six or seven inches in diameter into pieces eight feet long. One end of each piece was fashioned into the shape of sled runners. These were then placed about four feet apart. Two-inch-thick planks cut to the right length were then nailed with long spikes to the runners to make a top for the boat. A hitch was fastened to the front end of the boat so that a whiffletree or whippletree could be attached. This was a swinging bar to which the tugs of the harness could be fastened. (Every horse-drawn vehicle had to have a whippletree.) Heavy stones could be rolled onto this stone boat, then drawn by horses to a corner of the field or to a woodlot where they would be out of the way. Every farm usually had several piles of these large stones.

There was an old saying that stones "grew." Sometimes a plow would hit one in a place where there had been none a year or two before. This happened because there had been heavy rains just before the ground froze in the autumn; water from the rains had settled under the stones. When

The author in the 1920s as county school commissioner

The Author's High School Graduation Picture
"With grim determination carving a pathway to success."

The Dodge School

The Riegle Farmhouse — 1868-1971

Pioneer Schools

the frosts came, the wet ground under the stones expanded and pushed the stones a little higher. Thus the stones would be pushed a little closer to the surface each year. I remember that several times during the summers I worked for my brother Andrew, the plow was thrown out of the ground when it hit one of these submerged stones. When this happened, I had to back the horses to pull the plow back, or turn them around and have them drag the plow to the place where it had been thrown out.

Sometimes the stones were too large to haul away on the stone boat. When Father encountered one of these huge stones he would dig a deep hole next to it and push the stone into the hole with pries. The bottom of this hole would be below the frost line so it would never be in the way of a plow again. Once when Father was digging a hole in which to bury a stone, I found, to my delight, an Indian arrowhead he had uncovered.

Before any crops could be planted, the land had to be cleared of the big trees that had been "chopped" or were still standing. There was no market for the hardwood trees: maple, oak, beech, elm, and ash. The limbs were first cut off, the trees cut in lengths short enough to be rolled into piles and burned. Clearing the land was hard, backbreaking work. In order to make fences to divide the farm into fields, rails were split out of the best ash and oak trees. These rail fences lasted about thirty years but were gradually replaced by woven wire fences.

Digging a Well

After Father bought his farm, one of his first tasks was to dig a well. The first settlers had built their homes near a flowing stream or a spring. Our farm was a mile from the nearest creek. The spot chosen for the well was close enough to the barnyard that a long trough could carry water from the well to a tub or wooden tank in the barnyard.

To start the work, a circle would be drawn six or seven feet in diameter. A hole the size of the circle was then dug until the digger struck a water vein, which is a layer of gravel through which water seeps. This hole might have to be dug twenty, thirty, or even forty feet deep before the water vein would be found. Until the hole was seven or eight feet deep, the digger could shovel out the dirt. After that, the dirt was put into a pail or large bucket and pulled up by a helper with a rope. A horse could be used to pull the bucket of dirt to the top if the rope was run through a pulley fastened to a tripod erected over the hole. The helper scattered the dirt to make a mound a foot high around the well so the surface water would not run into the well.

After the water was found, the hole was lined with stone. This job was a painstaking one which had to be done by an experienced stonemason. Pumps made of wood and worked by hand were made in a Flint factory. A cover made of two-inch planks close together formed a top for the well.

Pumping enough water for all our farm animals was *not* one of my favorite jobs. To supply the farmhouse with water, someone had to carry it to the house in pails. This was another of my daily chores.

Two or three years before we moved from the farm, Father had a so-called "drive" well made, which he put only forty feet from the house. This type of well was made by driving a steel-pointed metal pipe, about two and a half inches in diameter, into the ground until water was found. Our well was nearly seventy feet deep. The name of the man who drove this well was George Nash, the brother of Charles Nash who became president of Buick Motor Company and later the founder of Nash Motor Company.

The first few years after the "drive" well was made, it was used for household needs only. Later my brother Fred had pipes laid underground to connect it with a water tank in the house and another in the barn. He then bought a gasoline motor to operate the pump, truly a labor-saving device.

By the time I was born, the farmland had been cleared of trees and stumps, the fences had been built, and the usual farm buildings had been erected.

CHAPTER II

Days of My Childhood

My earliest recollection is of a day when I was about four years old, the day Sister Addie took me to visit school. What makes me remember this event was something I did that caused my sister and me some embarrassment. It was a rainy day, and not knowing that a rule of all schools was not to talk unless asked a question, I piped up, "I wonder if it is raining down at the creek today?"

The schoolhouse still stands a mile north of our old homestead, on the corner of Henderson and Stanley roads, but it has been converted into a one-story dwelling. The creek is a mile east of our old home. It flows north to the Flint River and is the outlet of Harseler Lake, a lake four or five miles southeast of Davison. This little creek was just the right size for a small boy to use for wading and fishing.

We lived in a pioneer community, only thirty or forty years from a wilderness. The years of my boyhood were really the transition years between the pioneer and the modern age. Before 1825 the migration to Michigan from the East was but a trickle. The opening of the Erie Canal in 1825 started the great migration to the West. Before that time there were very few white settlers in Michigan. The first house in Flint was built in 1829. During the next thirty years most of southern Michigan was settled.

The first houses were usually made of logs. Once in a while an enterprising citizen would bring with him the metal machinery for a sawmill, find a suitable place on a river or creek, build a dam with a sluice for power, set up his machinery, and then be in business.

Because many people lived several miles from the nearest trading center or a store where the farmer's wife traded butter and eggs or apples for groceries and drygoods, some farmers dug wells beside the road and kept a trough full of water so that travelers could give their horses a drink. In payment for this service the farmer was exempt from "working out" on the roads or paying a road tax. One such tank was kept by Honey Bee Austin, who lived a mile north of Davison on the road now M-15. (He was nicknamed "Honey Bee" because he kept several hives of honeybees.) These water troughs in pioneer days were hollowed out of large logs, cut to about eight feet in length. As they became old, they became covered with moss like "the old oaken bucket, the moss-covered bucket that hung in the well." When our horses approached this water trough, they hastened their pace, especially if it happened to be a hot day.

The school day ended at four o'clock sun time, which was half an hour faster than standard time, or half an hour slower than the present daylight saving time. It was usually half past four before I arrived home from school, especially if the ground were covered with snow, and that was the time for evening chores.

My jobs were to keep the woodbox full and to gather the eggs. By six o'clock the cows had been fed, milked and bedded down, the horses had been fed and bedded down, and the pigs had been fed. By the time these chores were done, Mother would have supper ready. Supper was the big meal of the day. It usually consisted of fried smoked ham or shoulder, mashed potatoes, perhaps cooked cabbage or cole slaw, or cooked carrots or turnips. These four vegetables were the only ones that could be kept in a cool cellar. Because a cellar had to be warm enough to prevent the freezing of vegetables during the coldest weather, the vegetables often began to sprout new leaf growth, which meant they could not be kept more than a month or two. As spring grew near, the only garden foods in our diet were sauerkraut and home-canned tomatoes. For the mashed potatoes, Mother made milk gravy. Sometimes we had johnnycake (cornbread) or cornmeal mush with milk. Supper was topped off with pie or cake. The pies were apple, cherry, custard, pumpkin, or mince. Our mincemeat was made when we butchered hogs for our own use.

Winter Evenings

When the supper dishes were washed, the long winter evenings began. Father would read his newspaper, which may have been a week old, for it had to be brought from the post office. (No rural free delivery in those days!) To get our mail, someone walked the two miles to Richfield Center, a small village of a dozen houses, where the post office was kept in the general store.

My readers may wonder what we did for amusement or entertainment during those long winter evenings. Such modern conveniences as radio and television, or even telephones and electric lights, had not been dreamed of before 1900 in a farm home. The work in the barn had to be completed before dark because the only light available then was a lantern.

After supper and dishwashing, Mother would sit by the kitchen stove and knit socks or mittens or mend our clothes while Father read his biweekly paper. Before going to bed, Mother always read a chapter from the Bible.

For the children on the farm there was nothing much to do for recreation but read. By the time I was twelve, I had read and reread all our books many times. Our school had no library, so I could do no supplementary reading. There was a township library, located in the home of the township clerk who lived two miles from our farm. I remember visiting this library only twice, borrowing one book each time. We had in our home the sum total of three books: the Bible, *Pilgrim's Progress,* and a book of Bible stories. I read these books over and over, for I loved to read. Few homes of this period had more books than we.

Quilting Bees

The quilting bee was an integral part of the rural life of those days. Quiltmaking in pioneer days was a matter of necessity and economy. The cold Michigan climate demanded a lot of bed covering, and frugal housewives made use of every scrap of leftover fabric in quilts. At first, and for many years, the pieces were put together hit or miss in "crazy quilts"; but soon women began competing with more and more intricate designs, and a spirited rivalry developed among the homemakers of the day to produce beautiful and imaginative patterns.

Quilting bees were usually held in the afternoon of a winter day, when five or six women of the neighborhood were invited in to quilt. A quilting frame was set up in the "front room." These frames were made of four pieces of board one inch thick and two inches wide, made into an eight or nine-foot square with holes about three inches apart bored in the frame. The sides were held in place by pegs through the holes in the side pieces. The lining of the quilt was then stretched and sewed to the frame and cotton batting was then spread over this lining. In the making of a comforter, two or more layers of batting were used. The top of the quilt was then fastened to the frame. Comforters were tied with wool yarn; quilts were quilted, that is, stitched in an ornate pattern.

When I was twelve years old, I pieced a "necktie" quilt, so named because the various blocks were arranged in a way that made them look like bow ties. When my quilt was ready for quilting, Mother had it quilted by her friends at our house. These gatherings served as social events where neighbors could exchange the latest gossip, thus relieving the boredom so common in a lonely farm home. However, it was not unusual for a housewife to walk to a neighbor's farmhouse to spend the afternoon visiting.

Once in awhile we would walk or drive to the home of a neighbor, or a neighbor would drop in to spend the evening.

It was during the long winter evenings that I did my reading, and I craved more reading material. When I was ten years old I saw an advertisement in *Farm and Fireside* that offered one book by G. A. Henty for every two or three new subscribers to the magazine. One Saturday I rode old Barney, one of our farm horses, around the area and got enough subscriptions to earn four or five Henty books. These books were the beginning of my own library.

We usually went to bed rather early because even in the winter work on a farm was strenuous. When the nights were severely cold, Mother would heat a soapstone or some bricks on the kitchen stove, then wrap them in newspapers and a flannel cloth, and put them between the sheets about thirty minutes before bedtime. The bedrooms were cold, but each bed had a feather bed over the mattress, flannel sheets, and plenty of quilts and comforters for covering. Some families also slept under feather beds, but we didn't.

On cold winter mornings we usually dressed huddled near the kitchen stove. Father was the one who had to get up and dress in the cold and then make the fire. Every evening he would cut shavings from pine stumps because these shavings made a quick fire.

When I was growing up, my mother made nearly all of my clothes. In those days a small boy was dressed just like a girl, with short dresses and homemade panties. When he was about three years old, he was given his first pair of knee pants, usually made of denim or salvaged material from wornout- pants of an older brother. Shoes and rubbers for winter wear were about the only wearables purchased at a store. Once in a while for "Sunday best" I had a suit, consisting of coat and trousers, bought at a store. One of my Christmas gifts was invariably a pair of stockings or mittens knit by my mother. A straw hat for summer and a cap with ear flaps for winter were also "store bought," as well as ankle-length, fleece-lined cotton drawers and undershirts. Mother sewed a band of cloth on the bottom of each leg of the drawers to slip under my feet to keep the drawers from creeping up my leg. In some families, though probably not many, such underwear was sewed on the children in the fall and not removed until spring. However, Mother always kept an extra pair for a change when she washed my underwear.

Children of today would smile if they saw a picture of me ready to start to school on a winter day. My cap would be pulled down over my ears, the collar of my jacket turned up and held in place by a woolen scarf. My legs would be encased in gray knit stockings covering my knees and held in place by round garters; and my hands would be clad in hand-knit mittens. I would have a tin dinner pail in one hand and sometimes, but not often, a book in the other.

My dinner pail usually held a sandwich made of either fried ham or roast beef, or apple butter, between slices of Mother's homemade bread. There would also be a fresh apple and a cooky or a piece of pie or cake. Perhaps there was a lack of variety in the lunches, but Mother's delicious homemade bread made up for any deficiency.

Whittier's poem, "The Barefoot Boy," gives a good description of a country boy in the summers before 1900:

> Blessings on thee, little man,
> Barefoot boy with cheek of tan,
> With thy turned up pantaloons
> And thy merry whistled tunes.

We took off our shoes in May or early June and did not put them on again until late September or early October, except on Sunday or some special occasion such as a visit to relatives which entailed a ride on a train.

THE BLACKSMITH

Sometime during my early years, either when I went to a country school or later when I taught in one, I learned Whittier's poem, "The Village Blacksmith." A mile south of our house there was a village "smithy." The place was not really a village, just four corners with a blacksmith shop, an empty store, and two or three houses. The store had been kept by "Uncle Mathias" Schweitzer, called "Uncle" by us because his brother had married my father's oldest sister, Maria. The blacksmith shop was run by John Memroe. The physical description of Whittier's smithy fit our Mr. Memroe:

> The smith a mighty man was he
> With large and sinewy hands,
> And the muscles on his brawny arms
> Were strong as iron bands.

In those days a blacksmith shop was a necessary and important adjunct to a farming community. The smith was a busy man shoeing horses, welding broken parts of machinery, setting tires on buggies and wagons, and doing many kinds of repair jobs. Now, if a farmer breaks a part in a machine, he can buy a new part in an hour or two. Then it might take weeks to get a new part, so the blacksmith was called upon to repair many broken parts. Many were the times I stood beside him, watching "the sparks that fly like chaff from the threshing floor," as the poet put it, or listened to the hissing of the red-hot iron as it was thrust into a tub of water to temper and cool. Today the activity that was once Schweitzer's Corners is but a memory; only one house remains.

CHAPTER III

Schoolday Experiences

THE DODGE SCHOOL

I started to school in September of 1892 in a one-room school situated one mile north of our farm. Teachers were hired to teach a term, not a year. My first teacher was Marcena Knapp of Davison, a good teacher, well liked by her pupils.

There were two or three other beginners. When it was time for our reading class the teacher would announce, "First reader, one." At her signal of "one," we would turn in our seats, at "two" we would stand, and at "three" we would march to the front of the room and form a half circle around the armchair in which she sat. One of our first tasks was to learn the alphabet. The readers we used were published by Ginn and Company. *McGuffey's Reader* was still used in some schools, but our reader was supposed to be more modern. It began with short sentences such as "I see a cat," and "I see a dog," with pictures of a cat and a dog.

The second year we had a second reader, the third year a third reader, and so on, with the readers progressively more difficult each year. Many of the lessons were poems and excerpts from the classics. In this small way we were introduced to good literature, but that was as far as our acquaintance went, for there was no school library.

Our schoolhouse, being comparatively new, was larger than the average rural school building. Ten years before I started to school the old log schoolhouse, with its homemade desks and seats, had been torn down and replaced. The new building had two entries, with swinging doors opening into the schoolroom. The teacher's desk sat in an alcove on a raised platform between the entries. The stove was in the center of the room. The building faced the west on the south side of the schoolyard, which comprised one acre.

The space between the schoolhouse and the south fence, about twenty feet, was supposed to be the girls' private playground. There was a high, board fence extending from the schoolhouse to the east boundary, which gave the girls more privacy. Their toilet was a small building on their side of the high fence. The boys' accommodations were on the other side of the fence.

To the left of the schoolhouse was a large woodshed, and along the east fence in the boys' yard were the usual hitching posts for visitors' horses. In the front yard there stood a small, lonely maple tree which had been left when the schoolgrounds were cleared. To a pioneer, trees were enemies to be destroyed rather than things of beauty to be preserved.

The classroom was equipped with four rows of double seats, with desks attached, which were progressively larger from the front to the back, to fit the different sizes of children. The girls were seated on the south side and the boys on the north.

There were windows on all four walls, with only one in front. There were blackboards on both sides of the teacher's alcove. I cannot remember any pictures on the walls. If there were, they made no impression on me. There was, however, a set of colored maps; one of the Eastern Hemisphere, one of the Western, one of the United States, and one of Michigan.

Going to school was a routine affair. The school term began about the second Monday in September, with vacations at Christmas and Easter, and the last day coming after the first of June. Thanksgiving, Christmas, New Year's Day, Washington's Birthday, and Decoration Day were the holidays, always welcomed by the children.

We were lucky at our school because we had a bell in a belfry. This bell was rung at eight-thirty in the morning and again at nine to call us into the schoolroom. The first recess was from half-past ten to a quarter of eleven (no one spoke of ten-thirty or two-forty-five in those days). The lunch period was from twelve noon to one o'clock, and the last recess was from half-past two to a quarter to three.

School was opened at times by saying the Lord's Prayer or by singing from the *Knapsack*. The *Knapsack* was a compilation of the words of patriotic, religious and folk songs, compiled and printed by H. R. Patten-gill, an early superintendent of public instruction in Michigan. (A copy of the *Knapsick,* given by a friend, Ed Bremer, is a treasured keepsake.) Of course, we had no musical instruments. The teacher led the singing, and the children joined in as best they could, with results perhaps more noise than music.

Reading class came first, beginning with the first grade or reader, then the second, and so on. After the reading classes came the physiology or history classes. There were usually children of ages ranging from five to fourteen or fifteen. All eight grades had to be taught by the one teacher, which meant that there were only five, or perhaps ten, minutes for each class. After the first recess came the arithmetic classes. Following the lunch period, there were more reading classes for the younger children and language or grammar class for the older ones. After the last recess came geography and spelling. If there were an eighth grade class studying to pass the eighth grade examination, there would be a class in orthography tucked in, if time permitted.

Sometime during the day copybooks were brought out and everyone practiced penmanship. Sometimes this subject was neglected, or at least my father thought so. He was of the old school where "readin', 'ritin', and 'rithmetic" were the important subjects. He decided I wasn't learning to write properly; so when I was in the fourth grade, he bought me a copy-book to be used at home and saw to it that I practiced penmanship every evening until I became a fair penman.

The first year in school a child had only one textbook, the *First Reader.* In his reading class, he learned to read and to spell. In teaching writing, the teacher wrote a word or sentence on the blackboard or on his slate and the pupil would copy it with chalk or a slate pencil. In numbers, he first learned to count or add a little.

The second year, he came to school with a *Second Reader.* (In those days the parents furnished the textbooks.) He continued with spelling and writing. In numbers, he began to learn simple combinations, such as 2 plus 3, 3 plus 3, et cetera.

In the third year, he brought the *Third Reader* or perhaps the first book in arithmetic. During this third year, he was supposed to learn his combinations, addition, subtraction and short division.

The fourth year brought big changes. We had the *Little Geography,* a physiology book called *How to Keep Well* and a language book. In arithmetic, we learned long division.

The fifth grade was a continuation of the fourth, with perhaps not so much attention to reading but with the addition of a class in United States history, in story form. In arithmetic, we studied fractions.

The sixth grade brought us the big geography, as well as physiology and hygiene, and some grammar. Arithmetic was the continuation of fractions and the beginning of decimals.

In the seventh grade, we were supposed to complete geography and physiology and begin the actual study of U. S. history and grammar. Of course, we continued arithmetic and spelling. A few years later a seventh grader could take a county examination in geography and in physiology. If he passed with a mark of 75% or better, he was finished with these subjects.

The eighth grade was the big year for me, for this was the year to prepare to pass the eighth grade examination, if one planned on going to high school.

I remember the course of study so well, not because of a phenomenal memory, but because five years later I was teaching these same lessons from about the same textbooks in Marathon Township, Lapeer County.

MY TEACHERS

During the eight years I went to a one-room school there were at least eight teachers, probably more. Only two of these made any impression on me. The first was Marcena Knapp, a motherly person. If I had known about queens, I would have thought she was one, sitting in her armchair (throne) while two or three beginners gathered around her to learn their A B C's and to read, "I see a cat" and so on. When I started to school it was still the period when women teachers taught in the fall and spring and men "kept" the winter term. In the fall and spring the small children and the older girls went to school, but not the larger boys. It was only during the winter months that the older boys, who had worked on the farms during the fall and summer, came back to take up their schooling, sometimes to learn and sometimes to have fun. The name of one of these male teachers was Mr. Brooks. Another was a Mr. Rogers. They are but shadows in the distant past.

At the time I was in the third reader, we did not think in terms of grades, but rather readers. It so happened at this time that the older children had left school. Because the children were of my age or younger, women teachers were hired for each term. They were just a procession of shadowy figures; I can remember the names of three of them—one because I disliked her for some forgotten reason, one because she was still teaching when I became county school commissioner (age had not made her a better teacher) and the third one, Mae Calvery, a pretty girl eighteen or nineteen years old. She was like a bouquet of flowers; she brought freshness and beauty into the classroom. She was the first teacher who encouraged me to prepare for the eighth grade examination and perhaps to go on to high school.

None of my teachers, with one possible exception, had graduated from a twelve-grade school. None had attended a normal or teachers' training school. Some may have had one or two years of high school. At this time any boy or girl eighteen years of age could get a third grade certificate by passing a teacher's examination in the common eighth grade subjects plus an examination in a subject called "The Theory and Art of Teaching."

Before the turn of the century, one third of the teachers in the rural schools were teaching on third grade certificates. As late as the 1906-07 school year there were 260 qualified teachers in Genesee County, outside of Flint, including the superintendents and principals of the village schools. Of these, one held a degree from a university; four had normal life certificates; eleven had first grade certificates; one hundred and forty-nine had second grade certificates; and eighty-seven had third grade certificates. (This information is from my personal records, as the public school records were destroyed by fire in March of 1923.)

The average turnover in the teaching force in our county was once every three years. This does not mean that there were not some good, experienced teachers. However, it does mean that very few had any teacher training and few had any schooling beyond the ninth or tenth grade, and not many had experience enough to learn how to be a good educator.

It was a rural school with poorly trained teachers which I attended for eight years and have described. There was not one event or academic achievement that made any impression on me during the first seven years. I remember a few special days, the games we played, and my playmates of those formative years. However, I believe the schools did a better job of teaching patriotism and cooperation than they do today.

In 1892, the year I started school, it was only thirty-seven years after the close of the Civil War. Many of the men in public life were veterans of that tragic conflict, my father among them. My mother had a brother, John Bahnmiller, who died in the notorious Andersonville prison. I have lived through two World Wars, but the Civil War made a much greater and more lasting impression on the people than these later wars fought on foreign shores. Whenever two or three old soldiers met, they talked over all the battles from Bull Run to Appomattox. On every possible occasion they organized parades and celebrations, and they had committees to visit the schools to give patriotic talks.

On October 12, 1892, the 400th anniversary of the discovery of America, our school put on a gala celebration. A speakers' platform was built and decorated with fresh-cut boughs from maple and oak trees in their colorful fall foliage. The children recited poems, everyone sang patriotic songs, and a G.A.R. veteran gave a speech. I still remember the colorfully decorated stand, although I was only five years old. The day before this wonderful event took place, I was struck on my left temple by a baseball bat that one of the larger boys threw against the schoolhouse. It glanced off the building and hit me as I ran around the corner of the building, cracking the temple bone. I was carried home, where I had to rest for a week or ten days. I was brokenhearted to miss the program and Mother consoled me by saying I could go *next year!*

We also made a big occasion of Memorial Day, or Decoration Day as we called it. There was a small church a mile west of the school. Every child in school would memorize a "piece" to speak, and each would take a bouquet of flowers to the church to be placed on the altar. A G.A.R.

veteran would give a talk, after which we would give our recitations and sing a few songs. We would then pick up our bouquets and march to the cemetery to decorate the graves of Civil War veterans.

I remember one of these occasions vividly. Mother had made me a beautiful large bouquet of pink peonies and purple lilacs which I carried proudly to the altar. When the program had ended, we children made a grand rush to pick up our flowers. One of the older girls took my lovely bouquet and marched off with it, leaving me a scrimpy bunch of wilted flowers that no one would want. This was one day I never forgot.

The last day of school was always marked by a special program of speaking and singing. All the parents were invited; most of them came. I can still recite a poem entitled "Johnny McGee" that I memorized for one of these programs.

One year I was seated on the outside aisle next to a large map of Michigan. With no prodding from the teacher, I learned by rote the names of all the counties I could see without leaving my seat. This knowledge proved of great value to me when I began to print and sell school forms to the schools and counties in our state.

THE SCHOOL BOARD

The annual school meeting was always held on the second Monday in September. For some time my father was moderator or president of the school board. I recall going to one of these meetings with my father. The director or secretary read his annual report, which was followed by the report of the treasurer. Because the one-mill tax plus the Primary Interest Fund would not raise enough money to pay the teacher, buy the firewood, and cover the few incidental items, a small sum was voted to make up the deficit. As usual, a discussion was held before the vote was taken. During the preceding term, my sister Addie and another girl had drawn some fairly large maps of the United States and North America, using different colored crayons to color the various states and countries. The teacher liked their neat, accurate maps so well that she kept them and hung them on the walls. One of the men, who always objected to *any* spending, questioned why money had been spent on new maps. When he was told that two schoolgirls had made them, he looked sheepish.

Sometime during Father's term as moderator, the board adopted the Ginn and Company line of textbooks. Whether or not a former board had adopted American Book Company's books, I do not know, but I remember that the American Book Company sued to make the district use its books. The papers were served on Father as moderator. This caused a little excitement in our family because Father had to represent the district in court at Flint, the county seat, fifteen miles away. I do not remember any of the details of the suit, only that the Ginn and Company books were retained.

GAMES

Because our school was small—never more than twenty pupils of all ages from five to fourteen—sometimes there were enough players to play a ball game called "One Old Cat" with two batters, a pitcher, a catcher, and a baseman. Other games we played were Blindman's Buff; Anti-I-Over; Pom, Pom, Pull Away; and in the winter, Fox and Geese. When the weather was too stormy to play outside, we played guessing games or sang songs from the popular *Knapsack* mentioned earlier.

Because almost all the pupils were small, the teachers had no discipline problems, but once in a while we did things to vex her. One warm spring day three or four of us boys received permission from the teacher to go swimming in the Flint River during our lunch hour. The Flint River is a small river about half a mile across lots from the schoolhouse. Our "ol' swimmin' hole" was about two miles above the present Holloway Dam. At that time the river was a clear, sparkling stream with water pure enough to drink. We were having so much fun swimming that we didn't hear either the first or second bell. We returned to the schoolhouse an hour late. The teacher was so relieved to have us back that she did not punish us, for she had had visions of all of us drowning!

When school opened in the fall of 1899, we had a new teacher, the Mae Calvery I mentioned earlier. She may have had only one or two years of schooling beyond the eighth grade, but she went into teaching with great enthusiasm for her work. She brought a new outlook to our school. She tried to make her classes so interesting that the pupils would want to attend rather than go just because they had to. She was the only teacher who urged me to prepare to take the eighth grade examination.

Our home was a mile from the schoolhouse, but to farm children a mile was just a walk of a few minutes. Neither rain nor snow stopped us. There were several boys and girls who lived on our road, and often Sister Addie and I waited for them to walk along with us.

I can remember two desperate fights between playmates, but no particular harm resulted, and within a day or two they were good friends again.

There were woodlots not far from the road to school. In the spring I would stop to pick a bouquet of trillium, or lilies as we called them, and violets and adder's tongues for the teacher. On the way home I would often pick a bouquet of wildflowers for my mother.

CHAPTER IV

Life on the Farm

Life in those near-pioneer days was much different from farm life today. The home was much more self-contained. Money was really scarce; only such staples as sugar, salt, spices and yard goods were bought at the store.

Every farmer used his own wheat, which was ground into flour at a neighborhood flour mill, and corn from which cornmeal was ground. Every few months Father would load two or three bushels of wheat and perhaps a bushel of shelled corn into the buggy and drive seven miles to Columbiaville, a village northeast of our farm. Because he raised only winter wheat, he would trade some of the flour ground from his wheat for spring wheat flour. Mother liked the spring wheat flour because it made better bread. She was an expert breadmaker. She was the one always asked to bring "raised" biscuits to the Ladies' Aid, and hers were always made from spring wheat flour.

Father used to tell how, as a young man, he cut wheat and oats with a cradle. This was an instrument with a heavy scythe blade fastened to a frame, with five or six long wooden fingers six inches apart. When the scythe cut the grain, it fell on this cradle of fingers and the worker laid the grain stalks in a straight row on the ground. Another worker came behind him and raked the grain into small piles which he bound into bundles, using a handful of the stalks for tying.

About 1834, Cyrus McCormick invented the reaper, a two-wheeled vehicle drawn by two horses. However, it was not until 1847 that these machines came into general use. Father bought one of these reapers and I can remember when he still used it. The left wheel was larger than the one on the right side. The cutting bar was fastened to a triangular frame or table.

When I was seven or eight, Father bought a binder which cut and bound the grain. When I was ten, I was strong enough to gather the bundles and stand them in a shock where they were kept until they were dry. When dry, they were pitched onto a wagon and taken to the barn. At the age of eleven I was allowed to help get the grain to the barn; that is, I would load the wagon by placing the bundles with the butts pointing out and put bundles in the center of the load to keep the outside row from sliding off. Six or eight layers of bundles were thus put on the wagon to make a load. The man who pitched the bundles onto the wagon with a three-tined pitchfork placed them with the butts out, in even rows around the wagon. When the wagon was loaded, the one who had pitched the bundles, usually either my brother Fred or Andrew, climbed aboard and we drove to the barn. It usually took three to unload the wagon. One would pitch the bundles from the wagon to the mow; another would pitch them to me; and I would place them in even rows across the mow or, as the saying was, I "mowed" them away. Father usually left the grain in the barn for three or four weeks before a threshing machine was brought to thresh the grain.

The threshing machine was run by a steam engine. A crew of three men came with the machine, one to run the engine, one to draw water to make the steam, and one to feed the bundles into the machine cylinder where the kernels of wheat or oats were knocked loose from the heads of grain. In addition to the three men who came with the machine, Father had to furnish nine or ten other men, neighbors who came to help him. When these neighbors were doing their threshing, he helped them in return. It took two or three men to pitch the bundles from the mow to the table beside the cylinder, one to cut the strings that bound the bundles, two or three to stack the straw as it came from the machine, and two or three to tie bags to the spout where the grain came out of the machine and to carry it to the granary.

The set of revolving cylinders, which were made of steel, did not touch and were provided with short projections. These cylinders revolved very rapidly; only an experienced man was allowed to feed the bundles of grain into the cylinders, for if a finger or hand should be caught, the whole arm might be pulled into the machine. After the grain was removed by the cylinders, it was carried by revolving canvases to screens that separated the wheat kernels from the chaff. Below the screen a fan was placed in such a way that it blew any chaff or dirt away. The kernels then fell into another set of revolving canvases where they were carried to a spout which delivered them into a canvas bag.

Small boys were not permitted to work around the threshing machine. They could look on, but that was all. Usually threshing time came after school had started in the fall; I would be in school and would miss seeing the threshing unless I hurried home from school.

Threshing time was a festive time. As "hungry as a thresher" was a common saying. It usually took all day and sometimes late into the evening to get the job done. In any case, the farm wife on the farm where the threshing was being done served at least one meal and often two. Father never had any trouble getting neighbors to trade work with him, probably because of my mother's good cooking. Her dinners usually included a kettle roast of beef, mashed potatoes, brown gravy, cole slaw, perhaps corn on the cob, always fresh homemade bread, a side dish of home-canned peaches or pears, and all this was topped off with big pieces of fresh apple pie. To get the beef, someone had to drive a horse and buggy to the nearest meat market six miles away.

Father's original land purchase was of forty acres only. After a few years, he took advantage of an opportunity to buy twenty acres located nearly half a mile from our house. A few years later, when a neighbor who owned forty acres across the road to the south offered his farm for sale, my father sold the twenty acres and bought this forty, on which there was a small house and barn. We always called this barn the "little barn." It contained a stable where Father kept his sheep in the winter and a mow that would hold about ten tons of hay.

In the regular farm rotation of crops, Father would plant a field of wheat mixed with timothy seed; in the spring as soon as the frost was out of the ground, he would sow red clover seed. The haying time was usually during the first two weeks of July. The first year after the wheat was harvested, the hay that was cut would be mostly clover. The second year's cutting would be timothy hay, which was preferred for feeding horses. Father would fill the "little barn" with timothy hay. If it contained no clover, it would be called "number one" hay and would bring a better price than hay mixed with clover.

Sometime during the fall, a neighbor who owned a hay baler would move his machine to the "little barn" and bale or press the hay into tight bundles bound with wire. These bales, weighing from 100 to 125 pounds, would be sold to a dealer in Davison; they would then be shipped in railroad boxcars to cities to feed the horses owned by city dwellers.

Sometimes good hay would sell for $10 a ton. It was a cash crop and there was always a ready market for it. The money from such a crop could pay the taxes or at least be enough to make a down payment on a new tool.

Today a farmer would use a combine to cut and thresh his wheat and oats, without extra help. If he doesn't own a combine, he can hire the work done. If he wants to save the straw, he can cut, rake, and bind it into bales entirely by machinery and without additional help.

Father always grew a small patch of navy beans, which were threshed with flails after being spread out on the barn floor which had been cleared and swept clean.

We always had a large vegetable garden where he raised cabbage, string beans, peas, celery, cucumbers, potatoes, carrots, beets, and sometimes rutabagas and turnips. In our cool cellar we could keep potatoes all winter and beets, cabbage, and carrots part of the winter. Mother made pickles from the cucumbers. Celery would keep for a month or more if the bunches were packed in moist earth.

Father always raised enough carrots to fill a large bin, which took up about a third of the room in the cellar. Every day we fed a few carrots to the cows which gave the milk from which my mother made butter. The carrots gave the butter the golden color that butter always has when cows can get fresh grass in the summer. Butter made when the cows are eating dry feed only is white and has to be colored yellow with artificial coloring.

We usually had four or five cows in the milking stage. They had to be milked by hand, for milking machines had not been invented. The milk was poured into tin pans through a strainer to remove any coarse material that may have fallen into the pail during milking. These milk pans were "set" in the cellar, because in the summer that was the coolest place, and in the winter, the warmest. During the next twenty-four hours the cream would rise to the surface. Mother would then skim off the cream and feed the skimmed milk to the calves or pigs. She then put aside the cream to ripen or sour, and then put it into a churn, a glazed earthenware receptacle in which butter was made. Churns were about twenty inches high and ten or twelve inches in diameter. They had a cover that fit snugly, with a hole in the center through which a handle the size of a broomstick could be inserted. This handle was fastened to two crossed pieces of wood. The one who did the churning sat in a chair beside the churn and moved this handle up and down until the butterfat separated from the milk in the cream. If the cream were just right, the butter would "come" in twenty or thirty minutes. Mother would then put the butter in a wooden butter bowl to "work out" the remaining milk with a wooden butter ladle. In the summer she would store the butter in an earthenware crock; in cooler times she would form it into rolls. The crocks were made in different sizes and were weighed before being used and the weight painted on the bottom. When they were filled and taken to the store and weighed, the storekeeper could tell the actual weight of the butter.

When Mother took her butter to the store to trade for groceries, the merchant always kept her butter for his own use or sold it to his favorite customers. Much of the butter brought in by housewives had to be put into a barrel and sent to a butter-renovating factory to be renovated before it could be sold.

In the fall Mother always made a large crockful of sauerkraut. She would select a number of cabbageheads from the garden and slice the cabbage into fine shreds on a cutting board made for that purpose. This board was approximately eighteen inches long and twelve inches wide, with side boards about two inches high. A steel knife blade was fastened in this board at an angle, with a slot in the board beneath the knife. When this board was placed in a large pan with one end resting on the bottom of the pan and the other on its edge, it was ready for cutting cabbage. When the cabbage head was pushed back and forth over the blade, it would be shredded into fine pieces. The blade could be adjusted to make the shreds finer or coarser. The shredded cabbage was then placed in a crock or small barrel and covered. A weight, usually a large stone, was placed on the cover to keep it compressed. Fermentation then took place and the resulting product was sauerkraut. If the container were kept in a cool place the kraut would keep until used.

People talk about the "hard times" of the Great Depression, which started in 1929. When I was a child, people talked about the "hard times" of 1892 to 1896, when Cleveland was president. During those difficult years there was very little money in circulation. I can remember when Mother took butter and eggs to the store to be traded for staples or yard goods, she got 6 cents a dozen for eggs and 8 cents per pound for butter. If, after buying the items she needed, there were any cash due her, she did not get cash but a due bill which could be traded out only at the store which issued it.

Mother always had a small flock of hens and usually had one "setting" of ducks. She also raised a few turkeys. From the ducks she would get feathers for pillows. She would "pick" the ducks several times a year, or as often as the feathers became "ripe." When the feathers were pulled out from the breasts and undersides, they would grow back with the coming of warm spring weather. If they were pulled out too soon after they had grown in again, they would be bloody on the ends. When there were no bloody ends, the ducks were ready to "pick" again.

The surplus male fowl, roosters, drakes and gobblers, gave us fresh meat during the warm months when fresh pork or beef could not be kept. Sometimes my parents sold them for money to buy staples.

To make ends meet, everything possible had to be used. Our living room was heated by a base burner. This was a stove in which hard coal was put into a cylinder that opened at the top and led to within three or four inches of the bottom of the fire pot. The bedroom over the living room had a register in the floor to allow the heat from the room below to take the chill from the bedroom.

Making Soap

Wood was burned in the kitchen range. The pine trees which originally covered a strip a mile wide on each side of the Flint River had been "lumbered off" in the '70s or '80s. The blackened stumps still stood in many fields, although many had been pulled out to make the pine-stump fences that have now given way to age and decay. When Father heard that someone was pulling pine stumps, he would drive a team of horses hitched to a wagon to the place and bring home a wagonload of the stumps. They had no market value, but a handful of shavings cut from a pine stump would make a quick fire on a cold morning.

As nothing but wood was burned in the kitchen stove, the ashes were carefully saved in a barrel. In the spring the barrel was placed on a wide board raised high enough at one side so that a pail could be set under it, and two or three inches higher on the opposite side. On the upper side, the barrel was put nearly on the edge of the board, but on the lower side it was placed eight or ten inches from the bottom. Grooves were then cut from each side of the barrel to the center of the board. Room for a pailful of water was left at the top of the barrel, and when water was added it would trickle down through the wood ashes, dissolving the potash on its way. The resulting brown liquid that came out of the barrel and down the grooves in the board was collected in an iron kettle. Thus was obtained the lye that is necessary for the making of soap. If an egg would float in this liquid, it was considered strong enough to make soft soap. Every farmer had a large iron kettle holding thirty or forty gallons, which he used to heat water to scald pigs at butchering time, to cook hog feed, or to make soap.

When enough lye was collected to partially fill this kettle, it was set on an iron ring with four legs that raised it about eight inches from the ground. A fire was then built under the kettle. For several months before making soap, Mother would save grease from the frying of ham or side pork or from the remains left after trying out lard. She put this grease into the boiling lye and cooked it until it became thick. The result was soft soap, which could be used for cleaning floors or greasy dishes but had to be used with care because it was too strong for personal use. Sometimes she made hard soap by putting salt in the hot, soft soap. The salt made the soap rise to the top and solidify. It was then cut into bars and used for bathing and general use.

In the city of Flint there was a soap factory. Men from this factory drove into the countryside to buy wood ashes. In a compartment of their wagon they carried tinware, such as pans, basins, dippers, and the like, which were traded for wood ashes. A common yellow soap was also traded for ashes.

I remember that Mother also used wood ashes as a scouring powder to clean her silver and cooking dishes. She said the ashes "ate" or dissolved the stains. It was the potash in the ashes that did this.

Pack Peddlers

One of my earliest recollections is that of pack peddlers, usually elderly men of the Jewish faith. They would come down the road with a large pack of yard goods on their backs and a satchel filled with thread, braids and lace in one hand and a walking cane in the other. If one arrived in the evening, Mother would invite him to stay for supper and would let him sleep in a bed reserved for peddlers and travelers without a home. In payment for his bed and meals, Mother would get part payment on cloth for a dress for herself or my sister Addie Mae.

Making Cider and Apple Butter

In every rural neighborhood there was usually a cider mill, where apples could be processed into cider. One of these mills was located on State Road about forty rods north of Richfield Center. The apples were first ground into pulp which was then placed in a press between sheets of burlap. The juice pressed out of the pulp was collected in a tank below the press and channeled into barrels.

When autumn came and apples were ripe, it was time to make apple butter. To get ready for this project, Father would drive a mile and a half to the home of a neighbor named Cottrell to rent for 50 cents a day a large copper kettle. This kettle was used only to make apple butter. Early in the morning of this day Father would have taken enough apples, preferably sweet apples, to the cider mill to make a barrel of cider. The next morning he would set the copper kettle on a metal tripod seven or eight inches high, fill it with cider, and build a brisk fire under it. My mother and Addie would peel, core, and quarter sour apples to be added to the cider. Cider was made from sweet apples because they would not "cook up" for apple butter; the sour apples would. The contents of the kettle, apple quarters and cider, had to be stirred constantly to prevent burning and sticking after the mixture began to thicken. As some of the water was boiled out of the cider, more cider would be added. When the apple butter reached the proper consistency, it was ready for storing. Sometimes Mother added brown sugar if the cider used had not been made from sweet apples. This delicious, brown apple butter was then stored in large crocks or canned in Mason jars. It would keep in crocks during the winter months; in glass jars it would keep indefinitely. It made a delectable addition to our meals.

Apple cider is a pleasant drink until it begins to "work"—until the sugar begins to turn into alcohol. When Father had the cider made to use in making apple butter, he usually had an extra barrel that first became hard cider and finally turned to vinegar. Farm women used much more vinegar than housewives do today. They placed cucumbers in large earthen crocks and covered them with vinegar to preserve them. Peaches and pears were also preserved in vinegar. In pioneer days good cooks varied their menus in many ways by using the foods gathered from gardens and orchards and preserved in vinegar. The highest praise a farm woman could get was that she was a good cook.

In some rural homes hard cider was a common beverage, served on many occasions such as butchering time, grain threshing and sheep shearing time, and barn raisings. However, it was rarely served in our house. Father did not care for it and Mother drank no intoxicating drinks.

I remember one time when a member of their household tried drinking hard cider. Uncle Dyer was shearing our sheep in the barn and a pail of cider stood on a box in the corner. When no one was looking, a little boy eight years old took more than several sips of the brown liquid. When he began to act giddy and drowsy, his father carried him to the house, where his mother put him to bed. After he slept an hour or two he was all right and returned to the barn to watch Uncle Dyer finish shearing the sheep.

Butchering and Going to Market

The fall—no one spoke of it as autumn—was also the time for butchering. A litter of pigs, perhaps eight or ten, after weaning were fed skimmed milk and ground feed, usually a combination of corn and oats. The pigs had the run of a feed lot where they could eat grass and clover. Late in the summer they would be enclosed in a pen and fed corn. Pigs grow rapidly. When they were fat enough, about 175 to 200 pounds each, they were ready for butchering. Butchering day usually came during late November or early December. At least two of the hogs were kept for home consumption; the rest were taken to market, usually to Flint, a distance of fifteen miles.

The trip to Flint would start early in the morning, often before daylight. The journey took about four hours as the horses could not be driven much faster than a walk. Saginaw Street at that time was lined with hitching posts. Father would hitch his team to one of these posts and wait for buyers who would soon come by. Often meat market proprietors would take the entire load. Sometimes individuals would buy one whole hog. After the load was sold, the horses would be driven to Bachtell's Ten Cent Sheds, located on the northeast corner of the block where the Capitol Theater now stands. For ten cents a farmer could drive his horse, or a team of horses, into a stall with a manger. A feeding of oats and hay could be bought for 25 cents or a farmer could bring the oats and hay with him. Needless to say, Father always took the feed for the horses with him as money was always scarce. About sunset a tired man and some tired horses would return home. Once in a while I made the trip with him. It was always a gala excursion for me, but riding thirty miles in a farm wagon was rather tiring for a little boy.

The hogs that were kept for home use were cured or salted down. The side meat was cut into pieces of two or three pounds, then placed in a barrel and covered with a strong brine of salt and water. In this way, pork could be kept to eat in the summer. The hams and shoulders were carefully trimmed, soaked for a few days in the brine, and then hung in the smokehouse. This was a small building four or five feet square. A fire was then built of corncobs which would produce much smoke but no flames. It was a real job to keep the cobs making smoke and not flames for a week or until the meat was cured. The corncob smoke gave a delicious flavor to the meat. These cured hams and shoulders could be kept in a cold room until hot weather came. If some were left by the time summer arrived, Mother would cut them into slices and fry them as if she planned to serve them at the next meal. She then put the fried slices in a three-gallon crock and covered them with hot ham grease. In this way the meat would be preserved until eaten later in the summer. To serve it, Mother would reheat it, but this second heating took some of the good flavor from the meat.

Lard was tried out of the parts of the hog that were too fat to eat. These parts were found in the inner lining of the abdomen of the hog and outer covering of the stomach and intestines. The trying out was done by cooking the parts in water in a large kettle. When finished, with the water cooked out, the lard was kept in crocks until used.

Sausage, seasoned with sage and salt, was made of the trimmings and other odds and ends of pork. None of the meat was wasted. Mother very carefully cleaned the head, cooked it until the meat could be removed from the skin and bones, and then after seasoning it, put it in a cloth bag to squeeze from it any remaining fat or water. The result was a product called headcheese, to be served cold. As Mother made it, it was a most palatable food.

CHRISTMAS AT OUR HOUSE

Thanksgiving and Christmas were celebrated then as now, but they were not nearly so commercialized as at present. Sometimes Father would cut down a small pine tree from a nearby woodlot which Mother would decorate with strings of popcorn.

I remember one Christmas vividly, for my gift from my parents was an air gun! Of course, I had to shoot it at once. When I cocked it and pulled the trigger, the cap or top of the barrel flew off and hit a friend who was our guest. This man was a neighbor who had been invited to spend Christmas Day with us. Fortunately, he was not hurt, but I was in disgrace. This neighbor had a daughter who married John Hart, the father of Admiral Hart of World War II fame.

If we did not always have a tree at Christmas, we always hung up our stockings on Christmas Eve. Sometimes Santa left us an orange or a small bag of candy or two or three pieces of stick candy. And there was always that pair of mittens that Mother had knit on long winter evenings.

One Christmas there was a bright-red sled beside my stocking and another time a shiny "express" wagon. Perhaps Christmas meant more to us in those days with its simplicity than it does now with all the bright lights and tinsel.

My first recollection of attending church services was of the services held in the parlor of "Uncle" Mathias Schweitzer's house. Periodically, an Evangelican minister rode out from Flint to preach to a few of the faithful who gathered to worship. It was here that I was "sprinkled" when I was four or five years old. Later I went to church with Father and Mother to the German Church, a church of the Evangelical faith, which was a mile north and three miles east of our farm. Sister Addie and I first went to Sunday school in The Chapel, a church of the Protestant Methodist faith, located a mile west and a mile north of our home. When this Sunday school was discontinued, we transferred to the Methodist Episcopal Sunday School at Richfield Center.

The winters were long and cold, or so they seemed to a growing boy. However, there were some compensations. Nearby were several good hills that we could slide down after a snow. If a snowfall were heavy enough for sleighing, a ride to church in a cutter drawn by one horse or on a bobsled drawn by two horses was a diversion. One sleigh ride that I remember was when our school visited the Traver school three miles north. We had a spelling match, but as spelling was never my strong point, I don't remember which school won.

One winter, when I was nine or ten, my older sister Sarah and her husband, Frank Carr, moved into a house a mile and a half south of us. Because Frank had a job in Flint and could not get home except on weekends, I stayed with Sarah for several weeks and went to the Schweitzer School across the road from their house. The teacher gave me five cents a day for building the fire in the schoolhouse stove each morning. That was real money in those days for a boy my age!

MAPLE SYRUP TIME

However long the winter, spring always came. Among the good things it brought was maple syrup time. When Father cleared his farm, he left ten acres of woodlot. A few years before my birth, during one hot and dry summer, a careless farmer who lived north of us set a fire which burned out of control. Nearly all the trees in our woodlot were destroyed. However, twelve or fifteen large maple trees were saved, and Father was careful not to let them be cut for firewood.

Every spring when the days began to get warmer, he would scrub out the old iron kettle, gather up all the extra pans, kettles and crocks; find the bit and brace (or bit stalk); clean the spiles; and put them all in a wheelbarrow. A bit is a cutting or boring tool; a brace is a tool for holding and rotating a bit. The spiles were usually made of pine wood, about five inches long and three-fourths inch in diameter. A small hole about one-eighth of an inch in diameter was bored lengthwise through this piece of wood. The end was then whittled to a size to fit a one-half inch hole. This hole was drilled in the maple tree to a depth of two and one-half inches. If the weather were warm, maple sap would start running through the spile and drop into the pan which was placed on the ground under the spile. Sap runs best when the nights are cold enough to freeze, but the days must be warm enough to thaw. On a good sap day the containers would be filled with sap two or three times.

To make the maple syrup, Father would set the big iron kettle up against an old log, then fill it with sap and build a brisk fire under it. As the sap boiled away, he would pour in more sap. By evening he would have one or two pails full of a liquid which was almost syrup. The next day Mother would finish making the syrup by boiling it on the kitchen range. She would clarify it by adding a little fresh milk. This would cause any refuse that had fallen into the boiling sap in the woods to come to the surface as scum, which she would skim off. She put the finished product in glass Mason jars, in which it would keep indefinitely.

I always liked maple syrup time. If we had sap to boil on a Saturday, I was in luck. Some of our neighbors had large sugar bushes. They boiled sap in flat pans about four by six feet in size and eight inches deep over fireplaces made of stones or brick, with a chimney and a shed for cover.

However, with our twelve or fifteen trees, we did not need an elaborate setup. The seven or eight gallons of syrup we made helped make Mother's buckwheat pancakes a delicious treat. Sometimes Mother would invite a neighbor family in for an evening and we would "sugar off." That is, she would boil a quart or two of syrup until it formed sugar. Warm maple sugar was my favorite candy.

OUR SHEEP

As far back as I can remember, Father had a flock of sheep. Because money was scarce, to get his first flock he took a small flock, perhaps eight or ten, to double. One of our neighbors, the one who owned the apple butter kettle, let Father have the sheep, with payment to be made in four years by giving him twice as many sheep as Father got from him originally. This now seems to have been a big price to pay to get a flock of sheep. However, sheep have at least one lamb, and often twins, every spring. They begin bearing lambs when they are about a year and half old. In four years, if all the ewe lambs lived and were kept, a good-sized flock could be raised, probably twenty-five or thirty. After paying his debt, Father had the nucleus of another flock.

Once in a while a mother sheep would have twins and for some reason would refuse to "own" one of them. Father would bring this lamb to the house, where Mother would feed it cow's milk from a bottle. These lambs would become very tame and would follow us wherever we went. One day Father started to walk to the "Center" (Richfield), two miles away, to get the mail. When he was a short distance from the house, he heard a noise, turned around and saw a lamb following him. He stopped at a neighbor's, tied the lamb to a fence, and walked on. On his return trip, he untied the lamb and it followed him home. When the pet lamb was grown, it was returned to the flock.

Father never had to drive his sheep from one pasture to another. All he had to do was to approach the flock, give a customary call, and the sheep that had been a household pet would start following him. The rest of the flock would follow their leader.

A flock of sheep gave a farmer two dividends. In the spring, as soon as the weather was warm, Father would have the sheep sheared. My Uncle

Dyer Amidon, Mother's brother-in-law, did the shearing; he was the official sheep shearer for the entire area. The wool from each sheep was put into a special wool packing box, where it was tied with special wool twine into a square bundle ready for market.

A day or two before shearing time, we took the sheep to the creek a mile east of our house, where they were put in a pen beside the creek. Each sheep was then taken into the water and given a thorough bath to remove any dirt that was in the wool. This washing took nearly all day, but washed wool usually brought two or three cents a pound more than unwashed wool.

When fall came, the male lambs which had been born in the spring were put into a special pen, given extra feed for a few weeks, then taken to the market to sell. Sometimes in the fall, when fresh meat was scarce, we would butcher one of the male lambs for our own table. It was our custom to give our neighbors some of the fresh meat from any butchering, whether of sheep, hogs, or steers. When they butchered, they would reciprocate.

THE ORCHARD

We always had apples, cherries, pears, peaches, plums, and red and black raspberries in season. Before nurseries were established, where one could buy named stock, Father would graft named varieties on apple, plum, or pear seedlings. He grafted the trees in several of the orchards in the vicinity. Three or four of the pear trees he planted in our yard at least ninety years ago are still bearing fruit.

If the apple crop were good, he would sell a few barrels of them for cash. Northern Spies, Greenings, and Baldwins were the favorite winter apples. Fall apples were Red Astricans, Snows, and Sheepnose.

We had one tree of Russet apples. These Father sometimes put in a pit where they would keep until late in the spring. He made the pit by digging a round hole several inches deep and placing straw in the bottom. The apples were placed on the straw, then more straw was put over them, and the pit then covered with dirt. Potatoes were also kept in pits in the same way. When the pits were opened in the spring, the apples or potatoes would be as fresh as when put there.

In those days apples seemed to keep better in a cool cellar than they do now. Perhaps they were not afflicted with the diseases of today. However, Father did spray his apple and plum trees once a year.

Before winter arrived, Mother always had the shelves in the cellar filled with jars of peaches, pears, plums, cherries, berries, and tomatoes.

Because of the illness he suffered during nearly four years in the army and the hard work of clearing his farm, my father was never a strong man. Besides typhoid fever, he had had scurvy until some of his teeth fell out. He also had bloody dysentery, followed by piles which bothered him all his life. He retired from active farming when I was eight or nine years old. First my brother Andrew, then brother Fred, took over the heavy work. Father did most of the chores, planted the vegetable garden, picked the different fruits in season, and served as an extra hand during haying and harvesting time.

I had my own special chores, such as keeping the woodbox full, carrying water from the well, driving the cows from the pasture, and other odd jobs. I learned to milk a cow, but seldom had to do the milking.

About a mile from our house there was a quarter section of woodland which we called the "lake lot," so called because on the north side there was a small lake. Wild raspberries and huckleberries grew in this woodlot, and I often went with Father to pick them. After I grew old enough to hunt, it was my favorite hunting ground. By this time, the rabbits were the only game left in this part of Michigan.

When I was twelve, I got my first single-barreled shotgun by selling Larkin Soap. Upon the receipt of $10, the Larkin Soap Company would send a box of soap that was to be sold at retail for $20. My mother advanced the money for this venture. With the soap, they sent a premium; my premium was a twelve-gauge shotgun.

My First Business Venture

My second money-making endeavor brought me a combination bookcase and writing desk which I used during my high school days and for many years thereafter. I sold enough soap to repay my mother and earned money to buy needed clothes. In addition, Mother had all the soap she needed for a long time.

It was in this "make do" home that I lived for thirteen years. We were, by present standards, poor and underprivileged. Perhaps we were, but if so, we did not realize it. We had some "store" clothing, as I mentioned earlier, but most of our clothing was made at home.

We had the same disadvantages and the same pleasures as our neighbors. Neither my playmates nor I had cash allowances. Once in a while we went to Davison with our parents, on which rare occasions they might give us a nickel or a dime to spend. That was all. One Fourth of July Father took me to Flint to celebrate. This was one of the big events of my early life. He gave me a nickel or a dime at a time to buy firecrackers, ice cream, or lemonade, until I had spent the grand total of 35 cents. I had an unforgettable time!

CHAPTER V

Visiting Relatives

There were other memorable times. When I was five or six, Mother and Father took me on a trip to visit relatives. One of my brothers took us to Columbiaville to board a train to go north to Bay City. There we visited my mother's Aunt Sarah, whose daughter and son-in-law kept a tavern. After a few days in Bay City, we took the train to Harrison, where we were met by Uncle Elias Riegle, the youngest of the four Riegle brothers who served in the Civil War. All I can remember of this visit was that when we stood in his back yard we looked out at a circle of tall trees. The house may have been made of logs, as this part of Michigan was just being settled. (A few years later, Uncle Elias, or Eli as we called him, built a cobblestone house which later became the clubhouse of the Harrison Country Club.)

From Harrison we went to visit a cousin of Father's who lived not far from Gladwin. (Today there is a road near Gladwin named the Riegle Road.) This cousin had two daughters in their early teens. They were old enough to curl their bangs with a curling iron, which they heated in a kerosene lamp. Just for the fun of it, the girls curled my hair. When we started home, they gave me a pair of pigeons or doves, as I called them. One of these was soon killed by a turkey, but the other lived for several years, never taking another mate. When it died, I buried it in a box at the foot of a pear tree. This trip to Bay City, Harrison, and Gladwin was the longest trip I had until after my graduation from high school.

All of my mother's family except one sister lived on farms near Byron, Michigan. They were her brother Jacob Bahnmiller and his family and her sisters, Margaret Schweikert and Lena Wolf, and their families. We made an annual trip to Byron to visit. Someone would take us to Davison, where we would take a train to Durand. There we would change trains for Byron, where we would be met. This trip was only about fifty miles from home, but it took half a day to go each way.

As I mentioned earlier, Grandfather Bahnmiller brought his family from Württemberg, Germany, about 1854, when Mary, my mother, was five or six years old. Three of their six children were born in Germany: Margaret, Mary, and John. When the Civil War broke out, Uncle John enlisted. He was captured by the Confederates and confined in Andersonville prison, where he died. Mother always claimed that Uncle John died of starvation. My Grandfather Bahnmiller was killed by a falling tree soon after he bought his farm in Argentine Township.

My Grandmother Bahnmiller remained a widow for several years, until she came from Byron to Richfield Center to visit her married daughters, Sarah Amidon and my mother, Mary. At this time she became acquainted with a Mr. Kurtz, the grandfather of her son-in-law, Dyer Amidon, and changed her name to "Grandma Kurtz." By this marriage she became step-grandmother to her son-in-law.

Working for Uncle Jake

The summer I was twelve, I stayed at Uncle Jacob Bahnmiller's farm near Byron and helped him with the work, for which he paid me 25 cents a day, truly big wages for me. There was a little lake on a neighbor's farm just back of Uncle Jake's woods. Once in a while he took me with him to fish for bullheads. We could catch a dozen or more in one hour.

When I was working at Uncle Jake's, we were always up early in the morning. According to an old German custom, there was a lunch period at ten o'clock in the morning and another at three in the afternoon. At the afternoon repast a small glass of wine or cider was served. Uncle Jake had an apple grinder and a small cider press, so he could make cider whenever the apples were ready. In the fall, he always made a keg of wine, either from grapes he picked in his garden or from wild elderberries that grew at the edge of a swamp.

The summer I was thirteen I "hired out" to a farmer named Orentus Kurtz, whose farm was four miles northeast of our home. I was paid the magnificent sum of $5 per month plus board and room. The work was not hard, as it consisted mainly of light chores, such as loading wheat and oat bundles or cultivating beans with a one-horse walking cultivator. Several times I walked the four miles home on a Saturday evening. After I had worked two months, I cut my foot on a manure hook and had to quit work and return home. I used the $10 I had earned to pay my half on the price of a girls' secondhand bicycle that Sister Addie and I had bought the year before.

THE BLOCHERS

Grandma Kurtz's husband, John Kurtz, had a daughter by his first marriage who married Abraham Blocher, a cousin of my father. When Grandfather Kurtz died, his farm came into the possession of his son-in-law, Abraham Blocher. Abraham's father and my father's mother, Nancy Blocher, were brother and sister. They had another brother, John, of Buffalo, New York.

John B. Blocher was a tailor. When the Civil War began, he obtained Army contracts to make uniforms and shoes for the soldiers, which business made him a wealthy man. He and his wife, Elizabeth, had only one child, a son named Nelson. Rumor has it that Nelson fell in love with a servant girl in their household, that his parents objected to a marriage and sent the young man to Paris to forget his love or infatuation. The story goes that when he arrived in Paris, he registered in a hotel, went directly to his room and shot himself fatally. The grieving father had his son's body returned to Buffalo.

As a memorial to his son, the father hired a sculptor in Carrara, Italy, to carve an elaborate monument of the beautiful Carrara marble. This ornate monument, consisting of four life-sized figures, has as the central figure a statue of a young man reclining on a couch, with a book in his hand, as though he had fallen asleep. An angel hovers over his head. At his left stands a statue of his mother in the dress of the period; on his right is a statue of his father, very erect and formal in a cut-away coat. The inscription states that Nelson died at the age of 37 after a lingering illness.

This Blocher Family Memorial, housed in glass, is nationally famous. Thousands of visitors annually marvel at the artistry and craftsmanship of it. It is located in the Forest Lawn Cemetery in the heart of Buffalo, the cemetery where President Millard Fillmore is also buried. The complete story of this famous monument was written up in a national magazine a few years ago, but my copy was destroyed by fire in 1962.

Abraham Blocher always expected to get some of his rich uncle's money, but my father had no such expectations. When John Blocher died, he left his fortune for a home for retired Protestant ministers. My father was not surprised or disappointed, but Cousin Abraham was.

Recently my wife and I visited the Blocher Home in Buffalo and were escorted through it. It is a large stone building filled with beautiful antiques and objects of art from John Blocher's own residence, but because its elevator and facilities are antique, too, the building has been condemned. From the endowment and sale of surrounding lands there is sufficient money to replace it with a modern building for the aged. We saw the blueprints for the new building, which is probably under construction by this time. Because there were not enough retired ministers to fill the home, it is now open to elderly people of both sexes who can meet the charges.

CHAPTER VI

High School in Davison

The spring of 1900 I finished the eighth grade under the tutelage of my favorite teacher, Mae Calvery. I am indebted to this teacher because she encouraged me to take the eighth grade examination in order to go on to high school. Until she came to our school, we had not been told of such a thing as an eighth grade examination. I took this examination in Davison, but didn't do very well. However, I did well enough to enter the Davison High School as a freshman in the fall of 1900. My sister Addie was the main force behind my decision to go to high school. Incidentally, I was the first pupil from our rural school, the Dodge School, to take the eighth grade examination and attend high school.

During the summer of 1900, Mother and Father decided to turn the operation of their farm over to my brother Fred and to move to the village of Davison. However, they did not find a house to rent until the middle of October. Brother Andrew was then working a farm on shares which belonged to his father-in-law. This farm was located four miles from Davison. For the first six weeks in high school I stayed with him and rode the old bicycle eight miles each day.

About October 15th Father found a small house to rent on what is now Garland Street in Davison. The rent was $4 per month. We lived in this house until the following spring, when Father bought a house across the road from the rented one. We built a barn for "Old Meg," our driving horse. Those were the days when, if you didn't have a horse and buggy or a bicycle, you didn't go anywhere—unless you walked.

I remember the first day in the new school as though it were yesterday! There were five teachers in the school, one for the first and second grades, one for the third and fourth, one for the fifth and sixth, and two for the seventh, eighth, ninth, tenth, and eleventh grades! The teacher who taught the seventh and eighth grades also taught two high school subjects. There was no superintendent; the high school teacher was called the principal and he had general supervision over the whole school.

The school building was then on the corner of Davison Road and Main Street. All the pupils in the high school sat in one room. There were twelve to fifteen pupils in the ninth grade, ten or twelve in the tenth, and only one, Ray Whipple, in the eleventh. A middle-aged gentleman named F. W. French was the principal. He had an artificial leg but could walk without difficulty. We had a required course of study, with no electives. All ninth graders studied algebra, English, ancient history, and a class which might be called "reviews." Nearly all the pupils in the ninth grade were deficient in some of the fundamental eighth grade subjects, ₋aving come into Davison from one-room schools which had poorly prepared teachers. We started the "reviews" with a class in mental arithmetic. Our books were not furnished, but had to be bought at Peters Drug Store.

At lunch time of the first day, I rode my bike to a bakery where I bought six cookies and ate them sitting on a bench in front of the bakery. After that, I carried a lunch to school, as did all the pupils who lived in the country. I soon became acquainted with everyone in the high school, forming lasting friendships with almost all of them.

TEACHERS

Mr. French was a most exacting teacher. He always required complete sentences in answer to questions. Because I did not have a good foundation in mental arithmetic, I realize now that his class in this subject gave me a foundation that helped me later when I taught in rural schools and has been useful ever since. He even drilled us in the combinations and in multiplication so that we knew 9×7 are 63 and $9 + 7$ are 16 without hesitating. We were supposed to have learned such facts in elementary school, but few of us had.

He had a set formula for each set of arithmetic problems. If the problem were: "If a farmer took 25 bushels of wheat to market and got $2 a bushel for the wheat, how much money did he get?" We would have to answer: "If he got $2 for one bushel, for 25 bushels he would get

25 × \$2 or \$50." Problem: "If a woman got 80 cents for 4 dozen eggs, how much would she get for 6 dozen?" Answer: "If she got 80 cents for 4 dozen, for one dozen she would get as much as 4 is contained in 80 or 20 times, or 20 cents per dozen. For 6 dozen she would get 6 × 20 cents or \$1.20." Later, when I taught in rural schools, I had success by using this method, and when I taught algebra in high schools, I again found it of value.

Mr. French also stressed the value of getting each lesson as it came, because each one tied in with the one that followed. His favorite story was about Epaminondas and the phalanx he organized for Alexander the Great. This phalanx was invincible because it took one step forward at a time. Mr. French, to emphasize his point, would stomp a few steps forward with his wooden leg. He wanted us to remember that if we took one step forward with each lesson, we would always be ready for the next.

My favorite class was ancient history, taught by Horace Potter, who became my mentor and one of the best friends I ever had.

The school did not have an adequate library, but it did have a set of Redpath's *History of the World* which I read with much interest. We studied ancient history until Easter vacation, then finished the year in the study of botany. We made this change because we could get many varieties of plants and wild flowers in the spring, enabling us to analyze the flowers and assign them to their proper families.

Just before Christmas, Brother Will and his wife Clara, with their two children, Eddie and Beulah, came back to Davison. About two years before this, Will, with a little financial aid from Father, had bought forty acres in Garfield Township in Bay County. This land was covered with hemlock trees which he expected to cut and sell for enough money to get started in farming. During the winter of 1899-1900, Father lived with them for several weeks to help Will cut enough logs to build a log house. While this house was being built, they lived in a rented house nearby.

A week before I started to high school I went with Mother to visit Will and Clara. We went by train from Columbiaville to Pinconning, where we hired a liveryman to take us to Will's farm, about ten miles from the town. The charge for the livery was \$2. We stayed with them for three or four days. A neighbor took us back to the railroad station on our return trip.

Will and Clara both seemed in good health when we left, but a few weeks later we heard they had typhoid fever. When they recovered and were strong enough to travel, my brother Fred drove to their home in a double buggy and brought them to Richfield Center. Clara and little Beulah came to stay with us in Davison; Will and Eddie stayed with Fred and Ina. The two children then came down with typhoid. Beulah recovered, but Eddie died and was buried in the Dodge Cemetery. Will and Clara, discouraged by illness and tragedy, never returned to their farm in Bay County.

Life in a small town of three or four hundred inhabitants was not very exciting. The one drugstore had a soda fountain where teen-agers would meet. The evening train from the West came in about seven o'clock, and sometimes we would "meet" this train to see who had been to Flint, then a city of 13,000 or 14,000 people.

SPORTS

Our school did have a baseball and a football team, although there was no organized athletic program. There were no eligibility rules. When there were not enough high school boys to make up a team, eighth graders were allowed to play. I did not play baseball, but played tackle on the football team. Each player furnished his own uniform. In football this consisted of a pair of shoes with cleats nailed to the soles, or a pair of sneakers, a pair of padded pants, and an old sweater. No two outfits were alike. There were no helmets, no shoulder pads, and more importantly—no coaches. The only plays we used were end plays or line bucks. This was before the days of the forward pass, and the rule was three downs to make five yards. We played home and home games with Lapeer High School and with the Michigan School for the Deaf in Flint. I do not remember the scores, but only that after each game I was so sore and lame that it took me two or three days to recover. In the autumn of my senior year (we graduated at the end of the eleventh grade) I sprained my knee in the second game and was out of school for ten days. This ended my football playing.

Summer Vacations

Every summer from the age of fourteen on, I worked for my brother Andrew, whose farm was on the Coldwater Road just west of Richfield Center. The first summer (1901), he paid me 25 cents a day, plus board and room. Each summer thereafter he raised my wages 25 cents a day over the previous year and in 1905 he paid me $26 per month. A month was twenty-six days and I was paid for the days when it rained and we could not work in the fields. However, on rainy days we usually worked in the barn at extra chores. Brother Andrew was a very good farmer and a good employer. We usually got up about six o'clock and had breakfast at seven. We always heard the breakfast bell of our neighbor west of us, ringing when we were going to the barn. The neighbor's hired hand claimed that the breakfast bell of another neighbor rang at five o'clock. Even though we may have slept later in the morning than the neighbors, Andrew always had his work done on time.

Those were the years when more machinery was being used to take the place of manpower. When I worked for Mr. Kurtz, I walked behind a one-horse cultivator; Andrew had a two-horse cultivator that would cultivate two sides of a row of corn or beans at once. Although the hay and grain bundles were still pitched on the wagon by hand, hay forks and slings fastened to the top of the hayloft by ropes and manipulated by pulleys were used to unload the wagons. The use of internal combustion engines in farm tractors to take the place of horses was still one or two decades away. As I look back, it seems that the use of farm tractors and automobiles was probably one of the causes of the Great Depression.

Until the automobile came into general use, two of the principal cash crops on a farm were hay and oats raised to feed horses. When the city people began to sell their horses and buy automobiles and the farmers bought tractors, there was no market for hay and oats. Farmers plowed up their hay and oat fields and planted wheat, rye, and beans for human consumption and corn for beef cattle. The population did not increase fast enough to utilize the extra food produced. The result was that the market for food grains was glutted and prices plunged down to a point where farmers had no purchasing power. Business began to decline and this decline eventually brought on the Depression. After more than fifty years of unsuccessful governmental controls, the present world population explosion has begun to put the farmer once more in a competitive market.

To return to my high school days—a teen-ager's life then was entirely different from his life today. There were no automobiles, no motorcycles, no moving pictures, no drive-in theaters, no television, no recreation centers. On Sunday we went to church and Sunday school. Once or twice a year a vaudeville or medicine show would come to town. During my third year in high school, I joined a card club, where we played flinch. The club was made up of high school pupils and young married people, as there were never enough of any one age group to form a club.

We never once thought that we belonged to a "have not" group. We found our own pleasures in skating with boys and girls in the winter and in fishing, hunting, and swimming with boys in the spring and summer.

Graduation exercises were held at the end of the third year in high school. I recall that a Catholic priest gave the baccalaureate sermon and a Protestant minister the commencement address. There were only eight graduates!

After graduation, Roy and Willie Schumacher, John Gidley, Lawrence Burton, Noel Conger and I rented a cottage at Lake Napessing for a week, where we had a wonderful time swimming, fishing and bowling. There was only one bowling alley, a great attraction for me because it was the first time I had ever bowled. The lake was full of fish; one afternoon Noel and I caught more bluegills than we could eat in several days.

CHAPTER VII

High School in Flint

The following August Father sold our house in Davison and rented, for $10 per month, a house on East Street, Flint, at the end of Fourth Street. This move was made to enable me to finish high school. At this time, 1903, there were only two twelve-grade schools in Genessee County, Flint and Fenton.

When I presented my report cards to Mr. Kirkland, city superintendent of schools, I learned that it would take me two more years to graduate. I had studied physics in Davison High for one year, but because we had no laboratory, he gave only one-half year's credit in this subject; to get full credit I had to take physics laboratory for one year. For the seven months of ancient history and three months of botany I received only one-half year's credit for the history course and no credit for botany. Fifteen credits were required to graduate. After two years in Flint High School, I graduated with sixteen and one-half credits. That extra year in high school proved valuable to me in more ways than one.

My entry into Flint High School opened up a whole new world to me. During my last year in Davison High, the total high school enrollment was less than 35, with only two teachers for the eighth, ninth, tenth, and eleventh grades. In Flint there were approximately 400 pupils and 15 teachers in high school. There were 85 in my graduating class of '05.

Many of the pupils came from rural areas. Several from Atlas, Goodrich, and Burton rode back and forth on the interurban electric cars which ran between Flint and Detroit. Others from farms within a few miles distance drove a horse and buggy to school. A few students boarded with relative or friends in Flint.

I had had a year of Latin in Davison, but when I entered the second-year Latin class, which was called "Caesar," I found that my foundation in the language was not good, so I repeated first-year Latin. I also took German, English III, chemistry, and physiography. As I mentioned, to keep my half-year credit in physics I was required to attend two laboratory periods each week. These, with two chemistry laboratory periods, kept me busy for six periods a day for four days. Because there were only six periods in the school day, I had to do all my studying at home. I never had to prepare for the physiography class because Miss Carrie Lewis, our teacher, always explained the next assignment very carefully and if I paid strict attention to her remarks, I learned the next day's lesson.

Besides size, there were several differences between Davison and Flint schools. In Davison, each class period was thirty minutes or less and each teacher taught eight or more classes daily. (In Linden in 1908-09 I taught eleven half-hour classes a day.) In Flint High there were six periods of forty-five minutes, so no teacher could teach more than six classes a day. In Flint High all the teachers were college graduates. In Davison the principal and Horace Potter, his assistant, had first-grade certificates; the others had second-grade certificates.

THE SCHOOL BUILDING

Old Flint High School, located on Beach Street on the block now occupied by an auto ramp, was built in 1875 at a cost of $77,377.00. When I entered its portals in 1903, to me it seemed a most imposing edifice. There was almost as much difference between this building and Davison High as there had been three years earlier between the village high school and the one-room country school. However, it did not take me long to adjust to my new environment.

The high school building had three stories. When first built, the third floor was designed for the main assembly room; the rooms on the first and second floors were to be classrooms and laboratories. Several years before my time, the third floor was condemned as unsafe, so the freshmen were seated in rooms on the second floor and the other three grades on the first floor, with the laboratories moved to the basement.

Because the junior class, in which I was placed, was extra large, I was seated in a room with tenth graders. Miss Mary E. S. Gold was the homeroom teacher. Under her rule there was no nonsense. She was also my English history teacher, and a very good one, too.

I entered into all the school activities for which I had the time. The school was homogeneous. There may have been a little class consciousness, but the majority were from the middle class and I soon made friends with many of them.

SPORTS AND RECREATION

There were no organized sports. We had a football team and I tried out for an end position and made the second team. Each player, as in Davison, had to furnish his own uniform. I didn't try out for the baseball team. In the spring of 1904, we organized the first track team in Flint High. We had one track meet with Saginaw High in which I was scheduled to enter the half-mile, the quarter-mile, and the low hurdle races. We won two points. "Bubble" Lee Main was fourth in the shot-put. I should point out that at this time Saginaw was a city nearly three times the size of Flint.

Because there was little organized social activity in the school, we naturally drifted into groups. My group was the South Saginaw Street "gang" and our meeting place was the John R. MacDonald home, as Hazel MacDonald was the ringleader of the group. She later married Robert Knapman, a Flint man. We spent many pleasant Sunday afternoons at Hazel's house.

I can remember one sleigh ride we took to the home of one of the group who lived in the country. Something happened on that occasion that illustrates the great ethical change that has taken place since that time. After the trip, it was rumored that one of the girls had committed an indiscretion. The good name of the class was at stake, so a special meeting of the class was called, charges of misconduct were made, and a regular trial was held. The charges, the nature of which I do not remember, were not proved and the accused girl was declared innocent. The honor of the class was intact!

In our junior year we had a party in the old assembly room on the third floor of the high school. In our senior year we had a prom, held in the public assembly room in the Dryden Building, to which I took my sister Addie.

Mr. Kirkland resigned at the end of the 1903-04 school year. Mr. Alvin Cody, who had been principal for several years, was appointed superintendent, a position he held for nineteen years. Mr. C. G. Wade was appointed principal.

Years later, when I was County Commissioner of Schools of Genesee County, I always referred to Mr. Wade as the man who had had a great influence on my life. When he stood before a class, he had a habit of putting his tongue in the corner of his mouth when thinking intently. Because teen-agers are such imitative creatures, I acquired the same habit and later broke myself of this mannerism with difficulty. Later I told this incident to impress on my teachers the fact that they were in charge of impressionable children and that their every act could affect for good or evil the lives of the boys and girls under their tutelage. Today I wonder if the teachers still believe in this idea and conduct themselves accordingly?

DEBATING TEAM

In my senior year Mr. Wade organized the first debating team in Flint High School. James Lobban, Clyde "Spec" Simpson and I were on the first team. We debated with Detroit Central High in Detroit on the question: "Resolved: That some Southern states have been justified in keeping the Negroes from voting." We had the positive side, and lost the debate two to one. At that time, only the captain of the team did the rebutting. Our captain was "Spec," who had a reputation of being able to handle himself on any subject at any time. However, at rebuttal he became tongue-tied, so we lost the debate. Our second debate was with Saginaw High at Saginaw. The only change on the team was that Hubert Haller took the place of James Lobban. The subject was: "Resolved: That the United States should have a two-ocean navy." We won this debate. However, it wasn't until 1919 that the United States got a two-ocean navy!

CHAPTER VIII

Earning My Way

My brother Fred was a person who always seemed to be in the right place at the right time. Soon after we moved to Flint, he happened to stop in at the Genesee County Savings Bank (now the Genesee-Merchants Bank and Trust Company) and heard that they needed a janitor. He came to our house immediately and told me of the opening. The next morning I applied for the job and was hired at wages of $3.50 a week of six days. In the winter my week was seven days, as I had to stoke the furnace. I had to be at the bank by six o'clock in the morning—five-thirty if it had snowed during the night. I stoked the furnace, swept the floors, cleaned the spittoons, mopped the lobby, dusted the furniture, wiped the tops of all the desks with a damp cloth, and swept the sidewalk in front of the bank. After I had held this job for about a year, Mr. James Martin, the cashier, called me into his office and offered me a permanent job as collector. I told him that I wanted to graduate from high school with my class, and therefore could not accept his offer. He then asked me if I knew any young man who would like the job. I told him I could find someone. Immediately I wrote to Gyles Merrill, a friend of mine who lived in Burton Township, who had graduated the previous June. He was also a Sunday school classmate at Court Street Methodist Church.

When Gyles came into town, I introduced him to Mr. Martin and he was hired. This generosity lost me my job at the bank, however, as Gyles had to do the janitorial work as well as the collecting. He once told me that he received $5 a week for the two jobs. Much later Gyles became president of this same bank. In 1954, he was honored at an elaborate testimonial banquet at the City Club to celebrate his fifty years with the bank.

Bankers from all over the nation came; I was one of the few Flint men invited to this dinner.

When Gyles took my job, it left me with no income, but I soon found three jobs, one of which was with Miss Helen Walker, a spinster who lived on the corner of Liberty and Second streets in a large brick house built by her father. (The Walker school was named after him.) I kept her coal stoves filled, her walks swept and cleared of snow, and kept her water filter full of water—all for 75 cents a week. At this time Flint had no central water supply; all drinking water came from wells, except for a few families who filtered rain water.

I also earned 75 cents a week working for Mrs. David Crawford. Her late husband was the same David Crawford who ran a sawmill in Otisville in which my father worked to earn money to buy lumber for his first house. Mrs. Crawford remembered Father from the Otisville days; both she and her daughter Melissa showed great interest in my progress in school. (In later years my daughter Rosalie and Elizabeth Crawford, David's great-granddaughter, went to school together and became close friends.)

My third job was with a family on Fourth Street, where I tended the furnace and kept the walks clean.

In March of my senior year I wrote and passed a county teacher's examination and received a third-grade certificate which allowed me to teach one year in a rural school in Genesee County.

During the commencement exercises for the class of '05, the baccalaureate sermon was given by the Reverend Clarence E. Allen and the commencement address by Professor Benjamin Terry of Chicago University. Typical of most graduates, I was too excited to listen carefully to their words of wisdom. I do remember that in the yearbook under my picture was the following caption: "With a grim determination, carving a pathway to success." The graduation exercises were held in Stone's Theater, which was on the corner of Harrison and First streets where the Flint Journal building now stands.

In the spring of 1905, Mother and Father moved back to the neighborhood where they had lived for thirty-five years, where their children were born, and where all their friends lived. They bought a house in the four-corner village still called Richfield Center. They were genuine country folk who never enjoyed city living.

After graduation, I went to work for my brother Andrew, whose farm was only a quarter of a mile west of Richfield Center.

I had my teacher's certificate, but no school. Sometime during the summer, Addie's beau, Burt Petteys, whom she later married, told me that the Cyclone School in Marathon Township, Lapeer County, needed a teacher. Burt's father, Orson Petteys, was an officer in this district. Immediately I borrowed Father's horse and buggy and drove to Mr. Petteys' home to apply for the position. He took me to see the other two officers and I was hired to teach my first school.

CHAPTER IX

A Rural School Teacher

THE CYCLONE SCHOOL

I had come a long way since I left the one-room Dodge School to attend high school in Davison. Dodge School and the Cyclone School were ten miles apart, but they were identical in every way. Each had one large room, two entry rooms, a box stove, some seats and desks, blackboards, a few maps, a dictionary, a teacher's desk and chair, and a water pail, complete with one dipper for all.

My salary was $30 per month. For $2.50 a week I boarded with Mr. Albert Smith and his wife, Fannie, who lived about one-half mile from the schoolhouse. The Smiths had one child, a boy named Hugh, who was one of my "beginners." Each day I carried my lunch to school in a little tin pail.

Although I had a teacher's certificate, it was not valid outside Genesee County. I asked Mr. Fred Johnson, Genesee County Commissioner of Schools, to send my examination papers to the County Commissioner of Lapeer County, who gave me a transferred certificate. I have never known why he did this. Perhaps he thought the school needed a teacher or that I needed a job, for my marks were nothing to brag about.

The Saturday before schools opened, the County School Commissioner held a one-day teachers' institute in Lapeer. I probably borrowed Father's horse and buggy again to get to this institute, as Lapeer is only thirteen miles from Richfield Center. I shall never forget this institute, my first, conducted by Henry R. Pattengill, one of the most dynamic superintendents of public instruction Michigan ever had. He was not the state superintendent at that time, but was living in Lansing, where he was publishing a school newspaper called *Timely Topics*. He also published an orthography text and a civil government of Michigan textbook, as well as the aforementioned *Knapsack,* a collection of songs sung in practically every school in the state. After giving us an inspirational talk, Mr. Pattengill handed out copies of Whittier's poem, the first line of which is:

> Along the roadside like the flowers of gold that tawny Incas
>   for their gardens wrought
> Heavy with sunshine droops the goldenrod, and the red pennons
>   of the cardinal flower hang heavy on their upright staves.

He showed us how to study and then teach such poems to our pupils and get them to understand and see the beauty they portrayed. He instilled in everyone present a desire to go to his classroom and do the best job possible.

The following Tuesday I met my pupils for the first time and began to *practice* teaching. (There were no practice teaching courses offered then.) The classes included first through eighth grades. The hours were the same as in the rural school I had attended and left just five years before. Nothing was different except the building and the fact that I was occupying the teacher's chair. The school was called the Cyclone School because a year or two earlier a tornado had destroyed the old schoolhouse. Fortunately, there was no loss of life, as the pupils had been dismissed for the day a few minutes before the tornado struck.

At the institute in Lapeer the Commissioner had given each of his teachers a course of study which outlined in detail just what was taught in each grade. I followed the instructions carefully. I taught my three "beginners" in reading by the word method, just as I had been taught to read. A little later I tried to get them to help themselves by using phonics.

In arithmetic and "numbers" I remembered how Mr. French had taught the reviews class in mental arithmetic in Davison High. I drilled the second, third, and fourth graders in the combinations and multiplication tables until they knew them as well as I did. The different arithmetic textbooks had mental arithmetic problems which I had the children analyze in precisely the same way Mr. French had taught me. I used this analytical method in teaching addition, multiplication, and division as well as fractions and decimals. I tried to teach them the relationship between what they were learning in school and the problems of everyday living.

I don't know where I got the idea, but in all my reading classes, after a pupil had read a paragraph, I had him close his book and tell in his own words what he had read. With some of the pupils at least, this idea of putting into their own language the thought of the paragraph carried over when they later studied such subjects as history and geography.

Discipline was never one of my problems. To begin with, in my days of rural school teaching, none of the children was over fourteen years of age. Although one or two "tried out" the new teacher in some innocent way, I always put a stop to the first sign of wrongdoing at once, and that ended it.

Because it had been five years since I had studied the subjects I had to teach, except for some reviewing before I took the teachers' examination, I had to prepare each lesson carefully. Perhaps I studied as hard as the pupils. I was learning with the children and my new interest in the subjects may have helped to instill more interest in the boys and girls in my classes.

At noon and recess the children played the same games we played at the Dodge School. Sometimes I played ball, or anti-over, or "pom, pom, pull away" with them. They seemed to enjoy my participating in their games.

I recall that there were only two girls in the eighth grade of my first school and that both passed the eighth grade examination at the end of the year.

This community and the surrounding ones were still only one and a half or two generations away from pioneer days. General farming was still the order of the day. However, there were changes from those earlier days that made life easier and more pleasant. The grain binder, the hay mower, the horse-drawn hay rake, and a ground roller that the farmer could ride had taken much of the drudgery out of his work. He still picked up the bundles of grain and put them in shocks to be pitched onto the wagon by hand, gathered into cocks the hay that had been raked into windrows by the horse-drawn hay rake, and pitched the cocks onto the wagon by hand. Some farmers unloaded the bundles by slings and the hay with horse-drawn forks, but many still used hand forks to pitch the hay into the mows. Threshing the grain was still a neighborhood affair. Men walked behind a one-furrow plow and a one-row cultivator. Cows were milked by hand and stables were cleaned with hand forks.

Social affairs were limited. Once in a while someone gave a party or a square dance. I can remember going to one of the square dances. On the 22nd of February the Smiths, with whom I boarded, took me with them to a dance in Fostoria, a small village two miles north of the schoolhouse. The roads were in a deplorable condition because it was an open winter with no hard freezing. It took two horses to draw the buggy with three passengers, because of the deep mud. People were just beginning to talk about good roads.

I usually went home every two or three weeks. On Friday afternoon I would walk to Columbiaville, a distance of about four miles, where Father would meet me with his horse and buggy. On Sunday evening he would take me back the seven miles to the little town where he picked me up and I would walk the remaining four miles.

Once in a while I would board the "Huckleberry" train to Flint on Saturday and return to Fostoria in the evening. This spur railroad train running from Flint to Fostoria was a combination passenger and freight train. It came to Fostoria in the evening and went back to Flint the next morning. Although supposed to run on schedule, it rarely arrived at its destination on time. It had to pick up or leave freight cars at four or five stations en route. It got the name "Huckleberry" because delicious wild huckleberries grew along the right of way and it was said, probably in jest, that the train would stop so that passengers could get off to pick berries.

A SUMMER JOB

When school was out in late May, I got a job as collector in the Citizens Commercial and Savings Bank in Flint. I do not remember my salary, but it was probably $7.50 per week, just what my salary as a teacher had been. I was also the janitor, doing what I had done at the Genesee County Savings Bank during my high school days. As collector, one task was to take sight drafts, with bills of lading attached, to saloons so that the saloonkeeper could get the merchandise from the freight office. Each afternoon I took to a clearing house all the checks written on the other three banks that our bank had cashed. There I met collectors from the other banks and traded checks written on their banks for checks written on Citizens. Differences in amounts were carried on the books as debits and credits.

Flint River was then a clean little river where one could swim or fish. Pier's Grove was a picnic ground four or five miles up the river from Flint. Small power-driven boats ran excursions from just above the dam near the railroad bridge to this grove. One evening I went with eight or ten of my friends on a boat trip to the grove. Just as the last girl in our party, Mr. Cody's secretary, started to step into the boat, it pulled away from the pier and she fell into the water. Those nearest her tried to grab her but the boat had gone too far away. Without thinking, I jumped into the water and carried her to the boat. The river at this place was only four feet deep, so I was in no danger. However, the girl could not swim and by the time I reached her she was under water. The new suit of clothes I was wearing for the first time had to be cleaned and pressed! The next day she wrote me a letter thanking me for saving her life.

THE BROWN SCHOOL

When I took the job in the bank I had no settled plans for my future. In August, when my mother became very ill, she asked me to get a job teaching in a school near Richfield Center so I could stay at home. I was now an experienced teacher with one full year of "practicing"; I had no trouble getting a job to teach the Brown School, two miles west of our home.

Before I resigned from my job as collector, I wrote to Roy Schumacher of Davison, suggesting that he come to Flint and apply for my job. He applied, was hired, and he, too, later became president of the bank.

In August of 1906, I wrote and passed the teachers' examination for a second-grade certificate. My marks were much better than those of my first teachers' examination because I had learned more by teaching and studying with my pupils than I had in classes as a student before I tried to teach.

I taught the Brown School for two years. The first year my wages were $38 per month, the second year $42. As the methods I had used during my first year of teaching seemed to get good results, I continued to use them at the Brown School. The schoolhouse was almost a duplicate of the one I had attended as a youngster and the one in Lapeer County where I did my first year of teaching. The equipment was practically the same, typical of the rural schools of the period. I had to do the janitorial work. The older boys would help by carrying in the wood and the girls would sometimes help with the sweeping and dusting.

Wherever I taught, I made it a point to let the children know that I trusted them to behave properly whether I was in the room or out of it. They rarely betrayed this trust. One afternoon my sister Addie and my father's sister, Louise Riegle, came to visit the school. When I saw them drive in, I went out to greet them and tie their horse to a hitching post. After greetings, one of them said, "I'll bet your pupils are having a gay time in the schoolhouse!" The windows were covered with shutters that could be raised or lowered. When my visitors were where they could look in, I raised the shutters. Two or three of the children looked up when the light flashed through the shutters, but the rest continued studying just as if I had been inside the room.

Brown School had only eighteen or twenty pupils, with three girls in the sixth grade, no one in the seventh, and one boy, Thomas Lucas, in the eighth. All four were good students. At the end of the year Thomas passed the eighth grade and the three girls were promoted to the eighth grade. One of the three girls was Mattie Van Dyke, who never grew in stature after she was six or seven years old but who had a good mind and learned easily.

At that time the county school commissioner was required by law to visit each school once a year. Mr. Fred Johnson, the commissioner, had taught in Flint High and had succeeded Mr. John Tyler, who was the commissioner when I took my eighth grade examination. It happened that both times Mr. Johnson visited the Brown School I was teaching an arithmetic class in which we were analyzing mental arithmetic problems. Each time he complimented me on the way I was teaching. A few weeks after his second visit, he died suddenly. Horace Potter, who had taught some of my classes in Davison High, was appointed in his place.

Because it was only two miles to the Brown School, I usually walked to school and back, carrying my lunch. By the spring of 1907 I had saved enough money to buy a horse and buggy, a necessary purchase unless one wanted to walk wherever one went. The horse was a bay gelding that weighed about 1,100 pounds—just the right size for a good driving horse. I paid Elias Good, a neighbor, $160 for the horse. The top buggy was secondhand, but nearly new, and cost $40. I drove to the Durant-Dort carriage factory in Flint and traded the iron tire wheels for rubber tires. This was an outfit comparable to a Chevrolet car today. Before I bought Jim, as I named my horse, I borrowed Father's old "Mag" or my brother Fred's "Barney." One advantage a young man had in those days; if he were out a little late at night, he could tie the reins around the whip socket and go to sleep. He would arrive home safely, though the horse might be standing by the barnyard gate when he awoke. After I bought Jim, I could drive to school on stormy days and stable him in an empty barn a few rods from the schoolhouse.

One of the duties, sometimes pleasurable and sometimes disagreeable, of the country school teacher was to visit the homes of his pupils. A generation or two before my time teachers "boarded around" because wages were extremely low and the food and lodging were extra compensation. The length of time in each home spent in visiting depended on the number of children in the family. In my time, however, parents would invite the teacher to come for dinner and stay all night. As guest of honor, the teacher was given a special dinner, or supper as it was then called. Usually this was a pleasant occasion, as the farm women were good cooks as a rule. These visits gave the teacher an opportunity to get acquainted with the parents. This was long before the advent of the PTA.

At the end of my second year at Brown, the three girls who "skipped" the seventh grade passed the eighth grade examination with good marks. Hazel Jennings was one of these girls. She went on to Davison High, then graduated from the one-year county normal course and taught school for several years during my term as commissioner of schools.

CHAPTER X

Teaching in Linden and Montrose

Soon after school was out in the spring of 1908, Horace Potter, who had been my high school principal and was then Genesee School Commissioner, told me of a vacancy in Linden in the job of assistant principal of the high school. At that time Linden had five teachers and eleven grades. To this day I don't know why I did the strange and unwise thing I did. When I went to apply for the position, I took with me another applicant. He was Sterling Wickham, who had graduated with me from Flint High and had been teaching in a rural school. To get to Linden we boarded a train in Flint at nine in the morning, changed trains in Durand, and arrived in Linden about eleven. (Now one can motor there in thirty minutes or less.) We called on the various members of the school board. One of these was Dr. H. D. Knapp, who later became one of my closest friends. Sterling was an imposing-looking young man, six feet tall and weighing one hundred and seventy pounds. I was a mere five feet, six inches tall and weighed about one hundred and forty-five pounds. I was *sure* he would be chosen for the job, but several days later I received a letter from Mr. J. L. Kraft, the principal, saying that I had been chosen. He asked me to come to Linden to make plans for the next year.

Mr. Kraft had a first-grade certificate. When I called on him, he told me he was going to attend Kalamazoo State Normal for the summer term and asked me to go with him. I decided to go. This summer term was my first introduction to a college of any kind. Because I was expected to teach algebra and geometry in Linden, I took courses in these subjects, two classes each daily. Mr. Kraft had been instructed by the school board to prepare a course of study for all the grades in the school. We spent much of our spare time that summer at this task. The resulting curriculum was printed in due time by the *Linden Leader,* the local newspaper, and was used in the school for several years. The summer passed quickly. For recreation I played baseball on the normal school team and learned to play tennis.

When school started in September, I drove my horse from our home in Richfield Center to Linden, a distance of thirty-five miles. After two or three months, I found it too difficult to take care of a horse and sold Jim for the price I had paid for him.

In the 1908-09 Genesee County school directory John L. Kraft was listed as principal, John L. Riegle as assistant principal, Lulu Crane as grammar grades teacher, Carrie Wheaton as second primary teacher, and Iva McCreery as first primary teacher. With the exception of the principal, all the teachers had second-grade certificates. The first primary consisted of the beginners and the first and second grades; the second primary included the third, fourth, and fifth grades. The sixth, seventh, and eighth grades were called the grammar grades.

School was called at 8:45 each morning and ended at four in the afternoon, with two fifteen-minute recesses and an hour for lunch at noon. There were eleven class periods each day. My only free time was the first fifteen minutes in the morning. During the rest of the day I taught eleven classes, of which five were eighth grade, three ninth grade, two tenth grade and one eleventh grade. My salary was $50 per month; the second year it was raised to $52.50.

I found teaching in high school little different from teaching in a one-room school. In the English classes we studied the same classics, wrote themes, and studied the rules of rhetoric just as I had in Flint High School. I followed the same practice as I had in the rural schools of having the pupils read a paragraph and then tell in their own words what they had read. Because all the classes I had were in subjects I had not taught before, but had studied in high school, I spent hours every night preparing for the next day's lesson. Because it had been several years since I had studied these subjects, I believe I brought a freshness to each class that created a deep interest in each pupil. Discipline was never a problem, because the boys and girls were interested in their work. I can still see the students in an ancient history class—sitting on the edge of their seats, eager to recite. Only those boys and girls entered high school who *wanted* an education. It was several years later that a law was passed making it mandatory for children to attend school until they had passed the eighth grade or reached fourteen years of age. Probably not more than 20% of eighth grade graduates from rural schools went on to high school. Those who did go had to travel several miles in some instances to get to a high school. These farm boys and girls knew how to work; they usually had chores to do before and after school, yet very few of them were tardy or absent.

Algebra and geometry were two of the subjects I found easiest to teach. In algebra I used the same analytical method I had used in teaching arithmetic. If there were no oral problems in each division of algebra, I made up some. Perhaps my methods were not orthodox, but my pupils always were interested and they *learned* algebra.

In teaching geometry, I developed a method which I believe could be used by any teacher. First, one pupil would draw on the blackboard the diagram of the theorem to be proved. Another pupil would be asked to give the theorem and then give the proof. The next day another pupil would put the new diagram on the board and another would draw the diagram of the previous day's theorem, then others would give the theorems and proofs. Each day a new theorem would be learned; a new diagram would be put on the board daily, together with all the diagrams of all the theorems we had time to review. In this way we reviewed each theorem and its proof until any member of the class could go to the board, draw a diagram, then challenge any other classmate to give the theorem and proof. They made a game of this. Sometimes they would change the figure, drawing it upside down or making other changes in appearance. As along as the diagram fulfilled all the requirements of the theorem, it became almost impossible to challenge anyone who would fail to give the theorem and proof.

Later I went to the local print shop, purchased some 8-ply white cardboards, size 22 by 28 inches, and bound the sheets into a book with large rings. Each sheet was large enough to hold at least six or eight geometrical figures. The boys in the class then made an easel large enough to hold the cardboard book. Each day we added a new figure; each day we reviewed as many as time permitted. At the end of the year every member of the class could give every theorem in the book and its proof. I did not use the easel and book until my second year in Linden, but the preliminary work was done during the first year.

More than twenty years later John Green, one of the boys in my Linden geometry class, found himself stranded in Florida with no money. He found some children who needed tutoring in geometry, and he had no trouble putting his knowledge of high school geometry to work.

In 1908, organized sports had not come to small high schools. We did have a baseball team and played home-and-home games with one or two neighboring schools. Basketball was just beginning to be played by high school teams. There was a hall downtown large enough for basketball games. I was supposed to be the coach, but I probably knew less than the boys about playing the game, as I had never even seen a game played. We played two out-of-town teams, one at Durand and one at Clio. We could get to Durand by horse-drawn vehicles, but to get to Clio we boarded the evening train to Durand, changed cars in Flint, and from Flint took the interurban streetcar to Clio. After the game, the various members of the Clio team or other townspeople took us to their homes to spend the night. The game was on a Friday night; Saturday morning we returned to Linden by interurban and train. The total distance from Linden to Clio is about forty-five miles.

In the spring of 1909, the high school boys leveled off the schoolyard in front of the schoolhouse to make a tennis court, the first one to be made in Linden. This same year we also put on a play, which I coached, to raise some money for high school athletics.

In all my teaching experience I had no trouble with discipline. My two years in Linden were most pleasant as far as my relations with the pupils were concerned. However, the principal had some shortcomings which kept me in "hot water" most of the time. One day he would tell the students not to do certain things; the next day he would have forgotten what he told them and they would do the forbidden acts without censure. When school was out for the summer, I told the board members I could not work any longer with the principal, giving them my reason. They assured me they would make me principal or superintendent the year following—if I agreed to stay on as assistant principal for one more year. I was then only twenty-three years old and considered too young for the top job.

At that time I had not fully decided to make teaching my life work. During the summer of 1910, I seriously considered the idea of becoming a farmer. However, in April of 1910 I took the examination for a first-grade teacher's certificate, passed the test, and had the certificate endorsed.

MONTROSE

Soon after school closed, Horace Potter, my old high school teacher, told me of a vacancy in the principalship of the Montrose School, a ten-grade school. I applied for this position and received the appointment at a salary of $60 per month. There were four teachers in the school, including the principal. In my third year at Montrose we added the eleventh grade, which necessitated the hiring of a fifth teacher.

My three years as principal of the Montrose School were uneventful. Again, I had no problems of discipline. Most of the pupils were from farm homes. They came to high school because they wanted more than an eighth grade education. One boy, James Grill, lived four miles from the school; he walked those four miles to and from school every day and was never tardy or absent.

From my first day in Montrose, we began to make plans to have a twelve-grade school and arranged the program accordingly. The ninth grade had thirteen or fourteen pupils, but the tenth grade had only three, who were given diplomas at the end of the year. The 1910 ninth grade pupils became eleventh graders in 1912. To prepare for the added grades, new studies had to be added to the course of study, new books to the library, and plans for a laboratory had to be made. Geometry and Latin were two of the new subjects when the eleventh grade was added. Geometry posed no problem, as I had taught it in Linden for two years. Latin was a different matter. The new teacher hired to assist in the high school had never studied Latin; it was up to me to teach this subject because I was the only one on the staff who had ever studied Latin. In Flint High, I had two years of the language under Miss Henrietta Lewis, an old-fashioned task master and an effective teacher. Somehow I "got by" in teaching Latin by studying the lesson carefully for the next day. These boys and girls had been well drilled in English grammar, a fact which helped them in learning Latin. Incidentally, this was my only attempt at teaching a foreign language.

In Montrose we had no organized sports. There were never enough boys who wanted to play baseball in high school to make up a team.

When my contract with the Montrose district ended in June of 1913, the Board of Education hired Omar Potter to take my place. Omar was a younger brother of my old friend and teacher Horace Potter. (Years later in Flint, Omar and his wife Grace were my next-door neighbors and intimate friends.)

The end of the school year of 1912-13 had come quickly and it brought me a big personal problem. Word had come to me that I would be named the superintendent of schools in Linden if I wanted the job. I wanted the job, but I was not eligible because of a new law that had just been passed by the Michigan legislature. This law required the superintendent to have a life certificate if his faculty numbered six or more, including the superintendent. I was then teaching on a first-grade certificate. Up to this time I had not given much thought to getting more education.

To secure a life certificate in a hurry, my only recourse was to take a state examination in nineteen subjects. If I averaged 85% on this examination I would be granted a life certificate. Although there were choices of courses in one or two instances, there were several subjects, such as geology and zoology, that I had not studied in high school. I wasn't afraid of the common subjects and those I had been teaching, such as algebra, geometry, botany, and general history. There was a choice between physics and chemistry, both of which I had taken in high school but had never taught. My choice was physics.

Besides my teaching at least eight classes a day at Montrose, I had my duties as superintendent and as a member of the county board of examiners. This board consisted of three members: the county commissioner of schools and two members appointed by the county board of supervisors for a two-year staggered term. This board conducted two teachers' examinations and one county-wide eighth grade examination. The teachers' examinations were held in the courthouse in August and April. The eighth grade examinations were held in all the high schools of the county, with the superintendents of the various schools acting as examiners. The superintendents of twelve-grade schools could promote their own eighth grade graduates with an examination, but they often urged their pupils to take the regular state examination to test their pupils against the rest of the county. The examination in reading was based on a classic of literature designated by the State Superintendent of Public Instruction.

The county commissioner of schools also held an eighth grade examination in the courthouse for those pupils who lived in districts near Flint in which there was no high school.

The examiners were paid on a per diem basis. Each examiner took certain subjects and marked all the papers written on those subjects. There were from 300 to 350 eighth graders each year, and about an equal number of seventh graders who took examinations in physiology and geography. If the seventh graders passed in one or both of these subjects, their marks were carried over until the next year. Marking all those test papers was a tedious job.

A State Life Certificate

When school began in the fall of 1912, I dug out my old high school textbooks, bought new texts in geology and zoology, and began serious study for the state examination for a life certificate, held in March. This year was probably one of the busiest of my life, but when March came I was fairly well prepared.

The examination, which lasted five days, was held in the Capitol in Lansing. To get to Lansing, I boarded a train in Montrose at nine on Monday morning, changed cars in Durand, and reached Lansing about eleven o'clock. The examination began at 1 p.m. It was conducted by the State Superintendent of Public Instruction, Mr. Luther Wright, and his assistant.

This examination meant a great deal to me. I felt I *had* to pass it, as I had given my word to the Linden school board that I would take the job as superintendent the next year. Monday night I was nervous and had a restless night. I was tired on Tuesday, but managed to get through the day's work without much trouble. Tuesday night was worse than Monday night and I got less sleep. Wednesday was a difficult day but I managed to do fairly well in the tests.

I was rooming at the Kern Hotel with an older friend, Lee Russell, who was the superintendent of a school not far from Montrose. He also had to have a life certificate because his school had six teachers. He realized that I had to relax or I would not be able to finish the examination! Wednesday night he took me to a vaudeville show. The show happened to be really funny; I relaxed and laughed heartily until it ended. That night I slept like a baby. The examination the next day went off very well for me, thanks to my friend's insight.

Because we could finish the examination in August, I did not take the test in physics. The next summer I went to summer school in Ypsilanti, where I took a course in physics and one in psychology. In August I took the examination in physics and rewrote the examination in three or four other subjects in which my previous marks were rather low. My marks on the two examination averaged 93% and I was given a life certificate. I might add that this was not the easy way to secure a life certificate.

My last salary in Montrose as principal was $65 per month. My Linden contract as superintendent gave me $80 per month for ten months.

As soon as school was out in June 1913, we moved our household goods to Linden by freight, a distance of about 35 miles from Montrose. We rented a small five-room cobblestone house which still stands on North Linden Street.

I attended summer school that summer for two reasons; first, because I had to pass the examination in physics in August and second, because I had to teach the subject in September when school started. The instructor in physics was Professor Gorton, an excellent teacher. He had published a manual in which he showed how the experimental work in proving the laws of physics could be done with homemade material and how the equipment for performing the experiments could be made.

One of my first acquaintances that summer was Wilford L. Coffey, the commissioner of schools in Cheboygan County, who later became State Superintendent of Public Instruction. Because the rooming house where I was staying was so noisy I couldn't study, I moved, at his invitation, into his room after the first week. Our friendship lasted until his death some thirty years later.

Another friend I made was Roy Noteware, commissioner of schools of Mecosta County. He later became Deputy Superintendent of Public Instruction.

SUPERINTENDENT IN LINDEN

During the three years I had been away from Linden, affairs had not been going well in the high school. Rumors reached me of stunts and tricks by the pupils and dissention among the teachers. Before school opened, I had two nightmares in which I punished every one of the high school pupils. However, during my subsequent year and two months there, the only mischievous act I saw was done by a lively boy who later became a good dentist. He threw a paper dart across the classroom!

When the students told Miss Osee Jewel, their language teacher who was also assistant principal, of the stunts they had done the previous year, she said she couldn't believe such well-behaved young people could ever have done the tricks they claimed to have performed. Incidentally, Miss Jewel was the first teacher in Linden who possessed a certificate from the University of Michigan.

Of the five teachers on my staff, none were holdovers. Carrie Wertman, Nellie Hogan and Mildred Curtis had been in my classes in Linden when I was there from 1908 to 1910. Three others of that vintage taught in nearby country schools, as teaching was then one of the few jobs open to high school graduates.

Even though I was the superintendent, I taught a full schedule of classes, mainly in mathematics and science. It was this year that my tenth grade geometry class excelled, as told earlier. We were supposed to offer solid geometry in the first semester of the eleventh grade. This class consisted of three girls. I soon found that their plane geometry preparation had been so poor they could not do solid geometry the first semester. We spent the first semester in reviewing plane geometry and then, in the second semester, took up solid geometry, with which they had no trouble.

My first experience as a physics teacher was most satisfactory to me. The only equipment we had to start with was a Magdeberg sphere, a set of balances, and an air pump. The school board gave us a small appropriation to buy some equipment and the materials needed to make items described in Professor Gorton's manual. The members of the class became enthusiastic and greatly enjoyed this study of physics.

In a way, I was sorry to leave Linden. The school board did everything for the school that I requested. When I wanted something, I would talk matters over with each member separately; when they held a meeting they gave me what I wanted for the school. Everything we did seemed to work for the betterment of the school. For example, the pupils' desks in the high school were old and badly scarred. One day one of the ninth grade girls scratched her name on the top of her desk with a pin. When I saw this, I got out some sandpaper and made her sand the desk top until her name was obliterated. She didn't like to do this, but when the desk top was smooth and clean, I bought a can of varnish and a brush and varnished it. She then had the best-looking desk in the room. Within a few days nearly all the pupils sandpapered their desks and varnished them. From that time on, no new scratches were put on any desk. However, a few of the desks were so badly battered they could not be renovated. When the school board learned what had been done, they bought new desks for the high school so that all the pupils could have uniformly good-looking desks.

This school year passed quickly. Looking back, I think it was the most enjoyable of all my years of teaching.

I attended Ypsilanti Normal School for the 1914 summer term. This was necessary because I would have to teach chemistry when school began in September. The year 1914 saw the beginnings of great changes. World War I broke out in August; the world has never been the same since that fateful year.

For the 1914-15 school year the Linden school board added the twelfth grade to the high school and a seventh teacher to our staff. Zoe Spencer, a Linden girl who had been teaching in another school and who was a normal school graduate, came home to be our principal. She was an excellent teacher. Two other changes in the staff were made: Mae

Woodmansee, a normal school graduate, took the place of Mildred Curtis and Jessie Woolsey, also a normal school graduate, replaced Osee Jewel.

The class I had had in physics the previous year now studied chemistry. We had to improvise our own furniture and laboratory equipment, although the school board did furnish the funds to buy the chemicals we needed. This class started out well, but I was not destined to finish the year with them.

A New Door Opens

A few weeks after school opened, I received a letter from Horace Potter, my old teacher and mentor, asking me to come to Flint for a conference as soon as possible. I took the train to Flint to see him the next Saturday. He told me that he was going to resign as commissioner of schools of Genesee County to take a position as assistant cashier in the Citizens Commercial and Savings Bank in Flint. He wanted me to try to get the appointment to finish his term, which had about eight more months to run. This appointment had to be made by the county board of supervisors when they met in October. There were twenty-four members on this board, one from each township and one from each of the six wards of the City of Flint. I knew only a few of these members, including John Howe of Burton Township, Harry Potter of Davison, John Jennings of Fenton, John Johnson of Montrose, Charles Blackinton of Flint (father of a classmate of mine at Flint High) and Elmer Wheeler of Richfield.

There remained only two or three weeks for me to campaign for the appointment. I called on as many of the supervisors as I could and wrote letters to the others. When the day of appointment came, there were three other candidates: John Chapel, superintendent of Clio schools; Ed Mears, principal of Goodrich school; and John Rieman, the ex-superintendent of a school in Illinois who was then living on a farm in Burton Township. On the first ballot I received 11 votes, Chapel got 7 and 3 each went to the other two men. On the second ballot my total slipped to 8; Mr. Chapel received 11. I concluded that my chances of getting the appointment were ended. I reached over, shook Mr. Chapel's hand and congratulated him. However, on the third ballot I received 13 votes, a majority, while Mr. Chapel had only 7.

Before I left Linden, I wrote the University of Michigan, asking that an examiner be sent to our high school. He came, and shortly after I left, Linden High became an accredited high school.

When I resigned, the board hired Mr. A. J. Flint, a very good school man, to take my place.

CHAPTER XI

Educational Changes,
1900-1914

The years between 1900, when I entered high school, and 1914, when I was appointed commissioner of schools in Genesee County, had brought many changes in education to our county and to Michigan. In 1905, there were only two schools in the county, Flint and Fenton, with twelve grades. By 1913 Davison, Flushing, and Clio had been added to this list; within another year Montrose and Linden were added, with Mount Morris shortly afterwards.

In 1905, there were only four teachers outside Flint with two-year normal school life certificates and one with a university degree teaching in Genesee County. In 1913-14, there were twenty-four with life certificates, of which twenty were normal, two university, and two state life certificates. There were also nine normal school graduates who were given limited certificates; that is, after three years of successful teaching they were to be given life certificates.

In 1903, when Fred J. Johnson was county school commissioner, two consolidated schools were organized in the county. Two districts were joined to the Grand Blanc village district to form a consolidated school, and in Mount Morris one district was joined to the Mount Morris district.

The first county normal class organized in Genesee County was in 1907. Twenty pupils were enrolled. Katherine Schoenhals was the first director or principal. Minnie Oliff was the first critic teacher or assistant to the director. The first normal board was composed of Mr. Luther

Wright, state superintendent of public instruction; Mr. Alvin N. Cody, Flint city superintendent; and Mr. Fred J. Johnson, the Genesee County commissioner of schools.

The qualifications for admission to the county normal training classes were: (1) all applicants had to be seventeen years old; (2) applicants had to be either graduates of a ten-grade school, holders of a second-grade certificate, or have had two years of successful teaching experience. By 1913 this rule had been amended to read that applicants were required to have passed the eleventh grade or be holders of second-grade certificates, or have had two years of successful teaching experience.

The Genesee County normal school was discontinued in 1932. During the years it functioned it did a great job at elevating the quality of teachers in the county. During my term as commissioner, Ellen Anderson, Florence Colling, Ann Wiggins and Bess Penoyer, all dedicated to their profession, served as principal of the school.

The Michigan legislature of 1909 passed several laws that had far-reaching results. One stipulated that the school board of any school district which did not maintain a high school was required to vote a tax to pay the tuition to one of the three nearest high schools for children who had completed the studies of the eight grades, the amount not to exceed $20 per pupil per year. The parents of such children had to notify the board of education on or before the first Monday of June as to which high school the children chose to attend. This law immediately increased attendance at all high schools.

Another law specified that districts with 400 or more pupils had to maintain at least nine months of school. Districts with less than 400 pupils but over 30 had to maintain at least eight months, and all others not less than five months. I knew of no district in Genesee County that had less than eight months. Nearly all had nine months and all graded schools had ten. A third law passed read, "The district at any annual meeting may vote to close the school and pay the tuition and transportation to any neighboring school." This law may have had beneficial results on consolidation, because when a few schools did close, people learned that transporting school children was feasible.

Another law was passed providing for the organization of township unit districts by a majority vote of the qualified voters of a township. This law was used extensively in the Upper Peninsula, where county and townships were in the process of organizing. It was seldom used in lower Michigan. However, Grand Blanc township adopted this form of organization in 1921 and Montrose township in 1946 when Mr. John Carter was superintendent of schools in Montrose.

An interesting relic of early Michigan school history was the township board of school inspectors. This board consisted of three members, two of whom were elected at the annual township meeting. The township clerk was the third member, ex officio. The only power that remained to this board was to divide or consolidate school districts upon the consent of a majority of the resident taxpayers of each district. These boards of school inspectors were legislated out of existence when Michigan adopted a new constitution in 1909. The last listing of names of school inspectors in a Genesee County school directory is in the one for 1907-08.

The legislature of 1907 passed a law which provided that a county could establish a county school of agriculture which would give courses concerning the soil, plant and animal life of the farm, a system of farm accounting, and instruction in manual training and domestic science. No such schools were established in Genesee County nor, as far as I know, in any other county in Michigan. This law, however, may have contained the germ that sprouted into the Rural Agricultural School Act of 1917.

The school directory of 1913-14 gives some interesting information. In Fenton the corps of teachers, including the superintendent, was seventeen; Flushing had eight teachers; Clio and Davison each had seven; and Linden had six. These schools had principals of the high schools and all were four-year high schools. Montrose, Mount Morris and Otisville each had five teachers. Grand Blanc, Gaines and Goodrich each had four teachers and Swartz Creek had only three. These last seven schools had only ten grades and at the head of these schools was a principal, with an assistant. We added the eleventh grade in Montrose in 1912, as mentioned earlier, and in 1914 the first twelfth grade class graduated.

A New Era

Upon my appointment to the county office in October of 1914, we immediately moved to Flint to a rented house on West Fourth Avenue. A new era had begun for me. Perhaps it was also the beginning of a new era for the United States. I was born about the end of the pioneering era. The years from 1875 to 1890 have been called the "home building years," for it was during these years that the log cabins of the pioneers were replaced by modern houses with six, eight, or even twelve rooms. The lumbering off of the pine forests of northern Michigan and Wisconsin produced cheap lumber for the farmers' homes and the people who were building the cities. During these years, laborsaving machinery, such as the self-binding grain binder, the mowing machine, the horse-drawn hay rake, the steam engine grain threshing machine, and other devices had made it possible for farmers to increase the size of their farms and do their farming with less labor. The surplus labor supply was moving to the cities to work in the factories that were making the new farm machinery. The farmers also had more money to buy luxuries—organs, pianos, buggies.

It was during the early '80s that W. C. Durant started his road cart factory in Flint. This business grew into the Durant-Dort Carriage factory, one of the largest carriage factories in the world.

The spinning wheel had been replaced by woolen mills, although I can remember seeing Rebecca Amidon, a neighbor, spinning yarn to be used for knitting stockings for her children and grandchildren. A woolen mill to weave blankets and cloth was started in Columbiaville sometime during the seventies.

Notwithstanding all these changes, America was still made up of self-contained and self-centered communities. Men gathered around the cracker barrel in the neighborhood store; social life centered around the local church, the Grange, or the Gleaners. Young men married a school sweetheart or a girl from a neighboring school district. Once in a while a medicine show came to a town or someone showed pictures with a "Magic Lantern," the forerunner of motion pictures. The medicine show was a tent show put on by a seller of patent medicine. He brought along several vaudeville acts, but before, between, and after the show he urged his audience to buy his medicine, guaranteed to cure all human ills.

To visit a county fair or a Barnum and Bailey Circus at the county seat was an event long anticipated and carefully planned.

Until the turn of the century a high school education was out of the reach of the average country boy or girl. An itinerant music teacher gave music lessons to the farmer's wife or daughters on the organ or piano for 50 cents a lesson. Seth Knapp was such a teacher, who made his rounds with a horse and buckboard.

Pack peddlers wandered through the countryside with their offerings of yard goods, ribbons and thread. The tin peddler made regular visits to trade tinware for wood ashes to be used to make soap in a soap factory. Sometimes the pack peddler was replaced by a peddler owning a horse-drawn wagon. Hymie Winegarden, who with his brother started the New Orleans Fruit House, as well as other businesses in Flint, got his start in this way.

During the summer months, when farmers were too busy to drive to town, the village meat market man made regular weekly trips with fresh meat, and the village grocer made the rounds with a wagon loaded with groceries. In some communities the Atlantic and Pacific Tea Company sent out salesmen to sell its tea and coffee. They mounted a boxlike body, just large enough to hold the driver and his wares, on a buckboard frame and filled it with an assortment of teas, coffee and spices.

After the turn of the century, when free mail delivery was started, the mail carriers used the same kind of vehicle.

In 1893, a severe depression hit the nation. This depression was blamed on the Democrats because Cleveland, a Democrat president, occupied the White House. Expansion in the cities and on the farms was halted for several years. Business began to improve when McKinley was elected president. The Spanish-American War was fought in 1898, which probably helped to stimulate business. When the "boys came home" from following "Teddy" Roosevelt up San Juan Hill, they may have helped the start of the lifting of horizons of self-centered America.

The beginning of the twentieth century brought many changes to the United States. In the late '90s, electric railroads began to connect cities. By 1902 people could board a trolley car in Flint in the morning, get to Detroit in an hour or two, transact their business and arrive back in Flint for dinner, or supper, as it was then called.

The Buick automobile factory came to Flint in October of 1903. By 1905 Flint was a boom town. Automobiles caused a demand for good roads, which in turn caused more people to want to own cars. Indeed, the first ten or twelve years of the new century brought many changes into our lives; I have mentioned some that came to our schools.

World War I began in August 1914. This was a world-shattering event. To this day no one can predict what will happen because of the conflict of ideologies that were then loosed upon the world.

And so I came to Flint at the beginning of a new era. We did not realize it at the time, but the world of my childhood was fast disappearing.

Serving as County Commissioner of Schools

Upon entering my new office, my first task was to learn just what my duties were. I had been a member of the county board of examiners for several years, so I knew all about teachers' examinations and eighth grade examinations. The school laws were explicit in only a few matters. One of these was that the county commissioner was to visit each schoolroom in the county at least once a year. On this visit he was to see if the necessary aids to teaching were in the school. According to a school directory published in 1913, these aids were: a large dictionary, a set of school maps, a globe, a case for library books, a water tank, a comb, a towel, washbasin and mirror. Rarely did I find any of these items missing from a school.

The school law expressly said that on each visit the commissioner had to inspect the toilets. In meetings of the school commissioners we facetiously called each other the "official toilet inspector," as that was the only duty the law definitely stated as ours. The law read that if we found any toilet building not up to standard, we were to notify the school director and demand that he clean the building and make the necessary repairs. If he failed to do as directed, we had the authority to hire the work done and add the cost to the district taxes. Only once in my nine years as commissioner did I have to resort to this extreme measure.

My office was a room about twelve feet square on the second floor in the southwest corner of the courthouse. Besides my initial salary of $1,500 per year, all my traveling expenses were paid upon presentation of bills to the county board of supervisors. At the beginning of my first full term my salary was increased to $2,000 per year, plus traveling expenses.

My predecessor had made it a custom to keep the office open on Saturday and I continued this practice. Keeping the office open on Saturday enabled the teachers who had problems to tell me about them in my office; and the rural school teachers always had plenty of problems.

At that time a county commissioner of schools was allowed $400 a year for clerical help. My wife served as clerk. During the first three years in office, she kept the office open every afternoon when I was out visiting schools. During the latter part of my term, the office force consisted of one clerk, Mr. William E. Hamilton, who also served as truant officer. My gross budget did not exceed $3,500 plus necessary traveling expenses, which were considered on a mileage basis of 10 cents a mile for actual miles traveled.

With some trepidation I decided to make my first school visit a call on the Blair school in Fenton township, where John Crane was the teacher. John had been in the eighth grade when I first went to teach in Linden in 1908. There were two ways to get to the Blair school: one was to hire a livery rig in Flint and drive to the school; the other was to go on the train to Linden, via Durand, then drive to the school with a livery rig rented in Linden. I chose the second way. I do not remember much about this visit, except that John had good discipline and seemed to be doing a good job of teaching. I always found that if a teacher were a good disciplinarian the pupils would be working and learning. I probably visited another school that same day, stayed at the hotel overnight, and visited three or more schools in the vicinity the following day. That is the way I covered the corner townships, Fenton and Montrose.

When I went to call on the schools in Forest township, I hired a livery rig in Flint, visited three or four schools on the way to Otisville, then stayed all night there in the hotel. The next day I would visit several other schools on the return trip to Flint.

There were about twelve schools within a mile or two of the interurban trolley lines. These lines connected Flint with Saginaw to the north and with Detroit to the south. The local cars stopped at every crossroad. In those days a walk of a mile or two was commonplace.

There were 152 districts in Genesee County, with 225 teachers. Of these districts, 139 had one-room schools. I spent as much of my time as possible in these one-room schools. The visits to the village schools were short and perfunctory.

One wonders how much good could be accomplished by a visit of an hour and a half or two hours. After entering a schoolroom and being received by the teacher, I tried to make myself as inconspicuous as possible. Sometimes I would sit in the teacher's chair, but usually I sat in a vacant seat in the back of the room. I always checked to see if the necessary teaching aids listed earlier were present and in good condition. If any of the required items were missing, I made notes and later wrote to the director, calling to his attention the law which required him to buy such articles for the school.

Sometimes I would ask a teacher if there were any children who did not read library books. If there were a few, I would go to the bookcase, choose books suitable for their age and grade, talk to them about the books and try to get them interested in reading. Teachers later told me that this often resulted, for those children, in a new interest in reading library books.

I tried to interest the eighth graders in going on to high school if they passed the eighth grade examination. That this encouragement did some good I have had reliable proof. Forty years later I visited a farmer who lived in Genesee township, a mile from the Kiwanis Health Camp, to hire him to plow the camp garden plot. He asked me if I were the Mr. Riegle who had been school commissioner. When I told him I was, he made a remark which made me realize that some of my work was worthwhile. He said, "When I passed the eighth grade examination, you had me all pepped up to go to high school, but my dad wouldn't let me go." I shall never forget the wistful way he said it.

I always felt that if a teacher had good discipline she was doing a good job. A pat on the back with a word of praise was about all I could do to encourage her. If the discipline were poor, I gave suggestions for tightening the reins, then usually followed up with a second visit within the next few weeks to see if she had carried out my suggestions. Sometimes one visit to a school was enough; sometimes it took two or three.

Occasionally a teacher had to be replaced. However, during my term of office this happened only three times.

We always held a teachers' institute on the last Saturday before schools opened in the fall. At this meeting, attendance registers, class record books, Michigan course of study, and other supplies were given out, as well as report cards, attendance certificates, and library lists. In my instructions to the teachers, I always stressed the fact that on the first day of school the teacher was in command. The pupils expected her to be in command and would respect her if she remained in command. The quickest way to lose the respect of the children was to let them disobey and "get away" with it.

At the turn of the century, very few of the one-room schools had a library. However, soon after, the law was changed. School districts were allowed to establish district libraries, the funds to support them to come from penal fines collected in county courts. By 1914, all the districts had voted to establish libraries. The money was distributed according to the number of children in the school census.

In 1910, Genesee County adopted local option. Under this option, the people voted to close all saloons in the county and stop the sale of intoxicating liquor in the county. In a short time the fines from liquor law violations amounted to $1 or more per pupil.

YOUNG PEOPLE'S READING CIRCLE

Michigan had a Young People's Reading Circle Board which consisted of three members chosen at the annual meeting of the Michigan Education Association. This board reviewed all the better books for children published during the preceding year and added to the approved list fifty new books each year. The board had a manager in Lansing who kept an office where all the approved books could be bought. For several years the manager was E. T. Cameron, who had been commissioner of schools in Isabella County. I was a member of this board for the last three years I was in office. To make it more convenient for Genesee County schools, I gave the M. E. Carlton Company of Flint a list of the books approved each year. These books were kept in stock at the Flint store and sold at the same price as was charged by Mr. Cameron.

Then, as now, the annual census had to be taken during the last two weeks of May. This school census was taken on sheets furnished by the Department of Public Instruction. On one side was the school census; on the other side was the financial report of the district. After the director took the census and made out the financial report, he sent it to the township clerk, who was supposed to audit the report and check the census. Most of the clerks did a good job of checking, but a few just bundled them up without checking and sent them to me. Certain parts of these reports had to be sent to the office of the Superintendent of Public Instruction. Every year several of these reports were so poorly made that I had to take them back to the director who made them and audit his books.

Each district had three funds which could be used for specific purposes only. The library fund could be used only for the purchase of library books and the one-mill tax and primary interest fund for teachers' salaries only. The last two funds caused me little trouble, because teachers' salaries were being raised and most districts had to raise additional funds to pay them. However, the library fund had to be checked very carefully. Each year I would ask the teachers for a list of the books purchased during the year. I would then check this list against the director's report. On several occasions directors cheated. When this happened, I had the teacher make up a list of books suitable for her school library and then made the director buy them.

When all the reports were corrected and my report made to Lansing, I had them bound in a book with hard covers. Unfortunately the reports for my nine years in office were destroyed when the courthouse burned in March 1923.

In 1907, the state legislature passed a law that provided for the establishment of township high schools by a vote of a majority of the taxpayers of the township. In 1909, Mundy township voted to have such a school. Walter Allen was the first instructor. The high school was held in a room in a house in the small village of Rankin. The 1914-15 county school directory describes the course of study as follows, "The course of study, which includes the ninth and tenth grades, emphasizes the industrial side of education together with such academic high school training as will give a liberal English education to the young people." This Rankin high school died a natural death at the end of the 1914-15 school year because it had no community support and very few pupils. When I made my one and only visit to the school, I could see it had no future. Its physical surroundings were unattractive. It had no library, no laboratory equipment, nor any features that made it look like a school. It had had three teachers in its six years of existence and its enrollment had never exceeded eight or ten pupils. The last instructor had only a third grade certificate. No one mourned its demise.

TEACHER EXAMINATIONS

Teacher examinations for first, second, and third grade certificates were held on the last Thursday and Friday in April and the second Thursday and Friday in August each year. The examination in reading was based on a classic chosen by the Superintendent of Public Instruction. In April of 1915 the classic was *The House of Seven Gables* by Hawthorne and in August it was *The American Scholar* by Ralph Waldo Emerson. That year 35 third grade and 19 second grade certificates were granted. There were also 25 county normal school graduates that year. As I have pointed out earlier, the county normal did a fine job of raising teaching standards in our county.

For several years prior to 1915, attendance at summer school was one of the requirements for the renewal of a first or second grade certificate. No mention was made of credits to be earned, so to fulfill the requirements, a teacher could attend a week or two at summer school and observe in certain classes. In 1915 our board of school examiners changed this requirement to read "attend summer school and earn two credits." This rule caused comments and complaints; however, the final results were good. Several teachers who had been content to teach on a second grade certificate began to earn three credits in a summer.

Kalamazoo Normal School, now called Western Michigan University, gave in absentia life certificates. That is, if a teacher earned twelve credits in residence and twelve credits by correspondence, he could earn a life certificate. This could be accomplished in three years.

One teacher who had been teaching for fifteen or twenty years and was the principal of Otisville, teaching on a first grade certificate, was most indignant when the credit rule was made. He remarked, "That little whippersnapper Riegle can't tell me what I must do!" However, he complied with the rule and attended summer school in Kalamazoo in 1915. In three years he obtained his life certificate. After earning this certificate, he said to me, "John, if someone had kicked me out twenty years ago I would be somewhere today." Soon after he said this, he became superintendent at Hazel Park. Shortly afterwards he was killed in an automobile accident while driving to his summer home in Otisville.

CHAPTER XIII

The Challenge of the Job

4-H CLUBS

In 1914, my predecessor organized the first corn clubs. In November of 1914, I held the first corn show at the YMCA in Flint. In 1916, I organized the first potato clubs. In 1917, canning and sewing clubs were started. The canning clubs were a war measure. At my request, the home economics department of Michigan State University, then called the Michigan Agricultural College, sent helpers to organize these clubs. For the sewing clubs they sent a woman, whom I would take to three or four schools in one day so that she might organize the girls' clubs. For the canning clubs they sent Mr. E. C. Lindeman. He brought along an ordinary boiler used in boiling clothes and a two-burner gasoline stove. It was in the autumn and the pupils had prepared for our visit by bringing sweet corn and other foods that could be canned by the cold pack method.

Years later Mr. Sheldon H. LaTourette wrote a *History of Agricultural Extension Work in Genesee County, Michigan,* in which he stated:

> The real roots from which grew the permanent program of Extension Service are associated with a human interest story that is worth preserving. Starting in 1914, the office of school commissioner in Genesee County was held for a decade by a boy with a good education and a real vision of high standards in farm life. Besides taking care of the many details connected with his job from his small office in the old courthouse, and with only a part-time office girl, he found time to help promote the first consolidated high schools in this county which were also among the first organized in the state. Recognizing the need for organized work among farm boys and girls, as early as 1916 he started the first 4-H clubs in the

county. Some individuals who now have a state-wide and nation-wide reputation used to drive with him over miles of county dirt roads from one community to another helping establish and follow-ing up the work of canning clubs, clothing clubs, and corn clubs. Such men as Dr. E. C. Lindeman, Ray Turner, and Extension Di-rector R. J. Baldwin were among the aforementioned passengers. This school commissioner, now a successful Flint businessman, has never lost his love for and interest in the open country. His name is John L. Riegle, and he well deserves this tribute.

Year after year he witnessed the struggles to secure adequate finan-cial support for the Extension program at the annual meeting of the Board of Supervisors. In the fall of 1918, when our county had been without the services of a County Agent for a year, he sensed the need felt by many of our farm folks for such services, and the probable support for an Agent from the Supervisors. He wrote over to the College to the Director of Extension and asked him to bring over a likely candidate. Mr. Baldwin brought over Sidney Smith, who was hired and spent the next eight years in a strenuous program for the farm folks in the county.

My appointment as commissioner of schools in October 1914 was for eight months only, as Mr. Potter's term expired June 30, 1915. Soon after I took office, Mr. Byron Jennings, secretary of the Clio school board, visited my office to talk about the Clio superintendent. It seems that the superintendent was a good teacher, well liked by his pupils, but not a good disciplinarian. This put me in a difficult position, for the superin-tendent had been a candidate when I was appointed commissioner and was planning to run on the Democratic ticket at the coming April election, seeking my office. Soon after my talk with Mr. Jennings, I made an official visit to the Clio school and decided that he was correct in his complaints. I explained my position to him, because, in fact, I had no authority to do anything about the situation. At the April election, I won in all the pre-cincts in Flint and in all the townships except three.

My opponent had a three-year contract with the Clio school board. It was not a binding contract with the board but one which had to be renewed each year. Soon after the election the board met and refused to renew the contract. The superintendent resigned immediately. The pupils staged a strike and remained out of school for several days. There was a great commotion in the village and big headlines in the *Flint Journal.*

These headlines carried the implication that politics were at the bottom of the whole matter and that I was the root of the evil. The board immediately hired W. D. White, a very good school man, who was in retirement. He was an educator of the old school who believed that children went to school to study and learn. It took him only a few days to get the school settled down and back to the business of studying. Mr. White stayed in Clio for three years and when he left the school was in excellent condition.

In the spring of 1915, the year of the election to my first full term, I had a most disturbing experience. A young man who was teaching the grammar grades in a certain school came to me to report that stories were being told by some of the boys in the high school that the superintendent was practicing homosexuality with them on athletic trips. Immediately I visited the superintendent and talked with him about the charges. He denied the charges, but made one admission that caused me to believe the stories to be true. The next day I took the train to Lansing to discuss the problem with Mr. Luther Wright, the superintendent of public instruction. He advised that because it was only four or five weeks before the closing of school for the summer, we take no action in the matter. He further advised that I make the man promise that he would never teach school again if we took no action against him. When I went back to the teacher under suspicion, he gave me his promise that he would do what I asked of him. Later I heard that after school was out he got a job at the Ford Motor Company. However, several years later I received a letter from a school board secretary in western Michigan asking me "as a man and a Mason" if I could reccomend that man for a teaching job in their school. My reply was, "As a man and a Mason I cannot recommend him for such a position." That was the last I ever heard of him. This was my first and last encounter with a problem of this nature.

In April 1915, I bought my first automobile, a Ford sedan. It had a top with detachable side curtains, electric headlights, with the electricity for ignition sparks and for headlights being generated by a magneto. It was started with a crank in the front end. If a puncture or a flat tire occurred, I had to put a jack under the axle, raise the wheel, remove the tire so as to remove the inner tube and patch it. Every driver carried a patching kit in his car, together with tire iron, an air pump and a jack. If all went well, I got the tire back on the rim and pumped it up. Great care had to be taken to avoid punching a hole in the tube with a tire iron. If lucky, I could repair a puncture in thirty minutes. If a tire lasted for 1,000 miles without a puncture or 3,000 miles before wearing out, that was something to brag about. Tire chains were always carried in the car because getting stuck in the deep mud or sand was a common occurrence.

Soon after I bought my car, Mr. Wilford Coffey, assistant superintendent of public instruction, came to Flint and asked me to take him to Fostoria, a town about thirty miles from Flint. We left town about noon. Somewhere along the way we stopped to put on the tire chains. Everything went smoothly until we reached a clay hill just outside Fostoria. With Wilford's pushing and my driving, we managed to get up the hill. It took Mr. Coffey about an hour to audit the treasurer's books, which was his errand in Fostoria. We started home by a different route, first driving west because we wanted to avoid another encounter with that clay hill to the south. We came to a very muddy place in the road. When Wilford got out to push again, he noticed that one chain was missing. We surmised that it had been lost in the mud of the clay hill. Returning to the hill, we found the chain, replaced it on the tire, and finally reached Flint a full ten hours after we left for Fostoria that noon. Such were the joys of early motoring!

Before the next winter came, I had a custom-made top to replace the original one. The new top had isinglass (mica) doors that could be raised and lowered at will, a vast improvement over the old side curtains. Before I bought my second car, Ford was making cars with enclosed bodies with doors and windows of real glass. In all, I bought four Ford cars.

Because it was difficult to figure expenses on a car with no speedometer, the board of supervisors allowed me $400 per year for car expense.

A school commissioner had many demands on his spare time. He was expected to take an active interest in such activities as grange meetings, school picnics and socials, as well as to attend school board meetings when such matters as building new schoolhouses or altering the present ones to make the "standard" schools were to be discussed. I took these events in stride and indeed found many of them interesting.

I tried in many ways to be helpful to the country schools by doing things that would create in the children a greater interest in their school work. During the autumn days, while driving from one school to another, I would pass a clump of sassafras or other bushes on which the larva of moths, the prometha or polythemus or other moths or butterflies fed. Often I would stop to find cocoons which had been spun by the larvae of these moths. I would take these cocoons to a school and give the children a nature study lesson, explaining how these cocoons were made by the worm or larva of the moths which would change from the larva and emerge from the cocoon in the spring. I told how this moth would then lay eggs which would hatch into worms in a regular yearly cycle. This little talk never failed to arouse in the children an interest in nature study.

Often I would visit a school where the physical conditions of the buildings made it appear that no one cared how the school property was maintained. I would then ask the boys and girls, "Whose school is this?" The looks on their faces would show that none of them had ever given this question a thought. By asking them a few more questions, I would get them to realize that it was *their* school and because it was their school they should take better care of it and try to make it the best school in the county. To many a young teacher and to the pupils, this was a new approach and it produced good results.

My Goals

My first three years in office slipped by quickly and routinely. However, I have never been one to be satisfied with the status quo; I always have to have something to challenge me. When I was appointed school commissioner, the challenge was to improve the quality of the teaching in the rural schools, to encourage farm boys and girls to attend high school, and to make it possible for every rural eighth grade graduate to go on to high school. Other goals were to improve reading habits by seeing that good books were bought for the school libraries and in other intangible ways make the schools better or more interesting to the pupils.

But no matter what I did, I began to feel frustrated. Although the county normal school and the rule that every applicant for a third-grade certificate had to earn two credits at a state normal had done much good, there were many factors working against better teaching. Sometimes the school was too large, with forty or more pupils and eight grades in one room, with at least four or five children in each grade. In such instances, if a teacher could give six or seven minutes to each class, she was lucky. Sometimes the classes were so small there was no competition. But the biggest stumbling block of all was the rapid turnover in the teaching force. We had approximately 140 teachers in the rural schools of Genesee County; of this number, each year 45 to 50 were beginners. Each year that many left to be married or go to normal school or teach in a village or city school where salaries were larger.

Only a few more than half of the pupils who took the eighth grade examination in the spring passed each year. Several factors entered into this situation. One was the poor teaching; the other was that parents wanted their children pushed through school too rapidly. In a rural school it was easy to skip a grade. Another factor was that inexperienced teachers had no standard to go by—a child might be a good seventh grader or a poor eighth grader.

Eighth grade graduation exercises for all the district schools were usually held sometime in early June, usually in the Masonic Temple of Flint.

The eighth grade examinations were held in all the village schools, conducted by the village superintendent of schools. In Flint, the county commissioner conducted the examination. The superintendent of a graded school could promote his own eighth graders if he wished. However, all the schools with less than twelve grades, and some of those having twelve, had their pupils take the county examination.

Many of the young people who passed the eighth grade examination did not go on to high school, or if they did, went through the tenth grade only. There were several reasons for this. In 1919, Goodrich, Grand Blanc, Gaines, Swartz Creek, Mount Morris and Otisville had only ten grades, although soon after 1919 Mount Morris and Otisville added the eleventh and twelfth grades.

Distance from a high school was in many cases an unsurmountable difficulty. There were some who overcame this difficulty; I know of instances where, in all kinds of weather, some farm boys walked several miles each way to go to high school. Moreover, in most farm families education beyond the eighth grade was not considered necessary. Our rural communities were still too near the pioneer days.

After World War I began there was a shortage of teachers all over the United States. To keep the school open, we had to bring back into the classroom teachers who had not taught for ten or fifteen years. A few of these made good; others did not. One who was successful in her return to teaching was May Calvery Cox, the teacher who had inspired me in the eighth grade in 1900. (Many years later I was invited to the celebration of her golden wedding anniversary. As a present, I took to her the largest red apple I could find—a gesture which pleased her very much.)

This shortage of teachers brought higher salaries. Some school boards blamed me for this. However, I had *always* worked for better salaries in order to keep our best teachers. Fern Jennings, one of my rural teachers, answered this criticism in a letter to the Public Pulse column in the *Flint Daily Journal*. Her letter, in part, was as follows:

> Through the efforts of a certain school director, an attempt is being made to reduce the wages of rural teachers in Genesee County. School board members are being lined up and asked to form an organization or union for the purpose of reducing the wages 25%. Rural teachers must comply with these rulings or find positions elsewhere.
>
> In the letter which has been sent to all Genesee school directors it is stated that a strong teachers' organization backed by the county commissioner and seeking an exorbitant and unreasonable wage for teachers exists. I would question the truth of this statement, as I have never heard of the existence of such an organization.
>
> I do know, however, that our school commissioner has worked for better pay for rural teachers the same as other county superintendents have, knowing that the lure of better paying city and village positions is taking away the best rural teachers. But at the same time he has urged the teachers to become better trained and qualified for their positions so that they will be justified in asking and receiving higher wages. By doing this, he has aimed to better the rural communities.
>
> The question of high taxation confronts the farmer and he seeks to lower the taxes by reducing the teachers' wages, but will

this really be the means by which this task is accomplished? It is generally known that one gets what he pays for. If rural communities are really seeking a second-class article, they surely are entitled to no more than they pay for and there is absolutely no grounds for complaint. No one need be convinced of the fact that a poor teacher is not a paying investment but rather a means of great expense.

I would suggest that the school boards of Genesee County, in justice to the rural teacher and the rural community, establish a wage scale based on training, successful experience, and teaching ability.

(Signed)

FERN L. JENNINGS
Teacher of Holden School,
Thetford Township

The Michigan legislature that met in January of 1917 passed the Rural Agricultural School Act. This was steered through the legislature by Dora Stockman, lecturer of the state Grange. It provided that any three or more contiguous school districts, by a majority vote of each, could consolidate and build a high school where agriculture, manual training and domestic science would be taught. The state would pay $200 for each bus used in transporting the children and $1,000 to each new school to help pay the salaries of the superintendent and teachers of agriculture, manual training, and domestic science. However, when the bill became law, the attorney general ruled that we should not try to organize any new school under the act because of a defect in the law!

For reasons unknown to me, the Department of Public Instruction in Lansing was not interested in consolidation. Sometime in 1915 or 1916 three districts in Munday township were somewhat interested in consolidating because of small enrollments. In their interests, I visited the Superintendent of Public Instruction. He reviewed with me the steps necessary for consolidation, but his parting advice was, "You have to be careful of the after-clap." Nothing came of this consolidation interest, but it proved to me that country people were thinking of better schools.

At that time the legislature met only once in two years, so we had to wait until 1919 before we could take any action under the revised law.

The revised law gave me the challenge I needed. During the next four years I seemed to have a fiery zeal to carry out a dream I had, the dream to build a high school in reach of every child in Genesee County. However, this dream or goal of mine had a long, rocky road to travel before it became a reality.

CHAPTER XIV

World War I Brings New Challenges

April 7, 1917, the day Congress declared war, was a momentous day in the history of our nation. The United States had been at peace for fifty-two years, except for the little skirmish with Spain in 1898 and Aguinaldo's revolt in the Philippines a year or two later. We were still an insular, self-centered, agrarian nation. For most people, a journey of 100 miles or more was a big event. Europe was 3,000 miles away. World War I had been going on for nearly three years, with very little effect on our lives. Woodrow Wilson had been re-elected on the slogan, "He kept us out of war." All at once we had to organize for total war.

In many ways the organization that was perfected was much more effective than that of World War II. In World War II all rules and regulations were sent down from Washington, usually through partisan channels. In World War I the framework was made in Washington but the organization was developed at the local, grass-roots level. Before the war ended, literally thousands of people had been drawn together, each to do his share to get the nation prepared for war and make victory certain. The Genesee County effort is in itself a long story, vividly described and illustrated in a book entitled *Honor Roll and History of Genesee County in the Great World War*. (Little did anyone foresee that the future would force us to number world wars!)

The Genesee County War Board was the unifying and coordinating center of all the war work, from Liberty Loan drives through American Red Cross work to rationing. Mr. J. Dallas Dort was the dynamic leader who served as general chairman of the War Board. Mr. Roy Brownell was general director of the township organization. I was a member of the executive council of the War Board and assistant general director of the township organization. I was also secretary of the Board during the first few months, but had to give up this office because my work as commissioner of schools required too much of my time. The War Board organization was so complete that every one of the 152 school districts had a committee, with a chairman and two or more members.

The following quotation from *Honor Roll* tells of my part in the War Savings Stamp campaign, which took place in July of 1918. Sales of the War Savings Stamps and Thrift Stamps were begun by the federal government in January for the purpose of raising $2,000,000,000 (two billion dollars) for the war from the small savings of the public. Genesee County was given a quota of $1,783,000. Our county reached and exceeded every quota assigned to it. The book states:

> Tribute is due the school systems, both city and county, for the aid given W.S.S. sales throughout the entire years. Superintendent A. N. Cody and County School Commissioner John L. Riegle led the work in their respective territories with great success. The teachers enthusiastically took up the task and the result was that nearly every scholar enrolled became a W.S.S. salesman to his or her home or neighborhood. St. Matthew parochial school earned an honor flag for selling a larger percentage of stamps than any other school of its size . . .

In World War I there was no rationing as we had it in World War II, with stamps for food, tires, gasoline, and other commodities. Food conservation in World War I was put on an honor system. For the townships this work was done through my office. To quote again from *Honor Roll:*

> All teachers of the county and village schools were called to Flint for a meeting October 16, 1917, to organize to get pledges to observe Hoover Food Conservation rules. The teachers very enthusiastically promised to do everything in their power to carry out this comprehensive program. They took the necessary supplies home with them, and work of the campaign was begun November 29, 1917. In a house-to-house canvas by teachers and pupils, a total

of 5,514 pledges were taken, or about 90% of the households outside the city of Flint. Each housewife who signed the pledge was given an instruction card and a window card to display.

Again in the spring of 1918 a follow-up campaign was put on, at which time three leaflets and one instruction card were placed in every home in the county by teachers and pupils.

My office was also the headquarters for home demonstrations in conservation of food. Mrs. Kathryn Beekman was the county agent. She gave demonstrations in the preparation of foods using substitutes for the scarce items like wheat, meat and sugar. To quote from page 76 of *Honor Roll:*

> A third food-saving drive was planned for the first week of December, 1918, and preparations for it were well under way when the armistice was suddenly announced. Its further progress was halted to await Mr. Hoover's investigation of the food situation in Europe. Activity was not resumed and the State Food Department with all its subordinate branches became extinct on January 1, 1919.
>
> Compiled from reports furnished by:
> John L. Riegle, Chairman, Food Conservation Committee for
>   Genesee County
> Glenn R. Jackson, Merchant Representative for Genesee County
> Clarence A. Cameron, Food Administrator for Genesee County
> Mrs. Kathryn B. Beekman, Urban Home Demonstration Agent

On November 8, 1918, the word was flashed over the wires that an armistice had been signed. I was visiting schools in Clayton township when the news came. Immediately I drove to Flint, where I found that bedlam had broken loose. People of Flint and from miles around were parading up and down Saginaw Street. The tensions of eighteen months were released. When the parade ended, it was learned that the armistice had *not* been signed—that the announcement was premature. A dreadful dejection settled on the people. However, three days later the armistice was signed. Again there was a parade, but it was only an echo of the rousing first one. Within a few days the War Board and all the committees under it were disbanded and normal life was resumed.

Before the War Board disbanded it presented each member with a metallic badge or medal made up of bars chained together. The top bar bore the inscription "Home War Service Honor Board," next was an arrowhead inscribed "Flint, Michigan Volunteer campaign work." There were eleven smaller bars on my badge, one for each of eleven campaigns, namely: (1) Private First Liberty Loan, (2) Private First Red Cross, (3) Captain 2nd Liberty Loan, (4) Captain Three-in-One (to raise funds for the YWCA, YMCA, and War Camp Community Service), (5) Chairman 3rd Liberty Loan, (6) Private Second Red Cross, Flint, (7) Chairman 2nd Red Cross (in townships), (8) Chairman War Savings Stamps, (9) Chairman 4th Liberty Loan, (10) Chairman United War Fund, and (11) Chairman 3rd Red Cross. Sentimentally, I have saved this badge for my grandchildren.

Thus ended the war that was thought to be "the war to end all wars." It may have been the Pandora's box of Greek mythology. As a result, the Communists usurped power in Russia. No one in this year of 1971 can predict what the results of this takeover will be in the years to come.

CHAPTER XV

Working for Consolidation

While I realized that no action could be taken to establish a rural agricultural high school until the legislature could amend the bill, in the spring of 1919 I began to make plans and to talk about such new schools, even before the attorney general wrote his adverse opinion. Favorable sentiment quickly appeared in at least three communities: Gaines, Goodrich, and Grand Blanc. Many people became interested in the new concept. Among these were Morrice Myers, director of the Walker school in Grand Blanc township; Mrs. Thompson and Mrs. Inez Perry of Grand Blanc township; Alton Clark, director of the Mason school; Ed Evat, director of the Whigville school; and William Nutter, director of the Hoffman school. There were also the officials of all three schools in the Grand Blanc township and many others. The names of many of them have escaped me. I wish I could honor them all by listing them. Morric Myers was one of the most active; he often came to my office to visit and to make plans for the campaign that was to come. Grand Blanc was the most logical place for the campaign to start, as it was the most logical place in the county to get one of the new rural agricultural schools. In 1903, one rural school had been consolidated with the village school, and in 1907 a second was added, and horse-drawn buses had been used for sixteen years to transport the children from the farms to the central school.

THE STANDARD SCHOOL

In the spring of 1919, the county school commissioners of Michigan held a meeting at Michigan Agricultural College in East Lansing (now Michigan State University). The meeting, called by the Department of

119

Public Instruction, was under the leadership of Mr. George Otwell, head of the rural department and a great believer in and booster for the "standard school." A Mrs. Hutchinson, school commissioner from a county in the western side of the state, was to give a paper on "The Standard School," and I was to lead the discussion following her paper. She gave a good monograph which was received with much favor. Perhaps I was rude when I got up to lead the discussion, for I began with the statement, "Ladies and gentlemen, as long as I am school commissioner of Genesee County I will never give another standard school plate." I then proceeded to give my reasons for not wanting any more standard schools, declaring that from that day on all my spare time and energy would be spent in working for the establishment of rural agricultural schools. I went on to tell of the work I had already done and to outline my plans for the future. You may be sure that my talk was *not* well received. After I had finished my remarks, Mr. Otwell took the floor and criticized me severely for the stand I had taken. I was considered a heretic. However, there were several persons in the audience who told me privately that my stand was correct, but most of them thought I was too radical. Interestingly enough, two or three years later Mr. Otwell gave a hearty endorsement to the consolidated school idea when he attended a public meeting with me in Davison.

Some seventeen years later I met a cousin of my wife, Dr. Edwin J. Brown, who was dean of the graduate school in Kansas State Teachers College at Emporia, Kansas. He said that his class had just finished a study of rural schools in which they decided that the standard school plate did more harm than good. I told him I had come to that conclusion seventeen years earlier.

The "standard school" concept had its beginning in Michigan during the administration of Luther Wright as Superintendent of Public Instruction about 1913. The aims behind the idea of the standard school were excellent. The 1914-15 school directory gave these aims as follows:

> To arouse the spirit of improvement among the people as well as among the school officers and teachers and to lay out a field of definite achievement the Superintendent of Public Instruction provides the Standard School plan. A certain degree of excellence in environment, in comfortable and sanitary conditions, and in the ability and character of the teacher is fixed upon as necessary for a

proper efficiency of the school. Upon meeting the requirements, the State of Michigan will set a special mark of approval by awarding to the school a metal plate bearing the words "Standard School" and by conferring upon this school a diploma certifying to the excellence of the school. The specifications of the standard school will include yard and outbuildings, the schoolhouse, furnishings and supplies, the organization and the school.

To be a little more specific, the windows and desks and seats had to be arranged so that all the light came over the child's left shoulder and there could be no window in front of him. Heating had to be by a jacketed stove with a fresh-air intake. Two entry rooms had to be provided, with separate rooms for indoor chemical toilets. The walls of the schoolroom were to be appropriately decorated and provided with suitable pictures. The floor, desks, and all equipment had to be kept in good repair.

When I became commissioner, there were only two standard schools in Genesee County, and one of them did not meet the specified standards but had received the award mainly because of the excellence of the teacher. When I left the office, there were fourteen so-called standard schools. The idea was good but the end results were not always the best. They worked out satisfactorily when a new school had to be built, but when an old schoolhouse had to be remodeled the cost was about $1,000. After the metal plate was awarded, the school officers deemed the school perfect and that henceforward it would need no further care. It could almost fall apart before any repair work would be done. Furthermore, the "standard school" became a stumbling block to consolidation—my chief objection to it.

GAINES, GRAND BLANC, GOODRICH

As related earlier, even before final action was taken by the legislature on the Rural Agricultural School Act, we made our plans for action in the school districts in the vicinity of Gaines, Grand Blanc, and Goodrich. The Act was amended, passed, and given immediate effect sometime during the latter part of March of 1919. This Act provided that if a petition was signed by five taxpayers in a district, the director had to call a district meeting within ten days to vote on forming a rural agricultural school. Each district voted separately. The question carried if a majority of the taxpayers present and voting voted favorably.

During the ten weeks following the legislative action, I held twenty-eight night meetings in schoolhouses in Genesee County, mainly in the areas of Gaines, Goodrich and Grand Blanc. During two of these ten weeks I had tonsilitis and was confined to my home. Some of those meetings were most interesting. Those were the days when there were still some religious prejudices; however, at our general meeting in Gaines the Catholic priest and the Methodist minister sat on the platform and both urged the formation of the new consolidated school.

Usually the school board in each district led the consolidation effort. In the Cummings district, near Goodrich, the opposition of one family gave us trouble. For several weeks I tried to get the director to call a meeting of the voters to find out just what the sentiment was. When he failed to do so, at the suggestion of Mr. George Titsworth, he and I canvassed the district and found that a majority of the voters favored consolidation. The evening of the day of this canvass, we held a meeting at the schoolhouse and decided to force a vote. The next morning I wrote out a blank petition requesting the director to call a district meeting, filled in three special meeting notices that designated the date of the meeting and the question to be voted upon, and drove to the Cummings district. It took me only a short time to secure the five necessary signatures on the petition, because of the preliminary work done the evening before.

I found the director in his barn on a load of fodder. He read the petition and signed the three notices. I had brought along a hammer and some tacks. I proceeded to tack one notice on the schoolhouse door and the other two in conspicuous places in the district. We were working on a close schedule, as this was the last day we could call a meeting to vote the district into a new district in 1919. The time of voting at these meetings was from five p.m. till ten o'clock. When the voting day came, I found all the friends of consolidation at the schoolhouse. Just as I had expected, none of the school board members had come. At five o'clock I called the meeting to order and had the voters present appoint three tellers. I was a notary public and swore them in. The meeting was closed at ten o'clock and the ballots counted. The count showed eighteen for consolidation and three against. The opposition could have made the voting close. However, they knew they were defeated and only three came to vote.

Cummings was a key district which we needed to complete the organization of the new school in Goodrich. This was also the last day I could post notices calling the first annual meeting in the new, enlarged district. On my way to the Cummings school I had left one of these notices with Mr. William Nutter, director of the Hoffman school, properly filled out for him to post on the door of his schoolhouse—if the Cummings school vote were favorable. Before leaving the Cummings school, I posted the notice of the annual meeting on the door, then drove to Goodrich. It was a dark night, so I asked one of the Goodrich village board members to go with me to help post the notices, calling the annual meeting, on the three other schools that were to become part of the new consolidated school. His answer was, "John, I don't want to get mixed up in this, but I'll let you take my flashlight." The three remaining districts I had to visit were Ferguson, the Little Goodrich, and Goodrich village. Holding the flashlight between my knees, I posted the notices on the doors of each of the three schoolhouses and returned the borrowed flashlight to its owner before midnight. I could have made an affidavit that the notices had been posted in time, had it been necessary. I am not sure that my actions in the Cummings school election would have stood up in court. They were never tested, and the new school district was organized.

The Hoffman district was a fractional district, about half in Atlas township and half in Grand Blanc. Before the district voted to join the Goodrich group, we had promised the people who lived in Grand Blanc township that their property would be put into the Grand Blanc district. Within a few weeks after the first annual meeting in the newly formed districts, this promise was fulfilled.

I have no record, and my memory is not keen enough to recall whether we had any districts which turned down the first consolidation attempts. We had the key districts that enabled us to organize the three rural agricultural schools in Gaines, Goodrich and Grand Blanc, the first in Genesee and among the first six in Michigan. Before the Cummings school episode, I had posted the necessary notices calling the first annual meetings in Gaines and in Grand Blanc; and in due time these meetings were held and new school boards of five officers were elected in each place.

The new officers in Gaines were F. J. Moore, president; William Zeigel, secretary; D. P. Haviland, treasurer; and Albert Shepard and George Chase, trustees.

In Goodrich the officers were Dr. A. S. Wheelock, president; Dr. W. C. Reid, secretary; E. J. Pierson, treasurer; and William Nutter and A. Zimmerman, trustees.

In Grand Blanc the officers were Morrice Myers, president; L. Roy Perry, secretary; Walter Parker, treasurer; and Mrs. Alice Cheney and Mrs. Inez Perry, trustees.

All the officers in the three districts had helped in getting the schools organized. This helped immeasurably in getting the new schools off to a good start. Fortunately, all the schoolhouses in the three villages were adequate to take care of the additional pupils from the rural schools, so no new buildings were needed. Approximately 200 more farm boys and girls were now living in districts with high schools. Although the three village high schools were only ten-grade schools before consolidation, within the next two years the eleventh and twelfth grades were added in each school. Within the next two or three years all three became accredited by the University of Michigan. This was the beginning of the fulfillment of my dream of a high school for *every child* in Genesee County.

When I finished the strenuous campaign that resulted in the organization of the three rural agricultural schools, I was so tired that I would go to sleep sitting in a chair, something I had never been able to do before that time. Shortly after this exhausting campaign I had a second attack of tonsilitis. My family doctor, Dr. H. D. Knapp, told me that if I did not have my tonsils removed, they would kill me. As soon as I felt better, I went to Hurley Hospital, where Dr. William G. Bird removed my tonsils. Usually the patient went home the evening of a tonsilectomy, but I felt so weak I stayed overnight at the hospital. The next morning Dr. Knapp told me that if I wanted to get home within the next six weeks I had better go at once. This proved to be sound advice. The next six weeks found me in bed with inflammatory rheumatism. It was three or four months before I fully recovered. This illness put an end for a time to my work for consolidation.

During the intensive campaign for consolidation, some amusing incidents occurred. In the spring of 1920, Alton Clark, the director of the Mason school in Grand Blanc township, and I made a house-to-house canvass of the voters in his district to see how many of them wanted to join the new Grand Blanc village district. We counted twenty-four for consolidation and twenty-two against, but when the vote was taken, twenty-four voted against and only twenty-two for consolidation. We could not figure out which two voters had "deserted." About seven months later Alton came into my office, accompanied by an old, wizened little man. Alton was grinning from ear to ear. After introducing his friend, he said, "If we ever have another election in the Mason district, we can carry it for consolidation." The old gentleman chipped in, "Yes. My wife died a few weeks ago, so now I can vote as I please."

At the annual school meeting in July 1920, the Halsey school in Grand Blanc township voted to raise $1,000 to make their school a "standard school." At the request of the director, I met with the school board at the schoolhouse to tell them what changes they had to make to bring the school up to the qualifications for a "standard school." After explaining what had to be done, I advised them not to spend the money. I told them we were planning an election to make Grand Blanc township a township unit school. They didn't like my advice, but they followed it.

Soon after this meeting, petitions for forming the township unit district were circulated; the election was held, and Grand Blanc organized the first township unit school in the county. Five one-room school districts were discontinued to complete the township unit district.

During the school year of 1918-19 this school had four teachers for the ten grades. In 1919, with Glen Wakefield as superintendent, the eleventh grade was added and two extra teachers were hired to teach home economics, manual training, and agriculture. By 1922, they had added ten more teachers; the school had become a Smith-Hughes school and was given accreditation by the University of Michigan. Glen Wakefield, superintendent in Grand Blanc for three years, did an outstanding job in getting the new school organized with a good foundation.

During these same years Gaines and Goodrich followed the same pattern. Gaines, which had three teachers and ten grades before consolidation, added the two higher grades and four more teachers. It, too, became a Smith-Hughes school and within three or four years was accredited by the University. Mr. A. B. Lightfoot was the first superintendent of the consolidated school in Gaines.

Goodrich, before consolidation, had three teachers. It added five teachers, two extra grades, and the same three new subjects; and became a Smith-Hughes school and was accredited by the University. Mr. Ralph Sill was the first superintendent in the enlarged Goodrich school. In addition to being superintendent, he taught agriculture and manual training. In the 1920-21 school year, Paul Rood came to Goodrich as superintendent and teacher of agriculture and manual training. Mr. Sill went to Gaines to teach agriculture and manual training.

One Wednesday morning in the spring of 1920, I received a telephone call from a member of the school board in Grand Blanc, telling me that the schoolhouse had burned down. He asked me to come to a board meeting to be held that morning to make plans to bond the district in order to build a new school building. I attended the meeting and the plans were made. Shortly after that, the board hired a Lansing architect, a Mr. Holmes, and held a bonding election. In due time the new schoolhouse was built. The *Flint Evening Tribune* for Friday, December 30, 1921, contained a picture and a description of the new building. The article read in part:

> The opening of the winter term of school next Monday will find the new consolidated high school building at Grand Blanc village ready for occupancy. The opening of the new building will witness the full consolidation of the districts throughout Grand Blanc township. About a year ago the school taxpayers of the township adopted the plan to erect the central school building by a two-thirds vote.
>
> The new building was erected at a cost of $107,000. It embodies all the latest ideas in school construction. It is a handsome two-story building of brick, standing in a grove of fine maples on the Dixie Highway. . . .
>
> On the ground floor are separate rooms for the first six grades. The high school auditorium is on the upper floor. The latter has

sufficient seating capacity to handle all grades from the seventh to the twelfth. Adequate recitation rooms are provided, as well as fully equipped physical and chemical laboratories, a manual training room and domestic science and sewing rooms.

Three hundred and fifty pupils will be enrolled when the new school opens. Twelve buses will be used to convey the pupils to and from school.

The high school course will be the same as any accredited high school. Sessions have been held since the new building was started in various available rooms scattered throughout the village.

The superintendent, G. W. Wakefield, has a faculty of eleven teachers, with Hope Wakefield as principal of the high school.

In April of 1919, I was elected to my second term of four years as commissioner. Within a year after the organization of the new Goodrich district, the Bingham school voted to join the consolidation.

After the Grand Blanc township unit district was organized in 1921, there were *sixteen* less one-room schools in the county than there were in 1919. This was the beginning of the fulfillment of a goal I had long cherished—that every country boy and girl should have, first in Genesee County and later in all of Michigan, the opportunity to go to an accredited twelve-grade high school.

These new rural agricultural schools were the beginning of a revolution in rural education in Michigan. They brought the school to the door of every child in a district. Before this time, although the home district could pay tuition to a neighboring high school, no provision had been made to transport the pupils. Many boys and girls who lived in the country at a distance from a high school could not attend because of lack of money to pay transportation or to meet the expense of boarding away from home.

The new schools were also unique in that they provided courses in home economics, manual training and agriculture—courses which met the needs of farm boys and girls that few city or village schools offered.

On November 27, 1920, an article describing the new consolidated schools, with special emphasis on the Goodrich school, appeared in the *Michigan Farmer.* It stated:

The consolidated rural school has to do with our future generation of farmers, and in no line of business is education more needed than in the biggest business of all—farming. These schools will not only provide a better education for the boys and girls, but they will bring the whole community into closer relationship and make country life richer. Pupils attending them will not only be studying such courses as domestic science or home economics, manual training, and agriculture, which correlate their lives with the community. These schools also give them better teaching. In May, 1919, 1700 boys and girls from the rural schools of Michigan took the eighth grade examination from a list of questions prepared by the Superintendent of Public Instruction. 65% of this number received eighth grade certificates. In village and city schools 80% of all eighth grade pupils were promoted to high school.

In the winter and spring of 1920 I began to make plans for more consolidations in different parts of the county. However, a sharp depression settled over the nation, hitting the farmers especially hard. The World War I slogan "Food will win the war" had caused farmers in the West to plow up millions of acres of virgin land to sow wheat. The result was an overproduction of this grain. Also, during and after the war there was a great increase in the number of automobiles, trucks and tractors, with a corresponding decrease in the number of horses and mules. This trend induced farmers to raise more wheat, rye and beans and less hay and oats than before. Even the increase in the birth rate after World War I could not take care of the surpluses caused by overproduction. As a result, the farmers' income decreased and their opposition to increased taxes to support better schools strengthened.

During the next two years, voting on consolidation was held in seven or eight places. We voted on the question of forming township units in Davison, Richfield, Forest, Thetford and Montrose townships. In two of these townships, Forest and Montrose, we tried in two elections, but failed by small majorities in each attempt. At the time we voted in Davison township, in the eight rural districts there were only ninety-two pupils enrolled in the eight schools. One of these, the Wolcott school, had only *three* pupils—yet consolidation was rejected!

In the spring of 1922, after a hard-fought campaign, we finally got the fourth rural agricultural school, centered in the village of Swartz Creek. The Begole, Calkins, Grove, and Ryno schools of Clayton township joined with the Fletcher and Swartz Creek schools of Gaines township. The hardest contest came in the Grove district. The director, Harry Youells, was opposed to consolidation. After much persuasion by several members of the district, he called an evening meeting at the schoolhouse. Nearly all the voters of the district attended. I thought, from their reactions, that a majority favored consolidation. After the meeting, Mr. Youells sat with me in my car for an hour, discussing the question from every angle. He finally said, "Riegle, I won't help you, but I won't work against you." Before he left me he gave me a list of names of voters who would sign the petition necessary to call for the election. The next day I prepared the necessary petition and visited the people whose names he had supplied. All of them signed the petition as he had foreseen. I presented the petition to him and the election was duly called.

Since our first consolidations were made, the manner of voting had been changed. Instead of each district voting separately, the six districts voted as a unit. We won the election by a small majority. Soon after this, a suit was started in circuit court by Mr. Youells and others to overturn the election on the grounds that some people who had voted were not qualified. We won the court test. On the annual meeting day the consolidated school was organized.

The schoolhouse in Swartz Creek was only an overcrowded three-room building. The village had needed a new school building for a long time, but there was no leadership in the community. Three years after I left the office of school commissioner, the new district was dissolved. It was not until twenty years later, under the leadership of Edward Bremer, that the same six districts and one or two others reconsolidated. (In 1951, Mr. Bremer retired from teaching and became a salesman for the Riegle Press; he is still with us in 1971.)

For a few years the consolidated school idea gained in momentum. I was asked by several groups of people to explain the mechanics of organizing a rural agricultural school and to point out the benefits of consolidation. I spent nearly a week in Kent County working with Mr. Alan Freeland, the county school commissioner. We worked in eleven districts, with Rockford as the center. When I left for home at the end of the week, the outlook for consolidation seemed promising. However, one man disrupted the whole picture, destroying my work in Kent County. He happened to have a relative or friend who lived in the Grand Blanc township unit school district. This friend told him that the school taxes in Grand Blanc were $35 per $1,000 of assessed valuation. The truth was that the *total* taxes for all purposes were $35 per thousand; this included state taxes, township general taxes, county taxes, and two special assessment taxes for a town hall and a big county drain. In reality, the school tax was approximately $9 per thousand. It seems that people believe what they want to believe. No amount of explaining could erase this false information. The Grand Blanc resident had said the school taxes were $35 per thousand and that was what Kent County accepted as truth. The consolidated school was voted down, not to be resurrected for many years.

I also spent nearly a week in Midland County as a teachers' institute instructor with Byron Scollay, Midland County school commissioner. My topic in Midland, Coleman, and nearby schools was the same as in Kent County.

Several other communities also invited me to give talks on consolidation. In three of these, Byron, Hartland, and North Branch, rural agricultural schools were organized and maintained successfully.

Once in a while amusing things happened. The county commissioner of Lapeer County, at the request of the people in North Branch, asked me to give a talk in their village. Assuming the commissioner would go with me on the appointed day, I stopped at his office. He politely refused to accompany me; he just did not want to become involved in the consolidation question.

Another time I gave a talk at a large meeting of school patrons in the village of Snover. Nearly everyone at the meeting was in favor of consolidation. After my talk, the county school commissioner was invited to make some remarks. He said, "Ladies and gentlemen, if you believe in consolidation, you will vote for it; if you do not believe in it, you will not vote for it," and then he sat down. He was afraid to take a stand. In a year or two he would have to run for reelection and he feared that if he took a stand in favor of consolidation, he would lose the election. Had the election been the next day, very few of those who were present at that

meeting would have voted for him. This campaign for better schools failed
because there was no local leadership.

I have in my scrapbook a handbill advertising a meeting that I attended in Saranac, Ionia County, on Friday evening, December 9. No year
is given, but it was probably in 1922. It was headed "Consolidation of
schools, best solution of the present-day school problems. Discussion will
be led by Hon. John L. Riegle, from Genesee County, where many consolidated schools exist." I have no memories of the results of this meeting.

I can recall only one other talk I gave outside Genesee County. A
Mrs. Teft, commissioner of schools in Saginaw County, who had succeeded her husband at his death, invited me to go with her to a school
meeting in Hemlock. It was an interesting meeting, but I never heard
the results.

With a few exceptions, in these early days the county school commissioners gave only lip service to the idea of consolidation. They were
afraid to take a strong stand for consolidation and to work for it for fear
they would lose the next election. Perhaps they should not be blamed.
Most of them were elderly men and women; if they lost their jobs they
could not have found other employment nearly as remunerative.

However, there were exceptions. Commissioner Roy Noteware of
Wexford County organized two rural agricultural schools in 1919, and
Mr. Townsend, commissioner of Jackson County, organized the rural
agricultural school in Napoleon, also in 1919. Mr. Ben McComb of Tuscola County was another exception, and Will Lee of Macomb County became a dedicated advocate of consolidation. In the 1940s and '50s, he
consolidated all of his county. There were several others who should be
mentioned, but I have forgotten their names.

In 1923, I served on the legislative committee of the commissioners'
section of the Michigan Education Association. Alan Freeland of Kent
County was chairman of this committee. We had a bill prepared and introduced in the state legislature that would have given the voters of any
county the right to establish a county unit system for the schools of the
county. We had a meeting of all the school commissioners of the state in
Lansing. The county unit idea was debated pro and con. Nearly everyone
present promised to work for the passage of the bill. But when they went

home, many of them told their representatives in the state legislature, "Our present system is working all right; perhaps we had better not change it." I have always been positive that if this bill had become law, Genesee County (excluding Flint) would have adopted the county unit system. Dozens of people told me they would work for such a system.

Although I spent much of my time during the last four years in office on the organization of rural agricultural schools, I did not neglect my regular duties. I helped in organizing Parent-Teacher Associations and engaged in other activities that helped to make better schools.

In September 1921, all the village superintendents of schools of the county met in my office and organized a superintendents' club. Mr. Zar Storrs, the superintendent at Flushing, was elected president. I was elected vice president and Mr. John Goudy of Otisville, secretary. The purposes of the club were to promote closer cooperation among village schools, to have uniform courses of study and uniformity in teachers' wages and qualifications, and to work for anything else that would provide better education for our children. I remember one rule that was adopted and kept to the effect that no teacher would be hired in any graded school who did not have at least one year of normal school training. A program chairman for the club was appointed and meetings were held each month. After I left the office in June of 1923, the newly elected commissioner called a meeting of the club. Evidently she did not state the hour of the meeting, because two or three of the superintendents came in the forenoon and several others in the afternoon. There was no meeting. The club was dissolved, not to be reactivated for many years.

According to law, we had a meeting of all the school officers in the county at least once every two years. The last one held during my term was in 1922. The purpose of these meetings was to acquaint the officers with any new laws passed by the legislature and to explain the duties of the various officers. Much of the time at this last meeting was taken up with a discussion of the organization of rural agricultural schools and the proposed county unit system.

TEACHING IN NORMAL SCHOOL

When the spring terms of 1922 ended at Mount Pleasant Normal College, Professor John Kelley of the rural department took a much-needed rest to travel in Europe. President Warriner asked me to teach Professor Kelley's class in rural sociology for the summer term. I built my classes around the organizing and running of rural agricultural schools. It was a very pleasant summer for me.

I seemed to be fairly popular with the other school commissioners, for they usually made me chairman of the commissioners' section of the Michigan Education Association and once elected me treasurer of the organization. I was also on the Young People's Reading Circle Board for three years.

Sometime during my last term Ben McComb of Tuscola County and Charles Naylor of Lapeer and I were asked to arbitrate a dispute over the site for a new school in Otter Lake, a school fractional with Lapeer, Tuscola and Genesee counties. Their schoolhouse had burned. The "old-timers" wanted to rebuild on the old site; the younger people wanted to select a larger plot just outside the village. There really was no choice, as the old site was too small. We chose the larger site. Before our visit both factions agreed to abide by our decision. However, the faction for the old site reneged and took the matter to court, where the faction for the new site won.

Paul Rood was the second superintendent of the Goodrich rural agricultural school. He was a keen young man who had a degree in education from Michigan Agricultural College (Now Michigan State University). He always worked very closely with me. Even in schoolwork there is always a little humor. One Saturday Paul came to my office with a question which seemed most serious to him. This was the time when women were beginning to bob their hair, a trend that was causing a near scandal in his district. He asked me what he should do about the teachers' bobbing their hair. I asked him, "Have they bobbed their hair? If so, what can you do? Can you put it back on?" He decided that nothing could be done. The flurry soon blew over.

SCHOOL BUSES

The second year after consolidation, Goodrich became a Smith-Hughes school. Paul Rood was superintendent and teacher of manual training and agriculture as well. The school received extra state and federal aid because he held the dual office. One day he came to my office to discuss something that had a great influence on the future of consolidation. Up until this time, all districts had hired private individuals to buy and drive the school buses. Because the owners had a large investment in the equipment they used, they almost had a monopoly on the transportation of pupils. They kept raising their prices until the cost of transportation began to jeopardize the whole consolidation movement. At that time there were no factory-built buses. Each bus body had to be made to order and mounted on a truck chassis. Paul wanted to build a bus body in his manual training classes, then persuade the school board to buy a chassis, hire a driver, and have the district own and operate the bus. I agreed that he should build the body. When the schoolboard was approached, it developed that the board was not yet ready to take on the operation of a district school bus. Instead, they rented the bus body built in the manual training department to a driver for $200 a year. The next year Paul's classes built another bus body.

In June 1923, I had Professor Pittman, head of the rural department of Ypsilanti Normal School (now Eastern Michigan University) give the commencement address to the eighth grade graduates of the entire county. He stayed in Flint until the next day to visit the Goodrich school board with me. When we arrived in Goodrich, Paul had the school board assembled in Dr. Amos Wheelock's office. Professor Pittman had had experience somewhere in the West with schools which owned and operated school buses. With his help we persuaded the board to buy chasses for the two bus bodies and hire drivers for the school buses.

The first year the district owned and operated the buses the cost of transportation was cut in half. Some of the first drivers were teachers who welcomed the additional earnings. A few were high school pupils over eighteen.

I have always believed that what was accomplished at that Goodrich meeting, plus the building of the bus bodies by Paul's classes, saved school consolidation in Michigan. Within a few years all the rural agricultural schools in the state followed the example set by Goodrich. In Grand Blanc, private ownership of the buses had caused an acute financial problem; district-owned buses saved them from a bad situation.

CHERISHED MEMENTOS

One of my cherished mementos is a letter from Paul Rood, dated December 2, 1962, which says in part:

Dear John Riegle:

The clipping from the Lansing State Journal shows that what you started now gives half a million children in Michigan a ride to school. Congratulations!

Paul and Edna Rood

A few years ago, in 1965, when the Beebe School—the last one-room school in Genesee County—joined the Linden Rural Agricultural School, *my dream came true!*

That dreams *do* come true was attested to by an event that took place in 1964. When Mayme Anderson, principal of the McGrath School in Grand Blanc, retired, her school parents and teachers honored her with a dinner at the school. After the dinner a skit was presented entitled "This Is Your Life, Mayme Anderson," and I was asked to take part in it.

Back in 1918 Miss Mayme Michelson, a young teacher from the Upper Peninsula, had moved to Flint. She had come to my office in search of a teaching job and I had sent her to the Mason School in Grand Blanc where she was hired. After teaching in Grand Blanc for several years, she taught in Flint for a time, then completed her teaching career as a principal in Grand Blanc. In my part of the skit I re-enacted her first visit to my office and my sending her to the Mason School to apply for a job. She recognized my voice and the incident at once and seemed greatly moved by the recollection. At Christmas she sent me the following letter with her Christmas card:

Dear Mr. Riegle:

Thank you so much for coming to my party. I'm sorry I didn't think fast enough to tell the people of Grand Blanc how much they owe to you! It was your *dream* and your *hard work* that made it possible for Grand Blanc and its school system to grow the way it has. I tell people every chance I have.

Best wishes for a Merry Christmas and a Happy New Year.

Mayme A.

This letter gave me one of the greatest thrills of my life.

In June of 1959 *The Flint Journal* sent Mr. Homer Dowdy, a feature writer, to my office to get information on the organization of the rural agricultural schools in Gaines, Grand Blanc, and Goodrich for the June 28 edition. Because 1959 was the fortieth anniversary of the organization of these schools, the *Journal* generously devoted nearly an entire page to the story of these schools and the part I played in their history. (Mr. Dowdy, now vice president of the Mott Foundation Projects, gave me the information on the foundation which appears in the chapter on community schools.)

After the anniversary story appeared, I received many compliments, but the one that pleased me very much was a letter from Mr. Otis Smith, chairman of the Michigan Public Service Commission at that time and later a justice on the Supreme Court of Michigan. It read as follows:

> Dear Mr. Riegle:
>
> It was truly inspiring to read of your courage and foresight in connection with the school consolidation movement in Genesee County, as it appeared in Sunday's *Journal.*
>
> I recall that we talked about this on one or two of my visits to the shop. I felt very proud reading the article.
>
> Very sincerely yours,
> Otis M. Smith

By 1923 the movement of Flint residents into the suburbs had begun. It did not take long for the one-room schools to become overcrowded. The Lyon School on Flushing Road was one of these overcrowded schools. The building was really old, having been built originally for the children of Jacob Smith, the first white settler of Flint, and his Indian wife. I met with the Lyon school board to help them make plans to build a two-room building. This was the first new unit in the district which later became the Hoover school district.

The Beecher School had built its first two-room school in 1920. The Dye School on Corunna Road became the third school to feel the population squeeze. They, too, had to build a schoolhouse of two rooms.

CHAPTER XVI

Defeat Through Error

In March of 1923, I ran for re-election to the office of county school commissioner. My opponent was a woman who had been a critic teacher in a nearby county normal school; her home was in Clayton township. In her political advertisements she promised the farmers she would not work for consolidation. Election day was a nasty, windy day in March, with snow flurries. Everyone who was disgruntled with me because of my efforts for consolidation, as well as those whose toes I had stepped on when I had to decide against them in a disagreement in their school district, came out to vote. Many of my friends did not vote because they assumed I would have no trouble in being re-elected.

On the first tally of votes, I lost by eight. On a recount, I was ahead by thirty-five votes. Before the recount an agreement was made between our attorneys to abide by the recount figures, but when my opponent learned that she was trailing by thirty-five votes, she fired her attorney, who was her cousin, and hired another attorney. He took the matter to court with the claim that the ballot boxes were not sealed properly. This was a technicality, because the boxes were sealed. It was true that the city clerk of Flint had not furnished the proper seals. The election law had just been changed to require a freight-car seal, the type still used. The city clerk had furnished the old-fashioned seals. Judge Fred Brennan ruled in favor of my opponent. The board of election commissioners finished the recount and found that I had won the election by thirty-five votes. One of these men, Mr. A. E. Ransom of Flushing, who in 1891 was the first school commissioner elected in Genesee County, refused to sign my opponent's election certificate. She took the office knowing that I had received the majority of votes! This is the way the work to which I had dedicated myself wholeheartedly for nine years was ended.

CHAPTER XVII

Aftermath

A few days after the election the courthouse burned. All school records were destroyed. My office was moved to the second floor of Winegarden's furniture store and later to the Industrial Bank Building, now called the Metropolitan Building.

It was during the school year of 1923-24 that I did my last college work, an extension course in "The Junior High School" given by a professor from the University of Michigan.

My term of office ended Saturday, June 30, 1923. On Monday, July 2, I entered my own business, the printing firm of Ford and Riegle. I had been warned many times that if I continued to work for consolidation of schools, those who opposed me would "get" me. Taking their warnings to heart, I had formed the previous August a partnership with Ransom L. (Mike) Ford, an old friend, to start a printing shop in Flint. I knew nothing about printing, but Mike was an experienced printer. From early September he carried on the business while I was engaged in my regular school duties.

A few months after I left the county school office, I was appointed to the Flint Board of Education to fill a vacancy. I served on this board for nearly two years. During this period I was chairman of the committee that supervised the building of Whittier Junior High School.

At the spring election in 1925, I was a candidate for the full term. Strange as it may seem, at that time Flint was under the domination of the Ku Klux Klan. The head klansman sent a messenger to me with the word that if I would join the Klan I would have no trouble in being elected. I told this messenger that if I had to join the Klan to be elected to the Flint Board of Education, I would never serve on that board. Then one of their lower officers in the Klan came to me with the same message. My answer was the same as before. On the morning of the election every home in the second ward (my ward) was covered with handbills listing the Klan-endorsed candidates. My name was not on this list.

I lost the election. My only consolation in the loss of this office was that I defeated the Klan-endorsed opponent in my home precinct and in his home precinct. In the rest of the ward my name was "Mudd." This Klan-endorsed candidate served on the Board of Education of Flint for several years and later became a circuit court judge.

THE RIEGLE PRESS

In November of 1924, my partner, because of injuries from an automobile accident, was advised by his physician to quit the printing business. I then bought his interest and changed the firm name to The Riegle Press. In the spring of 1925, the first unit of the shop on Louisa Street was built. We moved into the new quarters in June. This first building was 32 by 66 feet, with full basement.

It was just at this time that I received a telephone call from President Warriner of Central Normal School in Mount Pleasant (now Central State University). He wanted me to come to Mount Pleasant to take the place of Professor John Kelley, who had just died, as head of the rural department. This was one teaching position I would have loved to accept, but I had invested all my savings in my business and had borrowed the money to build my new building, so I had to refuse.

At about the same time, Mr. Webster Pearce, superintendent of public instruction, drove to Flint from Lansing to offer me the job of assistant superintendent of public instruction. I had to refuse his offer for the same reason I gave Mr. Warriner.

To replace my friend "Mike" Ford in the shop, I hired Mame Buckrell, a very efficient typesetter, and made Edward E. Parish foreman of the printing department. I owe much of the success of The Riegle Press to his painstaking care of every phase of the work necessary to produce good printing.

Because I had been active in the Chamber of Commerce, the Kiwanis Club and other civic groups, I knew many of the businessmen of Flint and vicinity and my business grew rapidly, increasing each year by about $10,000. In 1929, the gross was $63,500. My profits during these years enabled me to buy a Packard automobile and build a brick house at 1613 Woodlawn Park Drive, where I still live.

DEPRESSION DAYS

In the fall of 1929, the Great Depression hit the world. It hit Flint especially hard because it is a one-industry town; business went down fast, like a sinker on a fish line.

In 1927, Mr. Wm. E. Hamilton, the Genesee County commissioner of schools, had brought me copies of a uniform series of forms now known as child accounting forms. The series was designed by the Michigan Superintendent of Public Instruction and had to be used in every school in the state. Putting these forms in print and selling them to both the city and rural schools helped to keep me from closing up shop, a fate of many businesses of that unhappy period.

Sometime in 1929 or 1930, a Mr. Brigham, who had been a salesman for the Hammond-Stephens Company, brought to my office copies of some class record and teachers' plan books. He persuaded me to put them into print by assuring me that he could sell enough of them to make it profitable for both of us. When I was county commissioner of schools, we had purchased similar books from the William Welch Company of Chicago. I have been told that Hammond and Stephens had been salesmen for the William Welch Company and left that firm to start their own business, taking the Welch forms as samples. Since these forms had not been copyrighted, we made some necessary changes to bring them up to date and put them in print.

I never found out whether or not Mr. Brigham would have become a good salesman if he had devoted enough time to his job. As the depression became sharper, his overdraft on his commission account became so large that I could not carry him and had to let him go.

Business semed to be better for the first six months of 1932, but when Roosevelt was nominated for president on the Democrat ticket the downward slide became worse. Businessmen feared for their economic future because of what had happened when he was governor of New York.

When Roosevelt closed the banks of the nation after his inauguration in 1933, the bottom dropped out of everything. For several months money was practically nonexistent even though some of the banks did open on a limited basis. When a check would come in from a school or county from a distance, we would deposit the check and then have to wait until it cleared through the New York clearing house before we could draw on it. It did not matter that the check was from a school or a county, whose officials do not write bad checks.

One day Chester Sibilsky, manager of the Detroit and Northern Savings and Loan Association, called to ask me to reprint a form we had printed several times for him. When I told him we could not print it because we had no paper and no money to buy paper, he asked me how much the paper would cost. When he heard that the paper would cost $35, he said, "Come down, John, and I'll give you the money." Needless to say, I made a quick trip to his office, ordered the paper, and had the forms printed within a few hours.

Sometime in June of 1933, I decided to try my luck at selling the child accounting forms by personal calls on school commissioners in the Thumb area of Michigan. My first call was on Ben McComb in Caro, an old friend. Ben and I had been appointed to our jobs by the board of supervisors in our respective counties in November of 1914. He gave me a large order. This was followed by another good order from William Sparling, the commissioner at Bad Axe. My call on the commissioner in Sanilac did not result in an order, but the two orders I did get gave me one of the biggest boosts I ever had. Later I told Ben and Bill that they saved my business.

SELLING AND CAMPING

These two initial sales gave me the idea that if I could sell to those commissioners, I could sell to other school officials. A few days after the Fourth of July I loaded an umbrella tent, a portable gasoline stove, some bedding and clothes and headed north in my old Packard, which, fortunately, had been paid for several years before. I took with me my son Don, age fourteen, and his two cousins, Kenneth and Russell Waterman, who were living with their grandmother after their mother died. We also took Skippy, our Boston terrier which Lee Lamb had given me because I kept him from resigning from the Flint school system when Mr. E. E. Lewis was superintendent.

The three boys had a great time on this camping trip. Each evening we camped near a river or lake. After breakfast each morning I would call on the schools within a radius of twenty or thirty miles of our camp. The boys would fish and have their catch ready to fry when I returned in the evening. After our evening meal we would move on to our next campground. We stayed several days on Indian Lake near the Big Spring, the spring immortalized by Longfellow in *Hiawatha*. Here the fishing was excellent. The boys had a good vacation while I covered the surrounding territory calling on schools.

On our way home we stopped in Mount Pleasant where I attended a meeting of the county school commissioners of the state. Many of my good friends were still in the group. I went to a meeting where Professor Walpool from the Michigan Agricultural College presented a plan to combine the teaching of physiology and agriculture into one class, thus saving the teacher's time in a crowded one-room school. He furnished mimeographed sheets of what he called "guide sheets" in the study of "Living Things." While he was talking, I had a pencil and paper in hand and was figuring out how much I would have to charge for them so my price would not be much more than the actual cost of the paper, the ink, and the stencils—if the commissioners decided to buy them. The professor had suggested that the commissioners mimeograph these sheets and send them out to their schools. I came forward with a price of 7 cents per guide sheet, a price which was acceptable to the commissioners present. Many of them assured me they would buy the forms from me.

Just as soon as I got back to the shop, I had some samples printed and sent to each county commissioner in the state. Orders began to come in at once; before the year was over we sold more than $5,000 worth of these guide sheets. With the orders for guide sheets came orders for child accounting forms. These sheets and the child accouning forms may well have been the salvation of my business in the bitter year of 1933. It was evident that without those orders I could not have kept my shop open, as business in Flint was at its lowest ebb and there was not enough commercial printing to keep our crew busy even on a half-time basis.

When the banks closed, the wholesale grocers had me print script to make change, as there was no small change in either silver or copper in circulation. It took a long, arduous journey to come to the day when we did as much business as we had done in 1929.

CHAPTER XVIII

Building a Business

I have always enjoyed the friendship of many good men, some of them former pupils of mine. George V. Gundry, who became an executive of the Buick Motor Company, and Judge Louis McGregor of the Michigan Court of Appeals, are two of the men who say I influenced their lives in a helpful way. Mr. Gundry, while serving as president of the Flint Board of Education, gave an address at a reunion of the Old Flint High graduates in which he paid the following tribute to me, much to my surprise:

> I firmly believe that whatever success I have achieved in my life is due to the influence that was brought to bear on me by John L. Riegle in my last two years of high school in Linden, Michigan. Mr. Riegle was superintendent of schools part of that time and he had a tremendous influence on my life, all for the good. My own father was not much help to me and I feel I received from Mr. Riegle the guidance and assistance that made my life for me.

I was deeply touched by this tribute. (It is always gratifying to have a bouquet tossed your way while alive to enjoy it.)

One of my contemporaries and my closest friend was Jesse Good. Although he was born on a farm two miles west of our place and distantly related to us, I did not get to know him well until he was elected county clerk of Genesee County in 1916, two years after I was appointed commissioner of schools. Jesse's office was on the first floor of the courthouse because it had to be readily accessible to the public; mine was tucked away in the farthest corner of the second floor. However, we soon renewed our early acquaintance and spent much time together in and out of the courthouse.

In 1919, Jesse and I built new houses opposite each other on the same street. We spent much of our leisure time together, first pitching horseshoes and later taking up golf together. We played hundreds of cribbage games. We took many fishing trips together to such places as Tawas Bay, Lakes St. Helen, and Houghton Lake.

In 1932, Jesse's eighth term as county clerk was ending. He had always been elected on the Republican ticket and was running for re-election. In October, all signs pointed to the election of Roosevelt and the complete Democrat ticket. As the day for election approached, Jesse grew more and more worried about his chances of finding another job. Sensing his anxiety, I told him that if he were defeated, he was to bring to me copies of all the legal blanks and election forms used in his office. I said I would put them in print and he could become a salesman for The Riegle Press. He was defeated, as were all the Republican candidates running for office.

THE LEGAL BLANK BUSINESS

Immediately we put into print all the legal blanks and election forms used in Michigan. The setting of the type for these forms was a stupendous task. There were over 600 of these forms, many covering four pages of legal-size paper, 8×13 inches. At that time there were four other printers of legal blanks in the state. These blanks could be reprinted by anyone, but there could be no variation in the forms, no matter who printed them. We called our blanks the "Good Line" of legal blanks, and in January of 1933 Jesse Good came into our firm as a salesman. He did fairly well in his new work, but he never especially liked it. Some men are not made to be salesmen; Jesse was one of these. People had always come to him for a service; it was most difficult for him to solicit orders. In October of 1933, he went to work in the office of the Groves Funeral Home, where he remained until his last illness in 1943.

It took several years for the legal blanks and election supply business to pay their way, but eventualy they became a stable part of our production. In 1944, we bought the Legal Blank Company of Grand Rapids, one of the oldest printers of legal blanks in the state. The original owners had died and a lumberman, who knew nothing of printing, had purchased it in a bankruptcy sale. When we bought the company and moved the stock and type to Flint, we also acquired their customers.

In 1935, an ex-Flint resident, Louise Stenger, who had been in the printing business in Rochester, New York, called on me seeking a job as saleswoman. I hired her and she began the work by selling job printing in the city. Soon we started her on the road selling to schools and dealers. The dealers, stationery stores and printers, bought legal blanks and election supplies as well as school forms. Her efforts helped to expand both divisions of our business.

When Louise visited a school, she would be asked to print passes, excuses, and other forms used in schools. Thus we began to print all the various forms that we now catalog. Louise worked for us until 1944, when a local stationery store owner coaxed her, by golden promises, to leave our employ to work for him. I have always been grateful to her for the work she did to build up our business.

By the time World War II started in Europe, The Riegle Press began to get back to the amount of business we had in 1929. However, our growth was limited by the paper shortage. After Pearl Harbor we were put on a quota; we could buy only as much paper each year as we had bought in 1941.

The National School and Universal Calendars

Twice each year for the past twenty years we have published a four-page circular called *The Riegle Press Messenger* in which we advertise our plan books, class record books, and other school forms. One edition, advertising the National School Calendar, was sent to every school board in the United States that maintained a high school. Another edition, stressing the Universal Calendar which covers the calendar year, was sent to several thousand stationers. These proved to be two successful pieces of advertising.

The National School Calendar, originally tailored to the requirements of school administrators but now used by many classroom teachers, is one of the largest-selling single items of our line. Annual sales now reach nearly 200,000 copies a year on this popular school calendar.

The origin of the National School Calendar dates back to 1936, when Philip Vercoe, then principal of Flint Central High School, brought in a copy of the National School Calendar. The first edition for the 1935-36 school year had already been printed by another local printer. We drew up a contract with Mr. Vercoe for The Riegle Press to print and sell the calendars on a royalty basis. After two or three years, Mr. Vercoe, much to my surprise, sold his copyright on the calendar to Ray Nash and his partner, who planned to push the sale of the item. This change of ownership was a big disappointment to me, because up to this time our firm had done all the advertising and selling of the calendars. Fortunately, however, we printed the books for Ray Nash on the same basis as we had for Mr. Vercoe. For various reasons, Nash and his partner could not sell enough calendars to make a success of their venture, so they let their contract with Vercoe lapse. Soon after this, we bought Vercoe's interest in the calendar. It was at least ten years after this before we sold enough of these calendars to realize a profit.

We had always tried to set up dealerships, especially school supply houses, to sell the two calendars. After World War II, we pushed this end of the business. Some of the dealers also began to buy our teachers' plan books, class record books, and other school forms. About 1952, business firms that specialize in taking photographs of school children in school started to buy our calendars as gifts to school administrators. This was the big boost we needed. When one of these school calendars was given to a superintendent or principal, other staff members who saw them wanted them and our sales multiplied rapidly.

THE NSSEA

About 1959, our firm joined the National School Supply and Equipment Association (NSSEA). This association has a yearly convention in the Palmer House in Chicago at which we exhibit all our printed forms used by schools as well as the two calendars. Our membership in the NSSEA has given us another big boost, as it has brought us many new dealers as customers.

Since 1948 we have built or purchased ten additions to our original shop, until we now occupy approximately 40,000 square feet of floor space, nearly a block square. Our annual business now amounts to nearly sixteen times our gross business in 1945. In 1962, we incorporated the business with the following officers: President and Treasurer, John L. Riegle; Vice Presidents, Donald W. Riegle and Edward E. Parish; and Secretary, John L. Riegle Jr. Our business has grown to be national in scope, with the National School Calendar to be found in nearly every high school in the United States.

Foreword to Book II

In order to get a clear picture of Michigan schools as they existed in my own time, I found it necessary to research the history of our schools from the time the state was admitted to the Union in 1837, together with inquiries into the territorial schools. Lewis Mumford wrote in his *The Conduct of Life:*

> Before every attempt to describe the world and life and time there stands an unspoken prologue; history itself. Without that prologue, the rest of the play would be unintelligible buzz and burr.

Yesterday is woven into the texture of today. What is, is the consequence of what was. Whenever there is change, it is from what was to what is coming to be. The change may be for better or for worse, but it always has relationship to the past, to the "unspoken prologue."

From the time I entered the primer class in a rural school in 1892 my life has been connected in some way with education in Michigan. This span covers 60 percent of the time since Michigan attained statehood. During these years this connection has been in a number of capacities: pupil, teacher, high school principal, village school superintendent, county school commissioner, member of the Flint board of education, and lastly a printer of school forms for forty-five years. During many of these years in the printing business I was a salesman soliciting orders from school officials. These contacts kept me informed of the needs and changes that should be made to make our school system second to none in the United States.

It is my earnest hope that Book II of this volume will be helpful to students and others interested in the history of the schools of Michigan.

—JOHN L. RIEGLE

CHAPTER I

Early Michigan History

FRENCH PERIOD

It was in 1634 that Jean Nicollet, a French explorer and woodsman, returned to Quebec from a journey to the Straits of Mackinac and Lake Michigan. He is credited with the discovery of Michigan, although the first white man to set foot on the soil of our state may have been Eitienne Brule, who returned from a trip through the West with a nugget of copper and a description of a country that could have been Michigan. The year 1634 was just one hundred years after Jacques Cartier had explored the Gulf of St. Lawrence and had discovered the St. Lawrence River. During the next thirty-four years only coureurs de bois or French fur traders visited the Great Lakes region. Occasional Catholic missionaries were on the waterways to the West at this time. Two of these, Father James Marquette and Father Claude Dablon, established the first permanent mission in 1668 at Sault Ste. Marie, founding the first settlement in Michigan. In 1671, Father Marquette founded another mission at St. Ignace.

For the next ninety-five years the French were the dominating force in what is now Michigan. In 1679, Robert Cavelier, better known as La Salle from the name of his family estate, built the first sailing ship, the *Griffin,* on the Great Lakes, above Niagara Falls. He sailed it across Lake Erie and up the Detroit River through Lake Huron to Lake Michigan. On its return voyage to Niagara, the ship was probably lost in a storm, as no trace of it was ever found.

Beginning in 1690, four wars were fought between France and England. The outcome of these wars was to determine the future fate of

North America. In 1701, Antoine de La Mothe Cadillac, aided by Count Pontchartrain, the French colonial minister, received a commission from the king of France to make a settlement on the Detroit River as a barrier against the English. Cadillac, with his thirteen-year-old son, fifty soldiers, forty Canadian traders and artisans, Father de L'Halle, a Recollect priest, and Father Vaillant, a Jesuit missionary, landed at the narrowest part of the river. They built a palisade on a site near what is now Jefferson Avenue and Shelby Street in Detroit and named it Fort Pontchartrain. The settlement that grew around this fort was named Detroit. This was the real beginning of the history of Michigan. On November 8, 1760, the French commander of Fort Pontchartrain surrendered this fort and Detroit to Major Robert Rogers, commander of the English forces. By the Treaty of Paris, signed in 1763, France relinquished all her claims to all the territory on the continent of North America.

That part of the territory north of the Ohio River, west of the Allegheny Mountains, and south of the Great Lakes became known as the Northwest Territory. It remained under the rule of England until the Treaty of Peace signed September 3, 1783, which recognized the freedom of the thirteen colonies. At that time there were very few inhabitants in the entire Northwest Territory. There were a few people at St. Ignace; nearly all the rest lived along the Detroit River or in Detroit.

During the French period, from 1701 to 1760, schools, if any, were kept by missionary priests. One of these was Father Simple Boquet. The first lay teacher in Detroit, thus first in Michigan, was Jean Baptiste Roucout. Born and educated in France, he migrated to Detroit in 1760. At first he conducted classes in his house on St. Jacques Street. In 1765, the church trustees bought this house with the provision that it should be used as a school building. Roucout was to have free lodging in the building as long as he served the parish and the school as Christian education director and as choirmaster. He held classes in this building for more than thirty years. There is no record of the subjects he taught, the methods used, or the number of children in attendance. This building was the first in Michigan to be called a "schoolhouse."

Subscription Schools

No effort was made by the English army of occupation to educate any children during their occupation from 1763 to 1796, when they finally gave up the territory. When the English moved out, settlers from the East slowly moved in. The first schools were known as "subscription schools." These had been in existence during the English occupation and were continued when people from the eastern states began to seek new homes in the West. Subscription schools were held in the homes of the teachers. To maintain these schools, each parent agreed to pay a certain sum for each child enrolled from his household. The teacher may have been an itinerant teacher, like an Ichabod Crane, who wandered into Detroit, or perhaps some young man who had sufficient education to qualify as an instructor. Based on the number of children he had in school, each father was expected to assume his proportionate share of the cost of firewood and candles. The average number of pupils in such a school was probably about twenty. Matthew Donavan, an Irishman reputed to have been an excellent Latin scholar, was one of these early teachers. His yearly income was probably about $500 to $600. He kept his school for eleven years, from 1794 to 1805. Another of these early teachers was Peter Joseph Dillon, who arrived in Detroit from Hamilton, Ontario, Canada, in 1798. His wife also taught school.

David Bacon was sent by the Missionary Society of Connecticut as a missionary to convert the Chippewa Indians. He was not a classical scholar, but he had received a good common school education. His schoolhouse was the first to be furnished with desks and seats, which were, of course, hand made. Tuition rates were from 10 to 14 shillings, depending upon the age of the pupils and the subjects studied. For reasons not clear to historians, his school lasted only about one year.

A Catholic priest from France by way of the Illinois Indian country, Father Gabriel Richard, who was to have a great influence on Michigan schools, arrived in Detroit in the spring of 1798. He was sent there as a missionary, but at heart he was a teacher. After his ordination, he had taught mathematics in a French parish college. He was forced to leave France because of the persecution of Catholics by the Revolutionaries. He immediately interested himself in educational work, but in June of

1805 a disastrous fire destroyed practically all the buildings in the settlement of Detroit.

In January of 1805, Congress established a separate territory of Michigan, with William Hull installed as the first governor. Detroit was made its capital.

TERRITORIAL SCHOOLS

In 1809, the first law to establish a school system was passed by the territorial legislature. This act provided for the division into school districts all the settled portions of the territory and for the enumeration of children between the ages of four and eighteen. Annual reports of the moneys expended in support of schools and in the construction of school buildings were required from each district. The territorial government was to levy a tax of not less than $2 and not more than $4 for each child reported within the ages mentioned. The sum thus collected was to be apportioned among the various districts, not in proportion to the number of children in each district, but in proportion to the sum spent the previous year for school purposes.

When the territorial government was organized, Father Richard began to cooperate with the authorities in every way he could, but especially in education, to make Detroit a better place in which to live. He probably established several schools in the city. His thinking was that these schools should be free so that the poorest child—French, Indian, or Yankee—could get the rudiments of an education. He also proposed that carpenters, blacksmiths, weavers, and shoemakers should be assigned to the schools to instruct the children in these crafts.

In 1808, a farm known as the Spring Hill Farm, containing 250 acres, was taken over by the United States government in default of a judgment. When Father Richard heard of this action, he began at once to plan a seminary which he hoped would become the head of all the schools in the territory. He planned to have it equipped with an air pump, optical and electrical machines, globes, maps, a carding machine and a spinning wheel. Not having funds enough to buy the farm, he rented it for $200 for the rest of the year. With the help of Angelique Campear and Elizabeth Lyons, he started two schools, one for boys and one for girls.

At about the same time, he bought a house and lot for $500 to which he moved his Academy for Young Ladies, under the direction of Elizabeth Williams. In his girls' school, he installed nearly three dozen spinning wheels and a spinning jenny. Academic subjects taught were reading, writing and arithmetic. One of the schools for girls had four Indian girls enrolled.

It was about this time that the federal government appropriated $400 for the education of Indian children, to be apportioned according to the number of Indian children admitted and taught in the academies. In 1809, upon Father Richard's return from Washington, where he tried to get the government to sell him Spring Hill Farm, he visited New York, where he bought an organ, a harpsicord, a printing press, type, and sixty reams of paper. In August, a printer whom he hired to come to Detroit, printed the first and only issue of a newspaper, the *Michigan Essay and Impartial Observer*.

After repeated efforts to get the War Department to sell him Spring Hill Farm at a reasonable price, Father Richard was forced to give up the idea and close his academy. The farm was sold at public auction for $5,000, a sum far beyond the educator's ability to pay. The War of 1812 put an end to all his plans.

In 1809, James Witherell, one of the district judges in control of Michigan Territory, drafted an education bill. This bill was to establish the school district as the basic administrative unit. The overseers of the poor, of which there were four in Michigan, were to form school districts most convenient for erecting schoolhouses and maintaining schools. These overseers were to serve as trustees. Each spring they were to take a census of all the children in the district between the ages of four and eighteen. They could change the boundaries of a district as they saw fit. They could appropriate a sum of not less than $2 or more than $4 for each child enrolled in the census. This act was never put into effect.

Before any further steps could be taken to provide schools for Michigan Territory the War of 1812 began. Governor Hull surrendered Detroit and Michigan to the British, who held the territory until September of 1813, during which time they destroyed every piece of public property in Detroit.

Lewis Cass of Ohio received an interim appointment as governor of the Michigan Territory. It was soon after his appointment that a survey of southern Michigan was made by surveyors sent from Washington, D. C. The purpose of the survey was to find bounty lands for the soldiers of the War of 1812. The surveyors' reports sent back to Washington called the entire area a swampland unfit for cultivation.

One of Governor Cass' first acts was to get the federal government to open a land office. His second objective was a plan to organize public schools. A new arrival in Michigan was the Reverend John Monteith, a graduate of Princeton Seminary. Governor Cass invited Father Richard and the Reverend Monteith to be members of a committee to plan schools for the Territory of Michigan.

The first step was the organization of a library association. Each member of the association purchased shares at $5 each. When ninety members had joined, the Reverend Monteith was sent to New York, where he bought 300 books.

The second step was the organization of a committee to begin work in the planning of a public school system. This committee was composed of Judge Augustus Woodward, William Woodbridge, Father Richard, and the Reverend Monteith. The plan this committee submitted to the territorial legislature incorporated an institution known as the Catholepistemead (or University of Michigan) with the Reverend John Monteith as the first president. The plan worked out was for a complete system of schools, from the primary level to the highest level of college. The university was to have thirteen professors, to be appointed by the governor and to be paid an annual salary from the treasury of the Territory of Michigan. The professor of universal science was to be president. He, with the other professors, constituted the governing body of the university. They had the authority to appoint all the teachers under them, to establish colleges, academies, schools, libraries, museums, and laboratories as well as to appoint all school officers throughout the various counties, cities, towns, townships or other geographical divisions in the Michigan Territory. All teachers were to be paid a fixed salary from the Territorial treasury. Public taxes were to be increased 15% and four successive lotteries were to be held, the proceeds from which the university was to receive 15%. Schools established under this plan were to charge tuition. To secure funds to build the first university buildings, a subscription list was made. The first day of soliciting, the sum of $2,500 was subscribed. The cornerstone of the first university building was laid in Detroit on September 24, 1817.

In September of 1817, the university, as head of the school system of Michigan, established the primary school of Detroit and specified that a schoolhouse be built on the grounds of the university. At the same time, the university appointed trustees and visitors for the primary school. Subjects to be taught in this school were reading, writing, arithmetic, English grammar, and elocution.

For the older pupils the university established the Classical Academy of the City of Detroit. The curriculum of the new academy required that the students be instructed in French, Latin, Greek, antiquity, English grammar, composition, elocution, mathematics, geography, morals, and ornamental accomplishments.

Unfortunately, the money pledged for the university building and the academy came in very slowly. The academy was opened in a house on the corner of Jefferson Avenue and Griswold Street, with Hugh M. Dickey, a graduate of Jefferson College in Pennsylvania, as headmaster. He was to be paid with tuition collected from his students. However, this first headmaster became ill and died in February of 1819.

The next teacher at the academy was Lemuel Shattuck, from New Ipswich, New Hampshire, who had been trained in the Lancasterian method. This method was based on the idea of having a large school with one headmaster and using the older children as monitors to teach the younger pupils. His success with this method was phenomenal. However, because of "hard times" and lack of support by the citizens, he remained with the school only three and a half years. His successor was John Farmer. Because support for the school was not forthcoming, Farmer left Detroit for Ohio after two years with less money than he had when he arrived. Thus ended the Lancasterian experiment.

In 1821, some changes were made which later developed into the fabric of our present school system. An act passed by the territorial legislature provided for a board of twenty-one trustees, of which the governor was a member *ex officio*. This board was given control of the university and was also given the authority to organize such schools, academies, and colleges as they deemed proper. These schools were to be supported by the income from lands especially set apart for educational purposes and by voluntary contributions from private individuals.

In March of 1823, Congress passed, at the request of Governor Cass, a bill which abolished the judges as the governing body of the Michigan Territory. This bill named the governor and a legislative council of nine members as the governing body. The President of the United States was to select the nine council members from a list of eighteen candidates elected by the people of the territory. The first election was held on September 4, 1823. This marked a turning point in the history of Michigan.

The first legislative council met in Detroit on June 7, 1824. One of the first tasks for this council was to devise a plan for public support of schools. Governor Cass recommended that the reserved lands, that is, Section 16 of every township set aside by an act of Congress in 1804, be leased and the money received from these leases be used to support public schools. If the money received from these leases proved insufficient, then additional funds were to come from tuition or direct taxes.

In 1827, a third act was passed which took the control of the common schools out of the hands of the board of trustees of the university and conferred those rights and powers upon the people, imposing upon them grave responsibilities. By the provisions of this act, every township containing fifty families was required to support a school. The townships having a greater population were required to maintain the school for a longer length of time and of advanced quality. This act was patterned after a Massachusetts law of 1647. The voters of the township could order a division of the township into districts, with a board of three trustees to manage local school affairs. The examination of teachers and the supervision of all the schools in the township were placed in a board of school examiners in each township.

In 1828, the law was amended to provide for the appointment of a Superintendent of Common Schools by the governor. By this law the district system was defined. It provided for a board of commissioners of common schools in each township, whose duties were to distribute all the money derived from the rental of the school section (Section 16) and to establish the boundaries of school districts. There were also to be inspectors of common schools who examined and licensed teachers and performed the functions of supervision.

JOHN D. PIERCE

Before much of the organization outlined by these laws could be put into operation, John D. Pierce was appointed Superintendent of Common Schools, a new constitution was written and adopted, and Michigan was admitted to the Union. This man, John D. Pierce, often called the father of the Michigan school system because of his great influence on education in our state, was born February 18, 1797, in Chesterfield, New Hampshire, the only son of Gad and Sarah Davis Pierce. George Washington was still president at the time.

My own father was born in 1840, only three years after Michigan became a state. When we consider these dates and events we realize how young we are as a people among the nations of the earth. It should also make us realize the debt we owe the pioneers, our grandfathers and great-grandfathers who carved the farms and homes out of the wilderness by backbreaking labor, built the schools, the churches, the cities and factories that have given us our "affluent society." This is as true for the whole United States as it is for Michigan.

When John D. Pierce was two years old, his father died. He grew up in a home where even the necessities were scarce and his schooling consisted of not more than eight weeks a year. However, he became an insatiable reader; he boasted that at an early age he had read every book within ten miles of Paxton, his home town. When he was eighteen, he decided to go to college to study for the ministry. After earning $100 by working for a neighbor, and with another $100 from his father's estate, he walked fourteen miles to the home of Enoch Pond for his first lesson in Latin, buying a Latin grammar on the way. He studied with Pond for a year, after which he enrolled in Brown University in 1813. Brown was under the direction of the Baptist Church but was well known for the liberality of its scholastic atmosphere. By teaching school three or four months of each year, Pierce was able to continue his studies and to graduate with the class of 1822. After studying theology at the Princeton Theological Seminar,y he was licensed to preach by the Congregational Society. He spent the next nine years preaching and teaching in Massachusetts and Connecticut. In 1831, the call of the West began to be heard in New England. Leaving his home in May, Pierce landed in Detroit in June. From there he went to Marshall, where he decided to stay and make his home.

In 1835, a convention was held in Detroit to write the first constitution for Michigan. Mr. Isaac E. Crary, a lawyer who lived in Marshall and was a close friend of Pierce, was a member of this convention and was chairman of the committee on education. Through Crary's influence, John D. Pierce was appointed to the office of superintendent of public instruction. These two men, Isaac E. Crary and John D. Pierce, together with a third man, Victor Cousin, a Frenchman who never visited America, laid the foundations for the educational system of Michigan.

The graves of Pierce and Crary are in a cemetery in Marshall. On the gravestone of Pierce are these words, which state that the object of the common schools is "to furnish good instruction in all the elementary and common branches of knowledge for all classes of the community, as good indeed for the poorest boy in the state as the rich man can furnish his children with all his wealth."

In 1831, Victor Cousin made a visit to Prussia. Upon his return to France, he wrote a report describing the schools of Prussia, a report which was translated into English by Mrs. Sarah Austin. This report is regarded by historians as one of the most quickening educational documents ever written. In 1835, a copy of this report fell into the hands of Messrs. Pierce and Crary. Its salient features were incorporated in the constitution of Michigan which was adopted in 1835, when Michigan Territory was asking Congress that it be admitted into the Union.

CHAPTER II

Schools Under the First
Michigan Constitution

Michigan was admitted into the Union in 1837. Provisions were made for a state superintendent of public instruction, a complete system of elementary schools, township libraries, and a state university. By the establishment of an independent Department of Education with its own administrator, Michigan became the first state to take this action. Thus John D. Pierce became the first state superintendent of public instruction in the United States.

The year 1837 may appropriately be called the beginning of the American renaissance in education. However, it should be understood that the system Mr. Pierce planned for Michigan was not one of spontaneous growth. The school system he introduced in Michigan had its roots in the schools of New England and Virginia. They, in turn, had been influenced by schools in England, Germany, Holland and France. The system he started in Michigan had to be made to fit into and be adapted to the pioneer society of a new state. The times demanded that there be a better organization of schools, including proper maintenance, supervision, and system of grading as well as the establishment of agricultural, industrial, and manual training schools, more liberal courses of study, better trained teachers and the corollary—normal schools—better textbooks and more adequate school libraries. These demands were uppermost in Pierce's mind when he planned the school system for the state. Unfortunately, he was influenced primarily by the school system of Massachusetts, where the organization had originally been based upon township units. Later, by 1789, the township units were divided into districts. It was the district plan Mr. Pierce adopted for the schools of Michigan.

Mr. W. B. Weeden, in his book, *The Economic and Social History of New England,* called the next three or four decades (after 1789) the "dark ages" of New England culture and education because of the poor schools maintained in some of the districts. Pierce's adoption of the Massachusetts district plan has always been a great handicap for Michigan schools, partially overcome when the legislature passed the K-12 law in 1961. It is to be hoped that the two worst disadvantages, really evils, of the district system, namely, unequal taxation and too many small, expensive districts, will be corrected by Governor Milliken's school reorganization plan which is stalled in the legislature as this book goes to print.

The renaissance in education was evidenced by the establishment of many new universities, colleges, and normal schools, by the publication of new textbooks and dictionaries, and especially by the concept of *free* schools. Free schools had been established in Pennsylvania around the turn of the nineteenth century, but at first they were for the children of indigent parents only, and thus bore a stigma.

The first constitution for Michigan was adopted in October of 1835. It was similar to those of the other states carved out of the Northwest Territory except for its provisions for education. That part of the document was in the hands of Isaac E. Crary and his friend John D. Pierce. As mentioned earlier, the report of Victor Cousin on the Prussian school system was carefully studied by these men and it had its effect on their planning.

Historians agree that it was through Mr. Crary's influence that Governor Mason had appointed Pierce as superintendent of common schools before the constitution was written. This position was of great importance because it gave him not only the task of organizing a complete new school system for Michigan, but also gave him the management of more than one million acres of school and university lands. Among these lands were the sections numbered "16" in every township, most of which were unsold at that time.

Mr. Pierce made a trip through the East to study the different school systems. When he returned home, he wrote a detailed report, presenting a plan for the organization of the schools of Michigan. In 1837, his plan was adopted by the legislature. His philosophy of education is best expressed in his own words:

> Let the schoolhouse and the church be planted, as they ever have been, in every village and hamlet throughout the length and breadth of our land, and no tyrant can ever arise that shall be strong enough to trample upon and tread down the rights of the people.

According to his theory, the state is a spiritual creation with supreme rights and duties. It must be protected and is under obligation to protect. To attain the welfare of the individual and the security of the state, the individual must be educated—and this must be done by universal and free education. This did not mean that private schools could not exist, but it meant that all who did not go to a private school should go to a free public school. In this system, the development of the individual was of supreme importance. This, Pierce said, was the letter and the spirit of the Prussian system. From other suggestions gained from his study of the Prussian system, Pierce spoke of the necessity of trained teachers, proper courses of study, better textbooks, libraries, better school buildings and the necessary appurtenances.

The system which this first superintendent of public instruction inaugurated is the system under which, with a few changes, the schools of Michigan operate today. Although he copied parts of the Prussian system, his plan made the local schools less centralized, with more power in the hands of the people. Under his plan, the school district was the unit of importance, the unit endowed with corporate power to erect school buildings and provide the necessary appendages for such buildings, to furnish a library, and to levy a tax for such purposes. Three officers were to be elected to a district board: a moderator, a director, and an assessor.

The next division in the plan was the township, which also had corporate powers and was to levy a tax equal to the money received from the Primary Interest fund. A board of school inspectors was to be elected by the people of the township. This board consisted of two members elected by the people, the third member being the township clerk, who was an *ex officio* member. It was the duty of this board to attend to the formation of new districts, inspect the schools and teachers, apportion the money received from the Primary Interest fund and from taxes, conduct teachers' examinations and grant teachers' certificates, and to make an annual report to the superintendent of public instruction.

Above the township was to be the county, with an academy of three departments. It was the duty of the county board of supervisors to secure a proper site and erect suitable buildings, subject to the approval of the superintendent of public instruction. Each academy was to have a board of trustees of seven members, six of whom were to be appointed by the board of supervisors and one by the state superintendent. This board was to have general charge of the academy and to select the teachers and professors. The board of supervisors was to appropriate a sum of money equal to that given from the university fund to finance the academy. The academy was to have three departments, one for those students who wanted more education than that offered by the common schools, one for classical education for those who wished to enter the university, and one to prepare teachers for teaching in elementary schools.

This county academy plan was one concept that did not work out as expected. It was an entirely new concept which, when tried, just did not work out successfully. The academies, which, under the School Organization Act, were under the dual control of the county and the University of Michigan, were the one phase of the school system which failed. Eight of these academies were organized, located in Detroit, Kalamazoo, Monroe, Niles, Pontiac, Romeo, Tecumseh, and White Pigeon. These academies, considered to be branches of the university, were supposed to bridge the gap between the common schools and the university. They had a short life, as they were forced to close when the appropriations from the legislature were not sufficient to support them.

When these eight academies were discontinued, many private seminaries were founded. The superintendent's report for 1852 lists 29 of these schools. As these were tuition schools, only the well-to-do could take advantage of them and consequently nearly all these private schools failed to survive.

The next step in the development of the new school system was the relocation of the University of Michigan, which was moved from Detroit to Ann Arbor.

Realizing that the public schools were in their infancy, Mr. Pierce submitted a carefully drawn plan of a model schoolhouse, a plan which was followed by many districts.

This general plan for the Michigan school system imbedded in the new constitution was implemented by the school laws passed by the first legislature after Michigan became a state in 1837. One of the first orders of business for the legislature after the constitution was adopted was to make rules for the formation of county and township governments. As soon as the townships were formed and had elected their first set of officers, the township board of school inspectors could proceed to organize school districts. Michigan at this time was to a great extent a wilderness. The basic idea with regard to education was to have a school within "the length of the legs of every child," which meant that every child should have a school within walking distance of his home. New districts were formed by the township board of school inspectors whenever in its judgment a new school district was necessary. However, there were limits as to the size of a district. No child could live more than two and a half miles from the school site and no district could contain more than nine square miles. The average size of a primary school district in Michigan was four square miles, making nine school districts to a township. These districts were to be numbered consecutively from "1" on. Fractional districts, that is, those in which parts of the district were in two or more townships, were numbered in the township in which the schoolhouse was located. Because of rivers, swamps and lakes, some townships had only eight districts while others had ten.

When a district was to be organized, it was the duty of the clerk of the board of school inspectors to deliver to a taxable inhabitant of such district a written notice of the formation of said district, describing the boundaries and specifying the time and place of the first meeting. It was then the duty of this taxpayer to notify all qualified voters in the district by person or in writing five days prior to the meeting date. Should the taxpayer chosen to notify all the other residents of the district fail to carry out the order of the inspectors, he could be fined $5. In such a case, the inspectors could then choose another taxpayer to follow this procedure.

At this first meeting, after organizing by appointing a chairman and a clerk, three officers—a moderator, a director, and an assessor—were elected for three-year terms. The annual meeting of the district was held on the first Monday in September. This date was later changed, first to the second Monday in July, and later to the second Monday in June.

All districts so organized became a body corporate, with the usual powers of a corporation, with a name, such as School District No. 1 of Richfield Township. The district could sue or be sued. It could carry on all the business necessary to maintain a school, including the purchase of a school site or the raising of taxes to build a schoolhouse. The school laws spelled out in detail the powers given to the districts and their officers. They are the same as those of today, with very little change. Among the changes that have been made is one that changed the title of moderator to president, director to secretary, and assessor to treasurer.

The duties and powers of the board of school inspectors were: (1) to choose a school site if the district could not agree on one; (2) to prescribe the rules by which a director could draw books from the township library; (3) to regulate and alter the boundaries of the school districts as circumstances warranted; (4) to reserve from the township treasurer all moneys appointed for the township library; (5) to purchase the books and necessary supplies for said library; (6) to make rules for the operation of the library and preservation of its books; (7) to appoint one of their number to visit each school in the township at least once each school term to examine the pupils and give advice to both teacher and pupils; (8) to make reports in triplicate to the township clerk on the first Saturday in October, giving the number of districts in the township, amount of money received by each, and other items required by the superintendent of public instruction. Later, when counties had a superintendent, these reports were sent to him, who in turn submitted them to the superintendent of public instruction. A ninth duty was to appoint district officers in a newly organized district if the voters failed to elect them.

CHAPTER III

The Primary School Interest Fund

Because of one of the most important acts of the Continental Congress and one of its last, Superintendent Pierce had at hand a very significant source of income to use in the big task before him, which was to organize a school system for Michigan. This act was the Ordinance of 1787, a charter for the government of the Northwest Territory. It may be well to examine in detail just what this source of income was. The preamble of this charter states:

> Religion, morality, and knowledge being necessary to good government and the happiness of mankind, schools and the means of education shall forever be encouraged.

This philosophy had a great influence on the future history of Michigan and the other states formed from the Northwest Territory.

To pay the debts caused by the Revolution, Congress made plans to sell the land in the Northwest Territory. As an inducement to people to buy the land, Congress promised that Section 16 in each township would be set aside for the advancement of education. These sections of land became known as the "school sections." When Michigan became a state in 1837 the state became custodian of these sections.

In some of the states the money obtained from the sale of these school sections was frittered away for the immediate use of the schools. In Michigan the legislature wisely entrusted the sale of these lands to the state superintendent of public instruction, with a directive that the money be placed in a trust fund, the interest from which would be spent for the maintenance of the common schools. The sale was by auction. Land could not be sold for less than $8 per acre, with a down payment of ¼ of the sale price, the balance to be paid in annual installments beginning five years after the sale, with interest at 7% per year.

The first year's sales amounted to approximately $40,000. The average price per acre was $12. In the first four years of the sale the total sales approximated $600,000. In 1841, because of hard times, one third of the contracts were forfeited. The minimum price per acre was lowered to $5, the balance to be paid at the pleasure of the buyer if the interest payments were made. In 1842, a review of all the contracts was made; the price was set at $5 per acre and the difference between what the buyer had originally agreed to pay was applied on the principal. The money received from these sales was used to construct the Capitol in Lansing and to build many badly needed roads. The state then issued bonds bearing interest at 7% per year as security. These bonds became and remain a perpetual fund. The interest paid on these bonds is apportioned each year among the school districts according to the number of pupils of school age in the district. This fund is known as the Primary School fund.

The constitution of 1850 also provided that all specific taxes, that is, taxes levied against the railroads, telegraph and telephone, express and insurance companies and toll roads, except those taxes received from the mining companies of the Upper Peninsula, should be used in paying the interest upon the Primary, University, and other educational funds and the interest and principal of the state debt in the order herein recited until the extinguishment of the state debt, other than the amounts due the educational funds, when such specific taxes shall be added to and constitute a part of the Primary School Interest fund.

At the close of the fiscal year September 30, 1870, the Superintendent of Public Instruction claimed that the state debt was practically extinguished since that part of the specific tax pledged for that purpose had outgrown the state indebtedness. The Supreme Court was called upon to place an interpretation upon this article of the constitution. The Court ruled in favor of the schools and the sum of $305,395.97 was added to the fund to be distributed to the schools. This raised the appropriation to schools to $1.06 for each child instead of the 47 cents per child paid in 1869.

In 1843, the sale of the land was taken from the jurisdiction of the state superintendent's office and placed in a newly organized land office.

Other sources of this fund were taxes on railroads, telegraph companies, insurance companies, express companies, and owners of plank roads. (Private companies built toll roads between certain cities, for example, between Flint and Saginaw. These roads were paved with lumber, which was cheap and plentiful. In one year the tax from the plank roads amounted to $88.33.)

Another source of money to be invested together with the Primary School fund was the proceeds from the sale of the so-called swamp lands. In 1812, Congress set aside from the government lands two million acres of bounty lands to be given to soldiers to encourage enlistments in the War of 1812. Mr. Tiffin, survyeor general of the United States, sent his agents into Michigan to survey these lands. Their report was that the land in southern Michigan was an unbroken series of tamarack swamps, bogs and sand dunes, with not more than one acre in a thousand fit for cultivation. Suitable bounty lands were then found in Illinois and Missouri. Why the federal agents made such an erroneous report is an unsolved mystery.

However, for Michigan schools the report was most fortunate. These so-called swamplands were transferred to Michigan in 1850 and were put under the jurisdiction of the land office. A large proportion of these lands were swamp in name only and were offered for sale. Much of this property was sold and became some of the most valuable acreage in the state for farming. After the cost of selling was deducted, one half of the amount received was put into the Primary School fund. The state issued bonds for this money and paid 5% annually on the principal fund. The bonds issued against the money received from the sale of Section 16 acreage paid 7%. By 1890 the amount of money from the swamplands totaled $846,778.52.

CHAPTER IV

Pioneer Life

The plan for our Michigan schools was implemented in the first constitution, adopted in 1835. The laws necessary to make the plan work were passed by the legislature that met in 1837, after Michigan was admitted to the Union.

Before tracing the pathway of the trials and errors of this plan and the laws enacted to make it work, it may be well to learn something about the citizens of the new state, where they came from, how they came, and how they lived. It may also be interesting to see what their thinking was in regard to education and what leading educators and authors of the textbooks considered essential.

According to the census taken in 1810 the population of Michigan was 4,782. In 1820 it was 8,765 and in 1830, 31,639. The rapid growth between 1820 and 1830 was caused by the advent of the first steamship on the Great Lakes, which reached Detroit on August 17, 1818. From that time on, steamships made periodic trips between Buffalo and Detroit. This growth was accelerated by the opening of the Erie Canal in 1832, which brought into Michigan an endless stream of settlers from New England, Pennsylvania and New York. Other settlers came on foot, by horse-drawn Conestoga wagons, or on horseback. By this time they had learned that southern Michigan was not a dismal swamp, as had been reported, but was good farmland covered by hardwood forests. They followed Indian traces or cut their own roads as they traveled to their new homes. Their first task was to clear the land of trees and stumps before they could build the log cabins which were to be their first dwellings.

These log cabins were approximately eighteen by twenty-four foot rectangles, eight feet high. The roof was covered by handmade shingles. Usually there was only one room, with a fireplace at one end and two windows and a door on the south side. The cracks between the logs were plastered outside and inside with clay mud. Much of the furniture was homemade. What factory-built furniture they had, such as beds, bureaus, and splint-bottomed chairs, they had brought with them from their old homes. Until their cabins could be built, they slept in tents or in the covered wagons that brought them there. Sometimes they even slept in Indian wigwams if there were Indians living nearby, as the Michigan Indians were friendly if treated properly.

When my father was born, in 1840 in Clarence township of New York, all farm work except plowing and dragging or harrowing was done by hand. Some farm motive power was provided by oxen and horses, but much of the farmers' work was done by manpower. Many of the tools, such as the fork, spade, scoop shovel, rake, hoe, plow, shovel, scythe, cradle and harrow had been used with little change for centuries. When farms became scarce in the eastern part of the United States, a young man could buy a Conestoga wagon, load into it all the tools necessary to start a home in the West, put in a mattress filled with straw for a bed, take his family and set out for a new home.

The first three decades after 1837, when Michigan achieved statehood, were spent in hewing the farms and villages out of the wilderness. The early settlers had to cut down the huge trees of oak, beech, maple and elm; chop off the limbs; then cut the logs with crosscut saws into lengths short enough to be rolled or hauled into large piles where they were left to dry. These piles were later burned in huge bonfires, for there was no market in those days for hardwood lumber.

Many farmers save a woodlot of ten acres or more. For years wood was the only kind of fuel available in village or countryside. Also, these woodlots were for many years a source of revenue from the sale of maple syrup and maple sugar that could be made each spring from the maple trees.

Before crops could be planted, the stumps had to be pulled, dug or burned out. All this took backbreaking, bone-breaking labor. My maternal grandfather was killed while clearing his land by a tree which fell the wrong way.

Building the roads, building the houses and barns, fencing the fields, and digging the ditches took the labor of every member of a family. Education and the finer arts of life were not thought necessary. The three R's, reading, 'riting, and 'rithmetic, which could be learned in school terms of two or three months in midwinter, were all the learning considered necessary for farm children. Notwithstanding the views of the early settlers on education, the foundation of our public school system was laid down in our first state constitution, adopted in 1835.

In those early days, most barns were built with a threshing floor running through the center, with a room on one side with stalls and mangers for the horses and oxen or cows. On the other side was a mow used to store hay or grain. The space over the room for animals was also used as a mow.

When the wheat was cut by a cradle, it was bound into bundles, drawn to the barn and stowed in the mow. When winter came, the farmer swept the barn floor clean and then threshed the grain by beating the wheat heads with a flail, an instrument of husbandry used since Biblical times. The straw was then pitched into piles and the wheat winnowed from the chaff by using a scoop to lift the wheat three or four feet from the ground, tilt it to let the grain fall from the scoop so the wind would blow the chaff away. It was during the 1840s that the first fanning mills were made.

The years from 1840 to 1860 brought streams of immigrants from Europe, especially from Ireland and Germany. They came from Ireland because of the potato famine in their homeland and from Germany because of political revolution. The Irish settled mostly in the cities, mainly Boston and New York; the Germans moved to the West and became farmers. As mentioned earlier, my mother's family came from Germany in 1854, settling first in the vicinity of Ann Arbor and later in Argentine township in Genesee County. These immigrants came in droves, and not only because land was cheap. One German wrote home to his relatives:

> If you wish to see our whole family living in a country where freedom of speech obtains, where no spies are eavesdropping,

where no simpleton criticizes your every word and seeks to detect
therein a venom that might endanger the life of the state, the
church and the home, in short, if you wish to be really happy and
independent, then come here.

The ferment that brought the people from New York and Pennsylvania
and New England and immigrants from the Old World to the states being
formed out of the Northwest Territory also brought about a revolution
in the lives and ways of the farmers.

The spinning wheel and the looms for weaving cloth were beginning to disappear as great mills for weaving cloth were built, especially
in New England.

LABOR-SAVING MACHINES

It was before the 1840s that the first machine was patented to take
the place of the flail to thresh the grain from the straw. This machine
was called a groundhog. The groundhog thresher was first patented in
England in 1788. Between 1790 and 1835 the U. S. Patent Office granted
267 patents for alleged improvements of the groundhog thresher. In
1842, J. E. Case, who was a groundhog operator in New York, purchased
six of these machines, took them to Oswego, where he loaded them on a
boat in the Erie Canal which took them through the Welland Canal,
across Lake Erie, up through the Detroit River, Lake St. Clair, the St. Clair
River, Lake Huron, and Lake Michigan to Chicago. There he loaded them
on a wagon and headed for Rochester, Wisconsin, which was the hub of
a new wheat-growing center. He sold five of the six machines on the way
to Rochester, where he became acquainted with Richard Ela and his
fanning machine.

Richard Ela, a native of Lebanon, New Hampshire, who settled first
in Plainfield, Illinois, then moved to Rochester, Wisconsin, was one of
the developers of fanning mills. His invention was a machine with fans
fastened to a shaft in a box in such a way that when the shaft was rotated
by a handle the fans blew the chaff away, thus separating the wheat from
the chaff. His fanning mills were the first to be used for this purpose.

The next step was to make a machine that would combine the
groundhog thresher and the fanning mill in one machine. This was accom-

plished in Rochester by Messrs. Case and Ela, with the help of Stephen Thresher, a local carpenter. At first these machines were powered by sweep-horsepower, that is, real horses, but soon steam engines came into general use. These early machines were drawn from farm to farm by horses at first, but not for long. Yankee inventiveness soon produced self-driven steam engines.

Cyrus McCormick patented his first successful reaper in 1849. Another inventor and manufacturer of reaping machines was William Deering, an immigrant from Maine to Wisconsin. In 1872, Deering added to his reaper a self-binding device invented by John F. Appleby, who worked to perfect his idea of a self-binding device while he was a Union soldier during the siege of Vicksburg. (My father bought his first binder when I was four years old; I can still remember the reaper he used before he bought the binder.)

It was during the 1870s that the first machines, called drills, were used to plant wheat and other grain. Before these drills were invented, a farmer would take a bag made of heavy cloth, put about a bushel of wheat into it, tie one corner of the bottom of the bag to the top and put the bag over his shoulder so its open end was where he could reach in and get a handful of grain. As he walked across the field to be planted, he would scatter the grain. To sow the grain evenly required both care and skill. After the grain was sowed, the farmer would cover it with dirt by driving a team of horses drawing a peg-toothed drag back and forth across the field. Before drags were invented, the seed was covered by the farmer dragging a large bush or limb of a tree across the field.

Thus during the few years from the time my father was born and the time I was born, the invention of the steel self-scouring plow, the reaper, the self-binding reaper, the drill and the threshing machine took much of the backbreaking labor out of farming.

While the farmer was being relieved of most of the strenuous labor, the housewife was also being helped. Large cloth-weaving mills in New England had replaced the hand-driven looms of my grandmother's day. Spinning wheels for making yarn for stockings and mittens lingered on in some homes until my time. In 1846, Elias Howe invented the sewing machine. Before this time all sewing had to be done by hand. About

1885 the washboard was invented. It was hailed as a great labor-saving device, but shortly afterwards hand-operated washing machines appeared and replaced the washboards to a large extent.

The labor-saving machines enabled farmers to increase the size of their farms and their incomes. They moved out of the log cabins of pioneer days into larger frame houses. The pine lumber for these houses came from the forests of northern Michigan and Wisconsin. The years from 1870 to 1900 have been called the "home building years."

The increased income enabled the farmers to buy such luxuries as parlor organs or pianos and to keep an extra horse or two for driving, hitched to a top buggy or a "surrey with a fringe on the top," as the song goes. I don't remember when my father bought our organ, but I do remember that my two sisters, Sarah and Addie, took lessons on it. If one of them played a wrong note and my father were in an adjoining room, he would immediately call the attention of the budding organist to her mistake. Although he never had a music lesson in his life, he had a good ear for music and loved to play his violin.

Another side effect from the increased prosperity of farmers, and dwellers in villages and cities as well, was the changes that came about in educational facilities. We have seen how the charter of 1787 for the government of the Northwest Territory stated that "schools and the means for education shall forever be encouraged." I have described the formation of primary school districts. Later graded or union school districts were formed, where high schools could be established. It wasn't until near the end of the nineteenth century and the increase of prosperity of the farmer that many farm boys and girls were able to get more schooling than that offered in a one-room rural school.

The early settlers of Michigan, in addition to building homes and farms, had to build schools. They had to accomplish this practically the same way they built their homes—out of a wilderness. The patterns for free schools were nebulous. In the eastern states from which many of the pioneers came the free schools were the "poor schools" or schools only for the poor or indigent. The children of all the rest of the people attended tuition schools. It wasn't until the late 1840s that free schools were considered for all children. In Michigan they did not become completely free until 1859.

By the middle of the third decade of statehood much of southern Michigan had been settled and cleared. Just when these pioneers may have begun to think of better times, the Civil War started. Michigan sent more than 9,000 soldiers to the cause of preserving the Union. My father was one of these, serving two years in a New York regiment before moving to Michigan and re-enlisting. My mother's older brother, John Bahnmiller of Michigan, died in the notorious Andersonville prison, reputedly of starvation. As happens after all wars, many of the returning soldiers came home with new ideas. One of these new ideas was to have better schools.

Even before Michigan was admitted to the Union, counties and townships were being organized. When the constitution was adopted in 1837 these townships proceeded to elect the township boards of school inspectors, whose members began at once to organize school districts. Because at this time the idea of equality was uppermost in the minds of the people, no qualifications were established for the membership of these boards. As far as the schools of the township were concerned, these boards held the supreme power. In setting up districts, the only directive in the school law was that the district formed should be as large and compact as practicable and that no pupil live farther than two and a half miles from the schoolhouse. After districts were organized and numbered, the most important duty of the school inspectors was the examination of prospective teachers and the granting of teachers' certificates. Section 85 of the primary school law stated that, "No certificate shall be given to a teacher who does not pass a satisfactory examination in the common branches, reading, orthography, geography, grammar, and arithmetic." Later, when union or graded schools were organized, the subjects that an applicant was to teach were added to the above list. The word "satisfactory" was the key word in the law. What was meant by "satisfactory"? Before an applicant was twenty-one, he need not even be a citizen of the United States. The law made no qualification in regard to the age of the applicant. For thirty years these school inspectors ruled the schools as autocrats. As was to be expected, they were subjected to much criticism. The schools themselves were also much criticized, as shown by the annual reports of the school inspectors to the state superintendent of public instruction.

CHAPTER V

Foundation of Modern Education

The year 1837, the year Michigan became a state, was one of the most propitious years possible for the birth of a state. During the next three decades great strides were being made along many lines. Transportation had been or was being revolutionized by canals, the steamboat, and the steam locomotive. Inventors were beginning to invent the "machines of plenty" such as the McCormick reaper and binder and the Case threshing machine.

The ferment that caused men to provide for physical needs and comforts also brought a revolution in the way the schools were organized. In the thinking of the state's early educators, three virtues—religion, morality, and knowledge—were deemed necessary to good government and the happiness of mankind. We must not forget that these words and these virtues were put into the Ordinance of 1787 by the men who helped to write the Constitution of the United States.

This educational revolution was the result of the teaching of Comenius, who brought realism to education in the seventeenth century, of Rousseau, who brought indivdiualism in the eighteenth century, and of Pestalozzi in the nineteenth century who brought the psychological method and the idea that education should be universal, of Herbart, a contemporary of Pestalozzi, who formulated a science of education, and lastly, of Horace Mann, who brought organization and administration to education.

To Herbart, the aim of education was morality and virtue. For centuries education had consisted of teaching by rote; the subject matter was authoritarian and for the privileged classes only. The influence of these great teachers brought many changes in education and in teaching methods. The greatest of these changes was the concept that schools should be *free* for every child.

EARLY TEXTBOOKS

One of the first results of this revolution in education and an item that gave it impetus was Noah Webster's spelling book, published in 1783, which combined what would later be found in a primer, a first reader, and a spelling book. Eight or ten thousand words became familiar to thousands of users of this book. The bright young person or the illiterate of middle age could learn to read with little help from others beyond that needed to learn the alphabet. Webster's spelling book became the schoolbook most used in America in the early part of the nineteenth century. By the early 1870s these sales had increased to a million and a quarter.

Aided by profits from the sale of his spelling book, Webster began work on his first dictionary, which was published in 1807. This book contained 37,500 words, 5,000 of which were English words whose meaning had to be changed or new American words such as squash, tomahawk, hickory, and so on. In his changes, he dropped the letter "u" from such words as labour. He established the use of "er" instead of "re" in such words as centre, which became center. A revised edition, containing 70,000 words, was brought out in 1828. The second edition of the revised dictionary, published in 1840, contained several thousand more words. After Webster's death, a third revised edition appeared under the editorship of Professor Chauncey A. Goodrich, Webster's son-in-law, which contained 114,000 words. No estimate can be made of the value of Webster's spelling book and dictionaries or of the effect they had on education in the United States.

The idea our founding fathers held that religion and morality could be instilled in the youthful mind is graphically shown by the new series of readers and other textbooks that were being produced. In the educational process, knowledge was the first requisite, but religion and morality were also to be emphasized. There were two new series of readers, five for the primary grades and one for grammar schools or academies. The first and second McGuffey *Eclectic Readers* appeared in 1836. These were followed by readers for the other grades and one for the high schools. By 1901 the readers had been revised five times. The estimated number of copies used between 1836 and 1920 was 122,000,000 copies. These famous readers contained selections from the Holy Bible, from classical English writings, and from fables to point out moral precepts. There is no question that the McGuffey readers had a marked influence on American youth. In 1928, they were republished in facsimile by Henry Ford. Recently a newspaper reported that a school district in Wisconsin had adopted the McGuffey *Eclectic Readers* for use in its schools. Unfortunately, in the thirty-one years I spent in close contact with schools I never saw one of those famous books. Two years ago an old friend, Ed Bremer, found a McGuffey fifth reader and sent it to me.

While searching for source material describing the early history of Michigan schools, my daughter-in-law, Dorothy Riegle, found five of a series of six readers written by Charles W. Sanders, A.M., the first five of which were for grade school and one for high school. She did not find a copy of the First Reader; from notes in the Second Reader I gained the impression that the First Reader contained words of one syllable only. The books she found were published sometime between 1838 and 1855; some of the copies may be revised editions.

When checking the annual reports from the union schools to the various superintendents of public instruction, I found that in the main those schools used Sanders readers. The McGuffey readers were rarely mentioned.

According to Mr. Sanders the oustanding purpose of his readers was to give a child the tools he could use in learning to read. With these tools he could learn to read without teachers if he should leave school at an early age, as many children did. Although the main objective of these books was to teach the child to read, special emphasis was placed on oral reading. In the second reader, in which two and three syllable words were used, special importance was given to accent and attention. The stories were supposed to be so interesting that the child would be sufficiently attentive to answer any questions the teacher might ask.

The third reader contained progressively harder lessons in reading and exercises in articulation and inflection. The new words of each lesson, with their definitions, were placed at the beginning of each lesson. The pupil was supposed to learn to spell them and to learn their meaning. In the front of the book, before the first lesson, there were definitions and explanations of the pauses: the comma, the semicolon, the colon, the period, the quotation marks, and the apostrophe. These the child was supposed to learn. Section II gave examples of elementary sounds of letters. Today when I listen to many public speakers and some radio and television speakers, I think what a tremendous help it would be to all if our schools would again teach articulation, enunciation, accent, and the place for pauses.

Dorothy Riegle also found several other books of nineteenth-century vintage, including a copy of Sanders' *New Speller, Definer, and Analyzer,* published in 1854. The preface to this speller states that in design it was threefold:

> It leads the learner gradually through all those elementary lessons in language, which are essential to a complete knowledge of the sounds of individual letters, and the various combinations of the same when employed to form syllables and words. With the forms and sounds of words, that is, with the *spelling* and *pronunciation,* it deals thoroughly; but it by no means stops there. It employs almost every possible expedient for the development of their *meanings* also; comparing and contrasting them with one another, unfolding their significations by formal definitions, and everywhere rendering prominent those distinctions which are likely to escape the notice of youth.

In the first section, the pupil was to learn the alphabet, both in script and in print. Only three or four letters were to be learned in a lesson. After this, he was to learn the vowels and consonants, then how these were combined into syllables and words. Next he learned the names for words according to number of syllables and whether they were primitive, derivative, simple or compound. He was also to learn the meaning of such terms as orthography, orthoepy, diphthongs, and the markings that showed the different sounds of the vowels. The four sounds of the vowel *"a"* were given as long, short, flat, and broad; examples of each sound were given. The substitutes for the consonant elements were taught and examples given. In all, nine pages were allotted to illustrating the different sounds of letters and their combinations. The first exercise consisted of words of two letters, next came three-letter words, then four, five, and so on. The book, designed to be used from the first grade on, contained 429 exercises. Most of the words were defined or another word of like meaning given. It would be interesting to know what the results would be if a school were to use this textbook now and to compare the results with those of a school using modern methods. It would seem that Mr. Sanders may have expected far too much of both teacher and pupil.

Another book, entitled *Spelling for Commercial Schools, Normal Schools, Colleges, Academies and High Schools,* gave six rules for spelling and a key to pronunciation and abbreviations. It had words for 225 lessons. Every word was divided into syllables and diacritically marked and defined. The year of publication was 1889.

One other book Dorothy found was a geography for beginners. It is most unusual because it is written entirely in rhyme. The rhyme describing Michigan reads as follows:

> Southeast the State of Michigan, in sight
> Of her dark water, is the town Detroit,
> Adrian, Tecumseh and the fair Monroe,
> Where River Raisin murmurs in its flow.
> And Ypsilanti on the railway keeps
> In Washtenaw, where Huron River sweeps.
> Ann Arbor then with Dexter we may view,
> Then Jackson comes, Marshall and Kalamazoo.
> Paw Paw is next and last of all St. Joe
> Where the dark waters of St. Joseph flow.
> And Hillsdale, Branch, and Niles, and Centreville,
> With Berrien, where St. Joseph's waters spill.
> From Shelby, west, is seated Pontiac.
> Near St. Clair Lake, Mt. Clemens seeks repose;
> St. Clair is where the St. Clair River flows.
> From Pontiac, west, Howell the first we scan;
> Then Bellvue comes, Hastings, and Allegan.
> Grand Haven, at the mouth of River Grand,
> Just opposite Milwaukee, takes her stand.
> Grand Rapids, with Ionia, up this stream,
> Where Lansing lives, as capital, I ween.
> Corunna, Flint, Port Huron, and Lapeer

Are in the counties stationed east of here.
And Mackinaw keeps in an open Strait,
'Tween Michigan and Huron, 'tis the gate;
Upon a dusky isle her bulwarks flame,
A fortress strong, and owned by Uncle Sam.

This unusual book, *The Poetical Geography,* by George Van Waters, was published in 1861 and contained the census of 1860.

Another interesting book which Dorothy came across is *Primary Arithmetic* printed in 1868 by E. E. White, M.A. According to its author, this arithmetic united "oral and written exercises in a natural system of instruction." The preface to this old book says:

> The true method of imparting to a child a clear comprehension of the value of numbers, the foundation of arithmetical knowledge, consists of three steps, viz.: (1) the perception of numbers represented by objects in sight; (2) the conception of numbers applied to objects not in sight; (3) the conception of numbers not applied to objects. A knowledge of the elementary combinations of numbers is best communicated in the same manner.
>
> A faithful observance of this *natural order* constitutes one of the characteristic features of this first book in arithmetic. Abstract numbers and operations are reached, in practice as well as in theory, as the final step. In this and other evident features, the book is a practical embodiment of the simplest and most vital principles of the inductive method of instruction.
>
> But the distinguishing feature of the book, as well as of the Series of which it forms a part, is the *complete union of Mental* (oral) and *Written Arithmetic.* This is secured, not by scattering a few miscellaneous slate exercises through the work, but by making every oral exercise preparatory to a written one and by uniting both as the essential complements of each other. Each lesson gives the pupil something to do, as well as something to study.

Pupils were to be drilled constantly in the combinations, both in addition and subtraction and in the multiplication tables. Nearly every lesson is illustrated with pictures of animals, fruits, tops, balls, and the like. Evidently Mr. French, my first high school principal, had been taught from this text or a similar one, for he required complete sentences for every answer in his class in mental arithmetic, a course required of all freshmen. I learned more arithmetic in his class in three months than in the eight years I attended a rural school.

CHAPTER VI

Successes and Failures in the Early Schools

Mr. Pierce, Mr. Crary, Governor Mason and the first Michigan legislature had performed wonderfully well in perfecting a plan for schools. The next step was to put the plan into operation and make it work. The success of the plan depended on the quality of the men elected to the township board of school inspectors. Probably volumes could be written about the successes and failures of the many school districts that came into existence during the first decade after the plan was made.

A brief account of the schools of Detroit township will give a picture of what could have happened in any district. The general primary school law became effective April 1, 1837, at which time the Township of Detroit elected three school inspectors. For some unknown reason this board failed to organize any school districts. In 1838, a new board was elected, consisting of John Farmer, James Joy and Henry Chapman. They divided the township into seven districts, which were organized immediately by each electing the three officers as provided by law. Under the law as first written, these districts were not eligible to draw state aid in 1838, but the third state legislature, which convened in June of 1838, passed an act that permitted state aid to be given to districts that had failed to organize in 1837. During 1837 no common schools were open in Detroit. Only a "free" school which had been maintained for several years by donations for poor children was kept open. Other Detroiters sent their children to private schools.

In June of 1838, the school inspectors of Detroit township held the first teachers' examinations and issued the first teaching certificates. During this year, five of the seven districts maintained school the necessary three months to obtain state aid. The expense of maintaining these schools was approximately $200 each, which covered teachers' wages, rent, fuel, and other necessities. The first distribution of money from the Primary School fund was made in June of 1839 to the seven districts on a per capita basis and amounted to 45 cents per child of school age. In 1838, an eighth district was organized in Detroit, this one being established for Negro children only.

By 1841 only one of the eight districts had built a schoolhouse. The others had maintained schools in rented quarters for a year or two, then closed them because of lack of funds. There is no record of what the school officials did with the money on hand, if any, or what was done with the money received from the state or from taxes. For two or three years the only schools in the city of Detroit were the twenty-seven private schools, which had a total enrollment of 714 children.

By 1842, under the district system, the schools of Detroit had fallen into such disrepute that the city council petitioned the legislature to pass a bill to make the city one school district. The legislature complied, and immediately the Detroit Union School was organized. The new law read that, "All schools organized in pursuance of this act, shall, under the direction and regulation of the board of education, be public and free to all children between the ages of seven and seventeen inclusive."

Even though the Detroit schools were free to all children in the city, Mr. Levi Bishop, then president of the board of education, in his report to the state superintendent of public instruction, complained of the irregularity of attendance, of tardiness, and of poor preparation of lessons. He estimated that more than a fourth of the pupils enrolled were absent each day. It was most annoying to the teacher, the class and the school to have in every class several "available candidates for the dunce block," as he put it, because of constant failure in recitations occasioned by tardiness, irregularity and truancy. These failures were caused by parents who had little or no interest in the education of their children. These facts appear in the superintendent's report of 1853, when Francis W. Shearman was the state superintendent. It took years to overcome these faults because there was no compulsory education until a compulsory attendance law was passed in 1871.

Mr. Bishop also noted that vocal music had been introduced into the Detroit schools to a limited extent, with good results. At first this brought much opposition from parents, who protested that they did not send their children to school to learn to sing. However, this opposition soon disappeared.

Regarding moral education, Mr. Bishop quoted from a report from the schools of Cincinnati:

> As the young mind constantly receives impressions for good or evil from the manners, habits, and character of its teachers, great care should be exercised to secure instructors whose moral worth as well as intellectual culture commands respect.

From this time on, under the wise management of the officers thereafter elected, the schools of Detroit became leaders in the educational field of Michigan.

In 1838, in all of Michigan there were 1020 school districts, with 28,764 children in the schools. These early schools were held in makeshift buildings, sometimes shanties. It was several years before all school children were housed in a log or frame building built expressly for a schoolhouse.

UNION OR GRADED SCHOOLS

Every district when first organized was a primary district. If a district had more than 100 children on the school census between the ages of five and twenty, the people could vote to organize a graded school district, establish a high school, and elect a district board of six trustees, provided the intention to so vote was expressed in the notices calling the annual meeting. To pass, the motion had to be carried by a two-thirds vote.

Two trustees were to be elected for a term of one year, two for two years, and two for three years. Annually thereafter, two trustees were elected whose term was three years. Later the number of trustees was reduced to five to avoid a tie. The trustees were given the power to classify and grade the pupils in such district and cause them to be taught in such schools or departments as deemed necessary. (This classifying could be delegated to the teachers under their authority.) The trustees could establish a high school when ordered by a vote of a district at an annual meeting. However, there was nothing in the law which specifically stated that taxes could be raised for the support of a high school. It was generally expected that any high school so established would be supported by tuition to be collected from both resident and nonresident pupils. It was held that the Primary School fund of the state was designed for the support of primary schools only.

The qualified voters of any school district having more than 300 children between the ages of five and twenty could, by a vote of two thirds of those present at any annual meeting, designate any number of sites for schoolhouses, including a site for a union school. (The terms union school and graded school and high school seem to have been interchangeable at that time.)

Section 152 of the Michigan school laws of 1842 also provided that two or more contiguous districts having together more than 200 children between the ages of five and twenty years, could severally, by a vote of two thirds of the voters present at the annual meeting in said districts, unite to establish a union school. The township board of school inspectors would then post notices to call a meeting in the new district to elect a board of trustees in the same manner as when a primary district changed to a graded district. These districts were called union school districts. The name "union school" district survives to this day in at least two Michigan cities, Flint and Jackson. When graded schools were organized to form a high school, resident pupils could be charged tuition because it was claimed, as mentioned earlier, that the Primary School fund was intended to support primary schools only.

Today we can hardly believe that 120 years ago there were *no high schools* in our state. A report by Levi Bishop, president of the Detroit board of education, printed in the 1853 annual report of the superintendent of public instruction, gives some interesting points concerning high schools. Detroit's public school system was organized by a special act of the legislature in 1842, when Detroit was the capital of Michigan. It seems that in 1852 one school was held in the Capitol building and known as the Capitol School. It was organized on the union plan with four departments and 700 pupils. This was evidently one of the first attempts at grading a school in Michigan. Mr. Bishop reported that the Detroit board of education had had several requests to allow classes to be established in the union school for the study of the classics, but they had not been able to grant the requests. He theorized that—

A public high school located in the central part of the city, into which the youth should be gathered by way of promotion from the other public schools, without regard to condition in life or the artificial distinctions of society, and with reference to merit alone, would be the crowning work of our public school system.

That attempts were being made to teach some subjects we now consider proper for high school is shown by the textbooks they used. Listed are Davies' *Algebra and Geometry,* of which I have a copy, Davies' *Bourdon and Legendre,* Watts' *On the Mind,* McIntyre's *Astronomy and Treatise on the Globes,* Parker's *Natural Philosophy,* Brockelbees' *Elements of Meteorology,* and Mayhew's *Bookkeeping.*

Although Detroit may have organized the first union or consolidated school district in Michigan, it was Jonesville that organized the first union or high school in the state. By this is meant that a central or union schoolhouse was built in which all the children in the district were brought together under one roof. The first union school, Jonesville, cost $3,400. It opened January 1, 1848, with A. S. Welch, M.A., as principal, with two competent assistants. The school had two semesters of 22 weeks each, with an enrollment of 220 pupils.

Ypsilanti became the second union school, when it was organized in 1849. Battle Creek voted to form a union school in 1847 by joining fractional parts of three districts, but did not organize the school until 1851, when the sum of $3,500 was voted to build the union building.

That the Battle Creek union school was thinking of a high school in 1852, or at least of high school subjects, is shown in their report which states that they had bought some maps and charts for illustrating physiology, chemistry, history, geography, chirography (penmanship) and the elementary sounds of the letters. The Battle Creek report also gave this interesting information:

Evening schools are opened for the instruction of the unclassified and those who cannot attend the day schools. The progress in them is heartening. The evening schools are superintended by the principal, who is assisted by his advanced class of students. This gives them an opportunity of putting into practice the theory they learn.

SCHOOLING FOR NEGRO CHILDREN

In the light of today's chaotic conditions in the public schools of our nation regarding the education of black children, it is intriguing to read of the early attempts in Michigan to furnish schooling for Negro children. In the annual report of the Superintendent of Public Instruction to the legislature of 1852—nine years before the Civil War—the report of Mr. Levi Bishop of Detroit says:

> As early as the year 1841 a school for colored children was required by law to be opened in the city, and it has been our policy to allow to the colored population equal advantages in this respect with the whites. The Colored School was kept in the basement of the African Methodist Church up to the year 1851. No rent was charged for the room by the proprietors of the church, who generously appropriated it to the purpose of educating the colored children. In 1851, we were required to rent a room for this school. The African Episcopal Church being offered the cheapest, and being the best room, was taken for $40 per annum. The School was taught by W. C. Monroe, at a moderate salary of $260 a year. It had, at the last term, 97 on its roll and is in a flourishing condition. Adults attend it with the children, manifesting a commendable desire to repair the defects, or supply the total want, of educational advantages in early life. This School is under our general rules and regulations and is in no way distinguished from other public schools of the city except in the color of its pupils.

Also, it was more than 100 years ago that a decision was made by the Supreme Court of Michigan relating to the exclusion of colored children from the public schools. A suit was brought against the school board of Detroit for refusing to admit a Negro child into one of the public schools, "The People ex. rel. Joseph Workman vs. the Board of Education of Detroit." The school board claimed they had the power to regulate the schools as they saw fit. They believed it was best that the colored children be placed in schools by themselves and had accordingly formed three such schools in the city and required all colored children desiring to attend school to attend one of these. The exclusion of colored children from the schools open to white children was claimed by the board to be a reasonable regulation. As they saw it, the prosperity of the free schools demanded this arrangement. The board also claimed they had the same right to separate children of different colors as they had to separate children of different sexes.

The plaintiff claimed that the general school law of 1867 expressly provided that "all residents of any district shall have an equal right to attend the schools therein, provided that this shall not prevent the grading of schools according to the intellectual progress of the pupils, to be taught in separate places when deemed expedient." This law, the plaintiff claimed, prevented any school board from making regulations to exclude residents of the district from schools because of race, color, religious belief, or personal peculiarities.

The Supreme Court held that the law of 1867 was of universal application to all the school districts of Michigan and that it was not the intention of the legislature to make an exception of Detroit. It ordered the father of the colored child be entitled to a writ of mandamus to compel the admission of a minor child to the public school in his district. (Heard May 5; decided May 12, 1869.)

NEW IDEAS AND LAWS

In March of 1838, Superintendent Pierce published the first issue of his paper, *The Journal of Education*. It was the first educational publication in Michigan. That month a joint resolution of the legislature provided that one copy of the paper be sent to each board of school inspectors and one to each school director. In the *Journal,* Mr. Pierce gave to the school officers of the state definite instructions on how to organize and operate a school district. He explained the duties of school officials and told how they were to be carried out. His *Journal* exerted considerable influence in shaping our public school system. To many people of that time, education at *public expense* was a new concept. One of Mr. Pierce's first recommendations to the legislature was:

> Let the Michigan law not only provide for the establishing of a common school in every school district, but also a normal school in every county, so that the teachers in the schools shall be trained in the art of teaching.

It took more than sixty years for the idea of county normal schools to germinate and become a reality. Another suggestion to the effect that a library be established in every school district fell on deaf ears.

During the first few years after the first laws were passed under which the schools were organized, amendments to these laws seemed to be negative instead of progressive. For several years after 1837, the year of the Panic of 1837, money was a scarce commodity. This panic hit the new states like Michigan very hard indeed. Retrenchment was the order of the day. In 1839, the legislature eliminated that part of the original school law which required counties to apportion to each township and each township to raise by taxation a sum equal to that which the township was to receive from the Primary School fund. Thus the law left it up to the township to raise sufficient funds to run the schools if it did not receive enough money for the three months of school required by law. It also gave a district the authority to raise up to $500 to build a schoolhouse and not to exceed $90 for school maintenance, by a majority vote of those taxpayers present at a regular school meeting. If a district could not maintain a school for three months from state aid and closed its school, it forfeited the right to more state aid. However, the legislature re-enacted the Rate Bill, a bill which had been in operation during territorial days.

If a school did close for lack of funds, two residents of the district with children enrolled in the school could call a meeting and by a majority vote of those present vote to keep the school open. The cost of doing this was prorated among the parents who had children in the school. The amendment of 1839 reduced the responsibility of taxpayers for maintaining schools. However, if a parent failed to pay his prorated share, it could be collected by the school assessor by distress and sale of goods and chattels the same as any other tax or assessment.

The legislature of 1840 reduced the amount of money that a district could raise to $100 to build a schoolhouse, unless the board of inspectors of a township certified in writing that a larger sum was required, and in no case could this sum be more than $300. Another amendment required that the total cost of fuel to be used be paid by the parents of the pupils enrolled in the school. Another change was the act that allowed a township to levy a tax of $1 (one dollar) for each child in the township of school age and apportion this tax on a per capita basis. By this year the number of children in the state had increased to 45,592, but the Primary School fund allotment was lowered to 42 cents per child.

The qualified voters in the regular district meetings, upon due notice thereof, could vote to establish sites, purchase or lease sites, impose taxes to buy sites, build schoolhouses or keep them in repair, provide appendages and appliances, and determine the length of time the schools were to be kept open. School finances, when left to the various districts, in many places became precarious. To remedy this situation, the legislature in 1841 passed an act to require the township supervisor to assess and collect a tax of one mill on all the taxable property in the district. However, in 1843 this tax was limited to $25. In 1844, it was limited to one-half mill and for each year thereafter, one mill. This tax was to be apportioned to the several districts in the township for the support of the schools. However, after 1844, $25 of this tax was to be set aside specifically for the purchase of books for the township library. The mill tax, together with the $1 for every child of school age in the district which could be raised by a vote at the annual meeting, plus the Primary School fund, plus the money from the Rate Bill was considered by most school officials to be sufficient to maintain a school.

When John D. Pierce's second term as State Superintendent expired in 1840, Governor John S. Barry nominated Franklin Sawyer Jr., a lawyer and the editor of a Detroit newspaper, as his successor. He was authorized by the governor to make a thorough survey of the whole educational system of Michigan. As a first step, he sent a questionnaire to every one of the 1486 districts in the state. Although many school directors failed to reply, the answers as a whole showed that the schools of the state were in very poor condition. This was caused by inefficient teachers, lack of proper supervision, low wages, poor discipline, inadequate school facilities, and lack of uniformity in textbooks. The male teachers ranged in age from seventeen to twenty; their wages averaged $16.21 a month. Female teachers were from fourteen to eighteen years old; their average wage was $1.27 a week. We must keep in mind that there were two school terms in the year. The winter term was for the larger boys, whose help was needed on the farms in the summer. The summer term was for the girls and the smaller boys. If a district had only three months of school, the time was divided equally between the two terms. Some of the larger districts were beginning to keep their schools open for four or five months, or even longer.

After an analysis of the returned questionnaires had been made, State Superintendent Sawyer recommended that the legislature provide for the appointment of deputy superintendents, one for each county, who would examine teachers, inspect the schools, and have general charge of education in his county. This was a good suggestion, but it was never acted upon.

Detroit had been the territorial capital of Michigan and remained the capital during the first decade of statehood. There was much opposition from the newer parts of the state to keeping Detroit as the capital. After several years of contention over the site for its permanent location, the legislature of 1847 decided that the capital should be located on Section 16 of Lansing township in Ingham County. The name "Michigan" was first given to the site, but soon changed to Lansing by the first session of the legislature which convened at the new capital on January 1, 1848.

Governor Felch had wisely withdrawn this section from entry and sale while the question of location of the capital was pending in the legislature. This section of land, under ordinary circumstances, would have sold for about $5 per acre. After Section 16 of Lansing township was chosen as the capital site, the sale of this land brought to the Primary School fund more than $100,000—a magnificent sum for those early days.

A NEW STATE CONSTITUTION

In 1850, a new constitution was written and adopted by the state. Under the first constitution the heads of the various departments had been appointed by the governor. Under the new constitution, these department heads were to be elected by the people. Thus the office of Superintendent of Public Instruction became an elective office and remained so for many years.

The new constitution provided that "The legislature shall, within five years after the adoption, provide for and establish a system of primary schools whereby a free school shall be kept for at least three months in every school district in the state." Because the methods of financing the schools were found not to be adequate in bringing this about, the legislature of 1858, after much debate, increased the mill tax from one mill to two. It took two or three years for all the townships to make this change.

In Superintendent Mayhew's annual reports for the years 1855, 1856, and 1857, which were published in one volume in 1858, he complained that many districts did not levy the $1 per pupil, which was called the "voluntary tax" and many also did not levy the two-mill tax required by law. This left many districts without funds to maintain a school for the statutory three months. He recommended that the legislature make stiffer penalties for failure to levy and collect taxes.

Another recommendation he made was that normal graduates be granted certificates to teach without being required to take an examination before township inspectors.

Realizing that one of the links in the chain of command in our school system was the board of school inspectors, he claimed that these inspectors were in many cases not capable of inspecting the schools and conducting the examinations for teachers. He theorized that in place of the three inspectors for each township a school commissioner should be elected in each senatorial district, whose educational qualifications would enable him to perform the duties of school inspector in a professional manner.

In these early reports of the superintendents, we can get a picture of how the educators were groping along on an uncharted trail that they hoped would lead to their goal of better schools. These officials were the first to see the faults and deficiencies in Michigan's new school system and the first to offer suggestions for making the many changes necessary for improvement. They were also influenced by the discussions in the meetings of the Michigan Education Association, especially in the school superintendents' section and later in the county commissioners' section.

CHAPTER VII

Libraries

Section 12 of the new constitution adopted in 1850, which had been part of the original constitution of 1836, provided:

> The legislature shall also provide for the establishment of at least one library in each township and all fines assessed and collected in the several counties and townships shall be exclusively applied to the support of such libraries.

Section 50 stated:

> A director of a school district may draw from the township library the proportion of books to which his district is entitled, keep them for three months, then return them to the township library.

He could repeat this procedure every three months. The first direct appropriation for the support of township libraries was the sum of $25 to be taken from the one-mill tax and given to the township board of school inspectors to buy library books. This amendment was passed in 1853.

The chairman of the board of school inspectors was the treasurer of the board and had general charge of the township library. He had to give a bond to the township in double the amount of library money to come into his hands during his term of office. If he failed in the duties imposed, the township clerk could begin suit to forfeit his bond. Any money thus collected was to be put into the township library fund.

That shenanigans were practiced then, as now, was shown by a report that the board of supervisors of a certain county had directed the county treasurer to credit the penal fines collected from all the courts to the general fund of the county instead of to the library fund. In many cases the fines were retained by the justices or other officers collecting them, with the plea that they were all absorbed in paying the costs of prosecution and collection. To correct these attempts or tricky maneuvers to divert the fines, the Supreme Court of Michigan ruled that no such use of the fund could be made legally and that all fines collected belonged to the library fund.

A new edition of Noah Webster's *Unabridged Dictionary* was brought out in 1847. During the term of Francis W. Shearman, the fifth Michigan superintendent of public instruction, who served from 1849 to 1853, he recommended that each township authorize the school inspectors to "apply temporarily the $25 now appropriated for the purchase of books for the township library to the purchase of six copies of Webster's *Unabridged Dictionary,* which should be enough to supply one copy for each district in the township." If there were more than six districts in the township, the rest could be supplied from the library fund the next year. Evidently this recommendation was not followed in many townships.

In 1857, when Mr. Ira Mayhew was serving his second four-year term as superintendent of public instruction, the legislature passed a law that enabled each district in the state to levy a tax of $4 at its annual meeting in 1857 or 1858 for the purchase of a dictionary for its school. If the district voted this tax, it was to notify the office of superintendent of public instruction. In Mr. Mayhew's report of 1858, he stated that he had ordered 2000 copies of the dictionary from the publishers, the G. and C. Merriam Company. They were to be delivered to Detroit during the months of January and February of 1858. The price of $4 each was 50 cents less than the regular wholesale price and $2 less than the established retail price. It was expected that the Michigan board of auditors would pay the freight on the books, but this they refused to do. The G. and C. Merriam Company advanced the freight charges, subject to adjustment. The dictionaries were distributed among the county clerks of the state, who in turn sent them to the townships. They were carried to their final destinations by freight, express, or stage coach, probably most of them by stage coach as few towns had railroad connections. In June of 1858, Mr. Mayhew sent a draft for $4,552.07 for the 1198 that had been delivered.

After that date, they could be ordered from a Detroit firm, Messrs. Doughty, Strow, and Company, or through the office of the state superintendent in Lansing.

In 1859, an act was passed to allow the people of a township to make an appropriation at its discretion from the two-mill tax for the purchase of books for the township library. In his annual report, Superintendent John M. Gregory devoted eight pages to the recommendation that *each school district* should have a library and to the reasons why the children should be encouraged to read the library books. In his report for 1860, he gave ten pages to the same ideas.

In 1860, an amendment to the law of 1850 was passed, making it possible for township library books to be distributed to form district libraries upon an application from a majority of the districts. The question was submitted to the voters at the spring election. Of the townships voting, 187 retained their libraries and 350 reported that they had established district libraries.

Under a law passed in 1859, the state Board of Education selected 500 books suitable for township or district libraries. These books were to be bound in durable bindings and lettered "Michigan School Library." They were to be bought under a contract with F. Reynolds and Company, booksellers in Detroit, at prices 25 to 35% less than the regular prices of the same books in cheap bindings. Dates were set between which the books could be ordered, to allow the booksellers to have them specially bound and lettered. Some of these books can still be found in some of the older school libraries. One, *The Life of Stephen A. Douglas,* is still in the Flint Public Library.

The law of 1859 giving the township the right to distribute the books in the township library to the districts voting to form district libraries repealed that part of the law which had given the board of school inspectors the right to take $25 from the mill tax for the support of township libraries. This new law left it up to the voters in the township to vote money at the annual meeting to support a township library. The records show that very few townships took this action.

The penal fines and all equivalents from military duty were the only moneys appropriated for libraries. In 1876, Mr. Daniel Briggs, the superintendent of public instruction, noted in his annual report, "There is no law in our statutes so generally and persistently violated as the one concerning the distribution of penal fines for libraries."

The legislature of 1879 provided that a township could vote to re-establish a township library if a vote were ordered by the township board of school inspectors at the annual meeting in April. If the township library were thus re-established, the several districts were required to return to the township library all the books in their possession unless such districts should vote at their annual meeting to retain their respective libraries.

The next change in the laws relating to libraries came in 1881. It specified that every township should establish a library, which would be in charge of the school inspectors. However, any district having not less than 100 children could, by a vote of two thirds of those voting at an annual meeting, establish a district library. Townships and districts were authorized to raise money for maintenance and support of libraries. They were to report to the superintendent of public instruction the condition of the libraries and the use of library monies. If these reports were not sent in or if the monies had been unlawfully applied, the offending district or township forfeited its share in the appropriations. After January 1, 1882, if a township board determined and reported to the state superintendent that the public would be better served by using said monies for general school purposes, then no forfeiture would occur. This provision was definitely one of the backward steps in the making of laws building our school system.

As the population of our state increased, many changes in the school laws had to be made to cope with this growth. In 1892, the limit of indebtedness that a common school could incur was increased to not more than $2,000. The purpose of this amendment was to allow the district to organize two departments and also to establish and provide a room for a library. This was accomplished by deleting from the existing law the words, "having a school census of not less than 100 children" and inserting the words, "having a school census of 75 children or more."

In his report of 1893, Mr. H. R. Pattengill bemoaned the fact that while in nearly all our cities and many of the villages there had been established working libraries, that is, books selected for different grades and different uses, in the rural schools the number of libraries showed a very rapid decline. In 1882, of the 7,000 districts in Michigan, 1,275 were supporting libraries. By 1892 only 750 had libraries, due to neglect in spending the library money properly. He recommended that the law be changed to prevent the township board from diverting the library money to any other purpose than the purchase of library books.

In 1897, an act provided that any school district could establish a library by a majority vote at an annual meeting and receive its proportionate share of the books in the township library as well as its proportionate share of the penal fines. This act revoked the power of the township board to divert the money for any purpose other than the purchase of library books. (The Dodge school I attended as a child did not establish a district library, but the second school I taught in Richfield Township, 1906-1908, had one.)

About 1910 local option made the sale of intoxicating liquors illegal in many counties. For the next several years the penal fines increased greatly due to violations of the local option law, the increase amounting to perhaps three or four times the penal fines before the passage of this law. This proved a big assist to school libraries. By 1920 nearly all the rural schools had libraries.

In 1931, by legislative act, the boards of supervisors of each county were given the authority to establish a county library and provide the necessary buildings and maintenance for the library in the general budget.

CHAPTER VIII

Coeducation and Union Schools

During the early years of our public school sytsem there was serious questioning of the value of coeducation in seminaries, in colleges, and even in the upper grades of the common schools. Many citizens were agitating for the state to establish a college for women. Mr. Mayhew argued that this was not necessary because there was nothing in any law passed by Congress in any grant to the state, or in any statute passed by the state legislature, that prevented women from attending the University of Michigan or the Normal School. He pointed out that in the original grant by Congress and by express statutory provision, the University was open to all persons resident of Michigan who pass the necessary scholastic and moral qualifications without regard to nationality, state in life, or sex. Those who favored separate colleges for women did not think it was in the best interests of the youths of the land to have the sexes mixed in a college or even in the higher grades of a school. In 1848, Mr. Mayhew argued:

> Its (referring to coeducation) manifest tendency is more fully not only to cultivate and develop their intellects, but to give them more rational views of human life and prevent the development of the prudery which is want to manifest itself in boarding schools composed exclusively of females.

THE UNION SCHOOL

Another subject being discussed pro and con was the union school. When the law was first passed permitting the formation of union schools, it meant just what the name implies—the uniting of two or more primary school districts. The law gave the school inspectors the authority to organize school districts, limiting the size of a district to nine square miles. There was no limit to the smallness of a district. An enterprising individual could buy some land through which a stream flowed. He would build a dam on this stream to make a millpond from which he could get the water power to operate a gristmill or a sawmill, or perhaps both. He would then subdivide his land and found a village to which he would give his name or perhaps the name of the village or city from which he came. As soon as there were enough children in the new village, the school inspectors would organize a school district.

Perhaps some other enterprising individual would subdivide some land on the opposite side of the stream or on the other side of the road from the first settlement and another school district would be organized. If a village were in a favorable location, it would grow rapidly. Even a third district might be formed in the same way. When such villages became large enough, they could incorporate and have two or three school districts within the corporate limits, each with a log or frame schoolhouse. When these first schoolhouses became crowded, the voters would consider the building of one schoolhouse large enough to take care of all the children in the village. This could be done by voting to form a "union" school. Under the law, when two or more contiguous districts had 200 children between the ages of five and twenty, they could unite to form a union school by a vote of two thirds of the qualified voters attending the annual meeting. This union school could then vote to build a new building adequate to house all the children in the new district. It would have several rooms, so that pupils of different ages could be separated according to age or scholastic achievement and be passed from one room or "reader" to another.

When the union school district of Flint was organized, it combined three districts whose boundaries could be contained in one square mile. Eventually five districts were united to form the union school district of the City of Flint.

In Genesee County six villages and one city grew up around millponds, although two of them, Atlas and Argentine, never grew large enough to have other than a primary school. (The old mill at Argentine is still in operation.) Most of the "millpond villages" in southern Michigan were founded in the three decades before the Civil War. During the war, immigration to Michigan slowed to a trickle, but as soon as the war ended a new boom started. Railroads began to crisscross the state. New villages sprang up at railroad intersections or where main-traveled roads crossed a railroad. These villages were more carefully planned than the earlier ones and the establishing of high schools began to be considered.

As the years went by, the word "union school" took on a different connotation. According to Mr. Mayhew:

> They may and should be established not only in cities and villages, but wherever the population is sufficiently dense, to bring a large number of children into one system of graded schools without embracing too much territory to be thus well associated.

Thus a union school could be established without the joining of two or more districts. Mr. Mayhew listed six advantages of a union school, namely: (1) they embraced a more extended and complete course of study; (2) they were cheaper than one-room or primary schools; (3) they made education accessible to the poor as well as to the rich; (4) they acted as normal schools to train pupils in the common branches to teach in the primary schools; (5) they admitted of the best methods of government and discipline; and (6) they performed the office of preparatory schools.

In 1858, to get a concensus of the thinking of the men in charge of the village and city schools, Mr. Mayhew sent a questionnaire to all the larger schools of the state. The questions embraced such items as the date the union school had been organized, size of the school site, cost and dimensions of the schoolhouse, number of rooms, value of apparatus, number of books in the library, departments in the school, number of male and female teachers, number of pupils, and course of study in use. There were also questions as to whether the school was coeducational or not and as to whether or not it was a preparatory school for applicants to the University of Michigan.

Replies came in from seventeen schools. Two of these, Bellevue and Cassopolis, reported that they had not established a union school. Adrian, Ann Arbor, Bronson, Coldwater, Detroit, Dexter, Dowogiac, Fentonville (now Fenton), Flint, Grand Rapids, Jonesville, Niles, Ontanogan, Port

Huron and Ypsilanti reported they had union schools. These fifteen schools were union in fact as well as in name. Only two reports mentioned grades or grading. Nearly all said they had three departments: primary, grammar, and higher. Ypsilanti had four departments: primary, secondary, grammar, and academic. Only three used the term "high school," referring to a department having a ninth and tenth or a ninth, tenth, and eleventh grade. From the list of textbooks used, it appears that in the department called "upper" the subjects taught were those which would later be taught in the ninth and tenth grades. Niles spent $30,000 for its union school, the largest sum reported. Two schools, Adrian and Ann Arbor, had preceptoresses in charge of the girls. This might mean that there were separate rooms for the boys and girls in the upper department. However, nearly all reports said the best results were obtained by mixing the sexes in all the classes. Nearly all the schools reported that they had four terms of ten weeks each, and three said they had three terms of fourteen weeks each.

CHAPTER IX

Superintendent of Public Instruction and Changes in School Laws

When the office of superintendent of public instruction was first established, no provision was made for any assistants or clerks. In Mr. Mayhew's annual report of 1858, he stated that during his first two terms, from 1845 to 1849, he performed all his various duties for the annual salary of $500. Under the new constitution of 1850, it became necessary for the office to be maintained in Lansing. A legislative act provided the state library was to be appropriated for the use of the superintendent of public instruction as his office and that the librarian was to act as his assistant and perform such duties as would be required by the superintendent, *free of expense to the state.* Even though the state librarian was a busy man, taking care of his own responsibilities, according to Mr. Mayhew he rendered faithful service by checking the mail of the superintendent and forwarding to him the letters needing his personal attention when he was away on official business. A bill had been introduced in the legislature the year before this report was made to give the superintendent of public instruction a room of his own and the power to appoint a deputy. This bill failed to pass. It was not until 1859 that the legislature established the office of deputy superintendent and gave the superintendent an office of his own instead of a corner in the state library.

The first deputy superintendent was Cortland B. Stebbins, who served until July 1, 1878. He performed many valuable services; in fact, it was because of his long and faithful service that the office was enabled to maintain a continuity of effort. Upon his recommendation, a law was passed to require a school director or secretary, when taking a school census, to give the name and age of the children and to attest to the truth of his census. It seems that some census takers had padded their reports in order to get more money for their districts. He also made a form to be used by the directors on which to keep their accounts, so that their reports to the state office would be uniform. He was also responsible for the law which gave equal rights to colored children.

When first organized, a school district elected three officers for equal terms. In 1859, the legislature amended the law to require all school districts to elect a moderator for three years, a director for two years, and an assessor for one year, the election to be held at the annual school meeting on the first Monday of September of that year (1859). From then on, one officer was to be elected each year for a term of three years.

These early Michigan legislators seemed to be much interested in schools and wanted to have money for the schools not subject to a vote of the taxpayers. For instance, they voted an annual tax on all dogs over two months old—one dollar on male dogs and three dollars on female. The money thus collected was to be apportioned among the school districts of the township according to the number of pupils in the district.

The 1859 legislature also provided that a district could raise a sum not to exceed $20 in any one year for the purchase of books of reference, globes, maps, or apparatus for the purpose of illustrating the principles of astronomy, natural philosophy, natural history and agricultural chemistry or the mechanic arts.

Under Section 41, the school director, within ten days of the annual meeting, was to take the census in his district of all the children between the ages of four and twenty (five through nineteen inclusive) and give to the township clerk a list of these children.

The district board was given the duty to adopt textbooks, but when once adopted they could not be changed within two years except by the consent of a majority of the voters at a regular meeting. The board was also given the authority to furnish books to needy children, whose parents could not afford to buy them. They could also exempt such people from paying the rate assessment and could admit their children to the school free of charge.

Another act stated that no more than $180 could be raised to build or purchase a schoolhouse of less dimensions than 24 by 30 feet and 10 feet between floors and a sum not exceeding $75 could be raised for the purpose of building or buying a schoolhouse constructed of round or hewn logs.

This same legislature also authorized a union school district having more than 300 children of school age to borrow money to pay for a site and erect buildings thereon and furnish same by a vote of two thirds of those present at an annual meeting or at any other regular meeting, but the whole debt of any school district could not exceed $15,000. This was a great boon to the union school districts because prior to this change in the law the amount of money that could be voted at a school meeting had been limited to a most inadequate sum.

During the first twenty-five years of Michigan school history, nearly all the superintendents of public instruction complained of the poor results of the work obtained from the efforts of the school inspectors. In 1862, Mr. John M. Gregory, state superintendent, suggested that better supervision could be obtained by the election of county superintendents to replace township inspectors. Five years later this recommendation was enacted into law.

During these early years the problems confronting the people in their relation to the schools were similar to those of today. Taxes then, as now, were uppermost in their minds. Today we have the question of assistance to nonpublic schools, or "parochiaid." In 1853, there was a petition signed by members of several religious faiths to divide the Primary School fund among the private and parochial schools in proportion to the number of children attending these schools. The contention was that schools could not be free unless the parent had the right to choose the teacher and the school of his preference and to draw from the public funds for *every* child so taught by the month or quarter, on producing such evidence as the law might require. A bill to carry out this plan was introduced in the legislature. Two committee reports were made. In one, the majority came out strongly against the passage of the bill. In the other, the majority came out just as strongly for its passage. That this bill aroused serious debate is shown by the ten pages given to the pros and cons in the 1853 annual report of Superintendent Francis W. Shearman. This has been a moot question ever since. The legislature of 1970, more than a century later, has acted favorably on a similar bill, but it still has to be tested in the courts before it can be put into effect. (Ed. note: Proposal C, the antiparochial school aid bill, became part of the constitution as a result of the November 1970 election.)

Many of the defects of the original plan for our school system which remain to this day were showing up over one hundred years ago. In his report of 1866, Superintendent Oramel Hosford complained that the district system was a *hindrance* to good schools. He pointed out that some of the older states were adopting the township unit system and recommended that Michigan adopt such a system. The first township unit bill had been introduced in our legislature in 1861 but failed to pass.

Another complaint of Mr. Hosford was that districts of less than 300 children of school age could not bond to build a schoolhouse. Each year such districts had to raise the limit allowed by law until they accumulated enough money to build a new building. He said that if the township were the unit instead of the district, the voters could bond to build a schoolhouse, vote more money for salaries in order to secure better teachers, and do a better job in grading the schools. He also maintained that county superintendents could do a more efficient job of inspection than the school inspectors were doing.

CHAPTER X

Annual Reports—School Inspectors— County Superintendents

When I told an old friend, Mr. John Dennis, who served as Genesee County road engineer from 1922 to 1948, that I was writing my life story and trying to show the changes in Michigan schools as well as the great changes in the lives of the people since our first schools were organized, he loaned me an antique book. This book, *Michigan School Report of 1867,* gives some interesting history of Michigan at that early date. It was because of this volume that I learned that there was a complete series of such books in the State Library in Lansing. From the year that Michigan bcame a state, 1837, the various superintendents of public instruction have made annual reports to the legislature, which are published in book form. Much of the information in these books is statistical, but in many of the reports there is a general discussion of conditions of the schools and of the thinking of the people, as they were reported to the Department of Education by the chairmen of township boards of school inspectors or by the county superintendents or other reporting officers. The Flint public library has copies of many of these annual reports, garnered from many sources. From their appearance, they have been rarely read; some of the pages had never been cut. One of the books had been used as a press to preserve leaves from different trees. It is from these old books that much of my information has been gleaned.

In 1865, the schools of Genesee County received $1,078.75 from the two-mill tax, $3,761.24 from the Primary School fund, $2,565.77

from the rate fund, and $391.15 from tuition of nonresident pupils. The county had $2,133 on hand at the beginning of the year. They raised $5,266.06 by extra taxes voted to pay teachers' wages, $4,091.20 from other taxes, $22.97 from library money (penal fines) and $2,838 from other sources not stated. They paid out for 45 male teachers $6,143.18, for 261 female teachers $1,547.54, for buildings and repair of schoolhouses $242.45, for library books $41.06, and for all other purposes $2,984.09.

There were nineteen townships in Genesee County; there are now eighteen as one was later detached from Genesee and added to Lapeer County. There were 155 school districts, with 8,763 children on the school census between the ages of five and twenty, 7,114 of them attending the public schools. The average number of months in the school year was 6.6 months. The number of volumes in the district libraries was 2,795.

The average wage per month of male teachers was $39.49; perhaps they taught for only six weeks or at the most, three months. Female teachers received the handsome wage of $16.88 per month, less than $1 a day for each day of work. In addition, they "boarded around" in the homes of their pupils, which gave them free board and lodging. These figures are for Genesee County only. Over the state, the average wage for male teachers was $41.77 and for female, $17.54 per month. In 1865, there were only 58 counties in Michigan. That year, and for many years, the mining counties of the Upper Peninsula paid the highest wages in the state.

DUTIES OF SCHOOL INSPECTORS

It was the duty of the school inspectors to visit every school at least once a year. They also had to submit a report of the finances of each school and of general conditions in the school to the state superintendent annually. Each district was supposed to send in its financial report on blanks furnished by the state superintendent's office. The inspector consolidated these reports and sent them on to Lansing. The state superintendents often complained of the difficulty of getting these reports from the schools.

Another duty of inspectors, as mentioned earlier, was to give teachers' examinations and issue teachers' certificates. One inspector admitted,

"There is a great deficiency in the present system of inspecting teachers and granting certificates. It is very rare for a teacher to be refused a certificate." In a note, one superintendent of public instruction wrote, "Reports show 770 applicants were refused teaching certificates in the state, about one in eleven of all examined." Many certificates were issued for six months only, some for a term only—a term being six weeks or at the most, three months.

There seems to have been no shortage of teachers. The 1865 report gives 155 as the number of school districts in Genesee County and 205 as the number of qualified teachers, both male and female. However, it seems that if a female teacher taught a spring term and a summer term, she was counted as two teachers.

The inspectors were requested to report on the general conditions and improvements of their schools, the qualifications and success or failure of teachers, the comparative success of male and female teachers, the adequacy of compensation, the conduct of the children, the interest of the local people in their schools, the condition of the libraries, the interest in reading, the manner in which penal fines were used, and the interest shown by the clergy, the lawyers, and other professional men in the township.

It appears that then, as in my time, some directors did not want to buy library books. In Tittabawasee township the inspector reported, "The library has been read down to a rather dilapidated condition. The works of Cooper, Dickens and Scott and writers of this order are read more than books of a more substantial character, but history and reputable books of travel are beginning to attract attention."

Some of these reports by inspectors are more revealing in what they do *not* say than in what they say. The report from Richfield township, in which I was born, reads as follows:

> The greatest difficulty I see in our township is too many little girls for summer teachers. They are wanting in judgment to govern and impart instruction; and many of the parents show but little interest in our schools. We want older and better-qualified teachers. The people are doing well if they get bright little girls for teachers for the wages they pay. One district with forty children

had seven months of school for $39.94 total wages, which is $5.74 per month. The average for 17 teachers for 41 and 1/16th months was $10.50 per month. If the teaching was no better than the pay (we trust it was) it must have been like the soap that the Rebels gave their prisoners.

Signed: S. J. Beecher

The inspector in Davison township complained that the parents objected to the visits by inspectors "even at the small pittance of $1 per day. They stand in their own children's lights. Admitting that the inspectors are incompetent, the teacher and the scholars do not know this and will be put on their good behavior and be stimulated by the mere influence of his office." This notation was signed by Ira T. Potter.

In all the reports the complaints were similar: poorly qualified teachers, too many young girls teaching (who had no discipline), the distinterest of parents and its corollary, poor attendance and poor support, no libraries or apparatus, and no special interest by the educated persons in the community such as ministers and lawyers. However, some reports enumerated good features such as new schoolhouses, outstanding teachers, the repair of old buildings, and the beginning of libraries.

When reviewing these old records, we must remember that Michigan in 1865 was a pioneer state. The Civil War had just ended. Much of the land had not been cleared or was just being cleared. Money was a scarce commodity. When we consider what these pioneers and their sons and daughters accomplished in the next fifty years, we can truly say they were the "salt of the earth."

COUNTY SUPERINTENDENTS

Several of the school inspectors of 1865 recommended that the office of county superintendent of schools be established. For thirty years educators had complained about the poor work done by the school inspectors. On three different occasions superintendents of public instruction had recommended changes to improve the inspection of schools and the certification of teachers. Responding to these complaints and recommendations, the state legislature provided by law for the election of a superintendent of schools for each county. The election of the first county superintendents was to be held on the first Monday of April in 1867 and every two years thereafter. They were to be elected at the same time and in the same way as the judges of the Supreme Court of Michigan. The term of office was two years, to start the first day of May following the election. The salary was to be determined by the county board of supervisors, but such compensation could not be less than $3 or more than $5 per day for each day actually employed. This number of days could not be less than the number of school districts in the county, plus one day for each township in the county for the examination of teachers. The county superintendent could also hold other teachers' examinations at other times. The wages for this official and the allowance of days to work were meager. For example, the county superintendent of Lapeer County was allowed 200 days at $3.50 per day.

This new school officer was authorized to grant three grades of certificates to teachers. A first grade certificate could be granted to any person who had taught one year with ability and success. This type of certificate was valid only in the county in which it was issued and was valid for two years only. A second grade certificate, good for one year throughout the county, could be granted to any person of approved educational qualifications and character. A third grade certificate licensed the holder to teach in a specified township for six months only.

The county superintendent could revoke a certificate for any reason which would have withheld the issuance in the first place or for gross neglect of duty, incompetency, or immorality, but no certificate could be revoked without re-examination unless the holder of the certificate failed to appear before the superintendent for such examination.

The superintendent of public instruction could issue certificates to any person on such evidence as might be satisfactory to him, which would be valid in any primary or graded school district in the state until revoked by the superintendent.

It was the duty of the county superintendent to visit each school in his county at least once a year, to examine carefully the modes of instruction and progress of the pupils, and to note the condition of the schoolhouse and appurtenances thereof. He was to counsel with teachers and school boards on all matters concerning the improvement of the teaching and any other item that would make a better school.

The annual reports made by the township school inspectors were to be submitted to the county superintendent. He, in turn, was required to combine these reports and make duplicate copies, one to be filed with the county clerk and the other sent to the superintendent of public instruction.

No county could elect a county superintendent of schools unless it had at least ten school districts. The 1868 annual report to the legislature shows that in the April election of 1867 forty-eight counties had the necessary number of school districts to enable them to elect superintendents.

Mr. L. C. York was elected superintendent of the schools of Genesee County, which at that time had 161 districts, with 1,030 children. He published a *School Journal* in which he reported on conditions he found in the schools of his county. One detail he noted was that nine tenths of the schools were opened with a religious exercise of some kind.

John D. Pierce, who had moved from Marshall to Ypsilanti after his service as our first superintendent of public instruction, was elected county superintendent of Washtenaw County. With the exception of Alpena County and one or two others, many of the counties north and west of Bay County and in the Upper Peninsula were still an unsettled wilderness.

One of the common complaints registered in 1868 was that there were too many small districts, which made the cost per pupil too high. There were many poorly furnished classrooms, with too few blackboards, maps, globes and charts. Also, many superintendents urged the adoption of uniform textbooks.

The regular custom was to have two terms of six weeks each, one in the winter for the large boys, with a male teacher who often held his job because he could "lick" the biggest bully, and the second term in the summer for the girls and the smaller boys, usually taught by a woman or young girl. The summer term was often poorly attended because of the heat. This was, of course, many years before compulsory education.

About this time, the state superintendents began to urge that all schools be made free and supported by taxation and that the school year be extended to six or nine months with three terms, the first term to be from early September to Christmas, the second from Christmas to April 1, and the third from April 1 to early July. Nearly all the county superintendents in their reports deplored the poor and irregular attendance.

The law establishing the office of county superintendent was a most important step in the *right* direction. Nevertheless, at once it became the object of intense opposition. As the township board of school inspectors had been established by the Michigan constitution, it could not be abolished by a legislative act. However, its most important duty—the conducting of teachers' examinations and issuance of teacher certificates—had been transferred to the new office of county superintendent. This loss of authority and prestige was a severe blow to the egos of the members of these boards. (Years later, when I was working to establish rural agricultural schools, I found that much of the opposition came from elderly members of school boards who would lose their office—their pride and joy—if new schools were organized.) About the only duty left to the township board of school inspectors was the collecting of annual reports from the various school districts and the forwarding of them to the county superintendent.

The annual reports put out by the state superintendents for the eight years in which Michigan first had county superintendents were full of praise for these officials. The following points in their favor were given:

1. They raised the standard of teaching by more careful teachers' examinations.

2. A better class of teachers was found in the schools. Lecturers in the teachers' institutes reported that their new classes were far in advance of those of former years. The county superintendents had managed to induce their teachers to perfect themselves in the subjects they taught as well as in the art of teaching.

3. More satisfactory and more reliable reports were sent to the Department of Education in Lansing.

4. The influence of the county superintendents was shown in the general interest in education, as evidenced by the increase in the number of visits by school officers of the districts.

5. There was increased interest in the schools by parents.

In some places the county superintendent was looked upon as an interloper. The state superintendent remarked in 1868 that no man could work as well or efficiently under implied censure as when he had the approval of his associates.

The improved condition of the schools and the advancement made in the various aspects of schoolwork were largely due to the untiring efforts of the county superintendents, according to the state superintendent. Knowing as they did that it would be impossible to have good schools without competent teachers and knowing that many utterly incompetent persons were employed to teach, they made it their first duty to remove such persons and replace them with persons better qualified. This was no easy task! Few persons could be found who were thoroughly prepared to teach; hence the county superintendents made a special effort to persuade teachers to prepare themselves. They advanced the standard of scholarship required to secure a teaching certificate. This caused great dissatisfaction, as might have been predicted, especially among those employed for years who lacked every qualification to teach but who were too opinionated or too lazy to make an effort to improve themselves in the subjects they taught and the methods of instruction.

The more experienced county superintendents made it a policy to retain every competent teacher possible and to persuade school boards to keep the same teacher for a series of terms. A constant change of teachers was, and still is, a great injury to a school.

Not everyone who was able to pass the examination proved to be a good teacher. Formerly such persons, upon showing themselves incompetent, were dismissed and the school discontinued. Under the new system, the difficulty was met by the action of the county superintendent in preventing such people from entering the teaching profession. If they did get in, they were easily removed and replaced by the superintendent of the county. In most counties the greatest harmony existed between the county superintendents and their teaching staff. The teachers prized a certificate that had cost them toil and they were gratified with the better results of their labor.

In the annual report of 1869, the state superintendent mentioned the *increased interest* in the public schools shown by people generally. He said it had not diminished but had greatly increased and was shown by improvement of school buildings and grounds, demand for better teachers, and readiness to meet any reasonable expense necessary to secure better schools. But the most manifest evidence of the increasing interest in the schools was the fact that men were engaging in earnest discussions pertaining to the best interests of the schools. The report pointed out that there was a time when such discussions would have been considered an eighth wonder of the world.

Increased interest in the schools was also shown by the longer length of the school year. Previously three months were thought to be time enough to maintain a school in a single year, and five or six months were deemed generous in the extreme. Now many schools were adopting a plan giving nine months for each school year. Where tried, the nine-month plan was found most valuable; pupils made much greater progress in their studies.

By 1870 the county superintendents were reporting that the school officers were visiting their schools more frequently than formerly. Previously district school officers seldom spent an hour within the schoolhouse itself. Little care had been taken in the selection of school officers; in fact, it had been no recommendation for a man that he was qualified for the position he was asked to fill. Indeed, this would have aroused the suspicion of the people and tended to defeat him in an election; the fear was that such a man would strive to secure better schools without regard to expense. *Cheap* schools had been the great end to be desired, but by 1869 more care was being taken to secure competent men as school officers. This change in attitude had come about through the efforts of the various county superintendents, according to the state superintendent, who reported:

> Wherever these men (county superintendents) labored earnestly and wisely, the district officers have become more efficient and the people manifest more interest in the prosperity of their schools and have a stronger desire that their children receive a good education.

Perhaps some of these changes were brought about because of the influence of our "boys in blue" who had returned from service in the Civil War and whose outlook had been broadened by their travels and experiences.

By 1870 nearly four years had passed since the organization of the system of county superintendency. The system had met with determined opposition when it was adopted and some of its enemies still remained violently opposed. Those who were hostile to the system argued that the wages of teachers had been increased (but they admitted that the better schools were taught by the higher-priced teachers) and that the county superintendents did not visit all the schools or if they did, their visits were too infrequent.

It was apparent at the time of the adoption of the system that too much territory had been given to many of the superintendents to enable them to do their work as thoroughly as it should be done. This was due to the lack of good roads and transportation facilities. Also, the time limits set for which they could be paid were not sufficient for them to do all that needed to be done.

Another class of complainers was made up of those who had been found lacking upon examination and who had therefore been refused teaching certificates. Naturally they favored the old system in which all applicants were granted certificates simply upon application.

The pressure against the office of county superintendent had been slowly mounting, with the resistance led by the school inspectors, whose power and prestige had been taken from them. The main argument against the office was that it was too expensive. This was but an excuse. In 1874, the legislature passed a law abolishing the office. In its place the office of township superintendent was created. That year, 1874, undoubtedly marks the lowest ebb in the affairs of education in Michigan.

CHAPTER XI

Township Superintendents and County Boards of School Examiners

When the powers and duties of county superintendents were turned over to township superintendents, the law listed no qualifications for a township superintendent. To be a teacher, a person had to be of good moral character, have the ability to teach, and had to pass an examination in the common branches of reading, orthography, geography, grammar and arithmetic. However, the township superintendent was permitted, because of his election to office, to teach in any school in his township without an examination.

His duties were to hold two examinations each year for teachers aspiring to teach in the primary schools of the township. These examinations could be either oral or written. Other duties were to visit each school at least twice each year to inspect the buildings, observe the teaching, consult with the school board regarding necessary corrections in teaching or in the physical features of the school. His compensation was $2 per day for time actually spent plus money spent for stationery, postage, and printing necessary to carry out his work. Union and graded schools were exempt from his jurisdiction. He was also chairman of the township board of school inspectors. The power conferred upon the township superintendent was mainly advisory, but grave responsibility was imposed on these officers. The job required men of special training, competent to advise teachers and school boards. They were supposed to be earnest, faithful, impartial and familiar with the needs of their schools. It was beyond the ability of most townships to secure such men to supervise; the ones who did were notable *exceptions.*

Mr. Daniel B. Briggs wrote in his report of 1876 to the legislature:

> The superivision that the schools in our rural districts stand in need of today will not and cannot come under the present system (township superintendents) and the reasons for it are evident. It cannot be realized without giving the superintendents increased compensation and a jurisdiction sufficiently extended to furnish them constant employment. Had the law of 1867 been retained and so modified as to do away with the vital objections that were made to it, our schools would have been in better condition than they are now.

He went on to say:

> The county system of superintendence is probably the best ever devised and the fact that this system prevails in nearly all the states is very conclusive evidence of it. Nearly two years have passed since the adoption of the township system of school supervision which superseded the county system that had a precarious existence for eight years. This change in school management has not only increased the labor and expense of this department, but has added greatly to the delay and uncertainty in securing the annual reports. Two years time is sufficient to demonstrate that it is much more difficult to establish and hold a communication with nearly 1,000 officials than with one-seventeenth that number.

In 1878, Cornelius A. Gower, the next superintendent of public instruction, stated in his report to the legislature:

> The great need of the ungraded schools of the state is a more efficient system of local supervision. The constitution provides for school officers for the district, the township, and the state. To make the system complete in its workings there should be added corresponding officers for each county. I think the great difficulty heretofore has been the idea that we must have a system of local supervision exclusively by a county officer or as exclusively by a township officer. When the county superintendency law was enacted, the township inspectors were ignored as useless as far as supervision was concerned. The county superintendent also rarely had anything to do with the district officer, while his relation to the state superintendent was purely clerical; he did not become a part

of the system. When, therefore, I say we need a county school officer I mean that such an officer or board should become a part of
the official school system.

Supervision is needed for several distinct purposes. First, for
the examination of teachers. This should be entrusted to none but
experienced educators of thorough scholarship and free from any
local or political prejudice. This examination cannot be completed
in a few minutes while the township superintendent is resting his
team in the plowfield, but it should be done with deliberation and
care. I think the authority should be a county board of three examiners. This would eliminate putting all the responsibility on one
man.

In his report to the superintendent of public instruction, the township
superintendent of Davison township, Mr. Enos Hollenbeck, gave his
opinion of the township superintendency in this statement:

I never had any confidence in a township superintendent
before I held the office and my personal experience has confirmed
my previous dislike.

He gave five reasons: (1) inability to please his neighbors; (2) the duties
were not numerous enough nor the salary large enough to keep him in
business; (3) the fact that the average township superintendent lacks the
ability to fill the office; (4) his efforts to get the teachers to give lessons
in penmanship, as some were practicing no definite system; and (5) the
new system was an abortive effort to reform "conceived in ignorance and
born in folly."

Another township superintendent reported in 1876, "No man can
retain the office if he refuses a teacher's certificate to anyone of an influential family in the district."

Nearly everyone agreed that creating the office of township superintendent was a *step backward.* In those years, when so many new ideas
were being tried, it seems that progress was very slow. The lawmakers
sometimes took two steps forward then one back, or even one forward
and then two back. Among the changes made were the following: (1879)
the two-mill tax was changed to one mill; the electing of school officers
was done by ballot (although the ballot may have been only a slip of paper
with the candidates' names written with pencil and the ballots collected
in a hat).

By 1880, educators began to realize that the law creating the township superintendents was a step backward. In this same year, the superintendent of public instruction recommended that all graded schools extend schooling through the tenth grade.

1881 — AN IMPORTANT YEAR

According to Superintendent Vernum B. Cochran's report, the year 1881 was one of the most important years in the history of Michigan schools. A thorough review of the whole body of laws relating to schools, especially those parts relating to the examination of teachers and the supervision of schools, was made. One law, effective July 1, 1881, was an act that abolished the office of township superintendent and put in its place a county board of school examiners. Because the township board of school inspectors was a constitutional office, it could not be legislated out of existence. The newly created board consisted of three members elected for three years, one each year. They were chosen by the chairmen of the township boards of school inspectors, meeting in the office of the county clerk, who was the clerk of the election, on the first Tuesday in August.

The school examiners then met at the office of the county clerk to organize as a board, by electing one of their number as secretary. The chairman of this board was the member whose term expired soonest.

After this new county board was organized, there was a joint meeting of the board and the chairmen of the township boards of school inspectors. The purpose of the meeting was to plan for better supervision of district schools. This meeting was held on the fourth Tuesday of August in the office of the Judge of Probate.

This new board was to hold three teachers' examinations each year. Prospective teachers were examined in orthography, reading, writing, grammar, arithmetic, the theory and art of teaching, and United States history and civil government. I have a copy of a book on Michigan civil government by A. M. Cocker, one-time superintendent of schools in Adrian, which was written in 1878 and copyrighted in 1884. It is a well-written book with much information about early Michigan government. My copy was once owned by Cleo Kelly, deputy county clerk of Genesee County when my friend Jesse Good was county clerk, from 1916 to 1932.

The school laws of 1867 required that examinations be required for only five subjects: reading, orthography, geography, grammar, and arithmetic. The fourteen years between 1867 and 1881 showed a distinct advance in educational requirements for teachers.

The certificates granted by the county board of school examiners were, for the most part, for a longer period and were valid in all of the schools of a county except in union schools where the school board could issue certificates. This change, of necessity, led to a better preparation on the part of the applicants and insured the same standard for all teachers in the county. The questions used in examination were sent to each county board by the Department of Education in Lansing. Realizing that there were many fairly competent teachers who could not qualify under the new system, the Michigan Board of Education advised the examiners to be more lenient in the first fall examinations for third grade certificates than would be warranted at a later date. Notwithstanding this leniency, an average of 26% of all applicants failed the first examination and 21% the final one.

The reports of 1882 show that the county boards of examiners had received a most favorable reception. (This was the year, incidentally, that the little log schoolhouse across the corner from our farmhouse was abandoned and a new frame schoolhouse was built one mile north of the old site.) These county boards soon weeded out many poor teachers who had kept their jobs for years because they were friends or neighbors of the men on the township boards of school inspectors. Better teachers soon commanded higher wages and a longer tenure.

However, it was not only in examinations that the county boards proved to be a power for good. Their relations to the township inspectors, the teachers and the schools were so intimate that their influence could be felt in all departments of supervisory work. Superintendent Cochran said in his 1881 report:

> Local supervision by the chairmen of the township boards was still a factor of prime importance because the value of a school depended largely upon the public sentiment of the community. The visiting inspector could do much in arousing and fostering this sentiment and through him and with him the county board could find ample means to bring itself into close sympathy with

the schools and teachers. It was hoped that the county board would be regarded as men desiring to be helpful in all that made for better schools and that the patrons of the schools would feel that a central agency was at work.

The work of the chairman who was entrusted with the local supervision in his township was: (1) to visit each school in his township at least once each term to examine discipline, mode of instruction, and progress of pupils; (2) to counsel with the teachers as to course of study; (3) to note the condition of the school buildings and grounds and suggest plans for heating and ventilating and general improvement; (4) to promote, subject to the advice of the county board of examiners, the improvement of the schools and raising the qualifications of the teachers in his township; (5) to notify the secretary of the county board of examiners of any school not being conducted in a successful manner; (6) to make such reports of his official labors as the superintendent of public instruction may direct or the county board of examiners may request; and (7) to perform such other duties as required by law or the superintendent of public instruction may direct.

Mr. Cochran further stressed that it was the duty of all who had the best interest of their local school at heart to see to it that the best men available were placed in these positions.

The year 1881 saw the beginning of many other firsts in Michigan education. Until the organization of county boards of school examiners there had been no standard requirements for the examination of teachers. In 1882, a standard was set at 75% average for a third grade certificate, 80% for a second, and 85% for a first grade with 75% as a minimum in five subjects: arithmetic, geography, grammar, orthography, and the theory of art and teaching. Until these standards were set, the applicant for a certificate was required only to pass a "satisfactory" examination, which could mean whatever the examiner decided.

In 1881, the legislature passed the first uniform textbook law. This law specified that the district should adopt uniform textbooks and outline the course of study. Before the passage of this law, pupils were taught from any book they happened to have.

A second attempt was made to pass a township unit bill, but this effort failed because of the opposition of the State Grange, a fraternal order of farmers.

Section 6 of Act 144 provided that all graded schools could have ungraded schools for retarded children. Before this, only districts of 5,000 inhabitants could have such schools.

Another first was that the superintendent of public instruction recommended that the curriculum of the smaller high schools be enriched by the study of Latin.

In 1885, a law provided for the establishment of a State Teachers' Reading Circle, governed by four members, two to be elected each year for a term of two years by the State Teachers' Association. The superintendent of public instruction was an *ex officio* member of the board. This governing board of five members was organized by electing a president, a secretary and a treasurer. A course of home study for self-improvement of teachers was adopted; textbooks were selected with reduced prices obtained from the publishers; and a depository was established in Lansing. These selected books were to be the basis for personal study. When the examinations for teachers' certificates were held, questions on the theory and art of teaching were based on the books chosen by the Reading Circle board. Credit could also be given to teachers who read books from the recommended list.

In 1885, an attack was made in a New York newspaper on the prevailing methods of college discipline. Military training in schools was also being discussed pro and con all over the United States. Is there anything really new today?

The legislature of 1887 made the secretary of the county board of examiners the visiting and supervising officer of all the schools of the county. In reality, he became a county superintendent, in fact if not in name. He could appoint assistant visitors. This law, which went into effect on September 26, 1887, took away from the township boards of school inspectors all their duties except that of forming new districts or dividing old ones.

The new supervising system seemed to be working out well in most counties, but complaints were made that in some counties poorly educated persons or failures in other professions had been appointed to the county board of school examiners with results far from satisfactory. However, in most counties the results were good and led to longer tenure for teachers, who were hired for the year and not for a term only. Other benefits were greater uniformity in textbooks, improvement in sanitary conditions, and better-trained teachers.

State Board of Education and State Certificates

In 1867, the act that provided for county superintendents of schools also authorized the state superintendent of public instruction "on such evidence as may be satisfactory to him, to issue certificates to license the holder thereof to teach in any primary or graded school in the state. Such certificate shall remain in force as long as the moral and professional reputation of the holder remains unsullied." This law, which did not require the superintendent to conduct any examinations, may have caused some criticism. To avoid any appearance of favoritism, Mr. Daniel B. Briggs, who was superintendent of public instruction from 1873 to 1877, recommended that the state adopt a plan of public examinations to be conducted at the capital by a board of examiners consisting of persons distinguished for their high character and ability. His report for 1873 listed the names of 136 teachers who held state certificates, five of whom received these certificates in 1873.

When the law which created the office of county superintendent was repealed in 1875, the authority of the superintendent of public instruction to grant state certificates, which was part of this law, was also repealed.

In 1878, Mr. Cornelius A. Gower, then superintendent of public instruction, recommended that the State Board of Education be empowered to hold examinations and grant state certificates. His thinking was that the prestige of the State Board of Education would thus be enhanced. At that time the Board had very few duties and the power to grant teachers' certificates would make it an integral part of the Michigan educational system. The revised constitution of Michigan of 1850 provided that in

1852 three members were to be elected to this board, one for two years, one for four years, and one for six years. At each biennial election thereafter one member was to be elected for six years. This board had general charge of the state normal school. Other duties included making a list every two years of unsectarian books suitable for township and district libraries, contracting with responsible bidders to furnish such books in suitable bindings and at stipulated prices, and the granting of diplomas to normal school graduates.

Public Act 231, passed by the legislature in 1880, authorized the State Board of Education to hold examinations and grant state certificates good for ten years. This method of obtaining teachers' certificates did not become popular. By 1889 only 43 certificates had been granted in this way. As a means of making state certificates more popular, the legislature in 1889 passed a law to require the State Board of Education to hold two examinations each year for state life certificates. When first enacted, this law applied to all graduates of the University of Michigan and of the incorporated colleges of the state. Two years of teaching experience were required for all applicants except those who had graduated from the University or an approved college.

An act of 1893 stipulated that any college whose students wanted to take an examination for a state life certificate had to provide a course in the science and art of teaching of at least five and a half hours per week, which course was to be approved by the State Board of Education. The applicant would have to pass a satisfactory examination in this course. The subjects in which applicants were to be examined for life certificates were: orthography, reading, penmanship, arithmetic, algebra, geometry, grammar, geography, United States history, general history, civil government, theory and art of teaching, physics, physiology and hygiene, botany, zoology, geology, chemistry, rhetoric, general literature, and the school laws of Michigan. Graduates of the literary department of the University and of incorporated colleges were exempt from the provision requiring previous experience in teaching.

In 1893, the act was changed to specify that the State Board of Education could grant certificates without examination to any person who had received a bachelor's, master's, or doctor's degree from any college in

Michigan having a course of study actually taught in that college of not less than four years, in addition to having had the preparatory work necessary for admission to the University of Michigan, upon recommendation from the faculty of such college. The recommendation had to state that "in their judgment the applicant is entitled to receive such certificate" and also state "that the applicant has had a course in the theory and art of teaching." The certificate then granted would be a life certificate if the applicant could furnish proof that he had had three years of successful teaching prior to the recommendation. If no such proof could be furnished, the certificate granted was valid for three years. A life certificate could be granted to the applicant any time thereafter upon his furnishing proof of three years of successful teaching.

The state superintendent's report of 1894 gave the name of Luther L. Wright, who later became a state superintendent of public instruction, as one who had passed a satisfactory examination and had received a life certificate. The same report gave the names of Fred L. Keeler, who later became a state superintendent; A. M. Freeland, later a county commissioner of schools and a member of the State Board of Education; and E. E. Gallup, later a director of the Smith-Hughes Act, as applicants who had received endorsed first grade certificates. In our early history, teaching while learning was often the pathway to the top positions in our educational system for many of our early educators. These men may not have known all the answers, but they had the actual experience to enable them to make correct judgments.

Should anyone like to see just how difficult the questions for a life certificate were, a set of the questions can be found in the annual report of the superintendent of public instruction for 1894 and in subsequent reports. It was such a life certificate that I had to have before I could take the position of superintendent of the Linden schools in 1913. The legislature had just passed a law requiring superintendents of schools with six or more teachers to have a life certificate. By this time, two subjects, Latin and German, had been added and the applicant could make choices of writing an examination in physics or chemistry and in Latin or German. I chose physics and Latin. The examinations were given in Lansing in the office of the state superintendent and covered nineteen subjects. It took from noon Monday to 5 p.m. Friday to write the examination. Two examinations were given each year, one in March and one in August. The marks were carried over from March to August. If an applicant failed in one or more subjects in March, he could attend summer school to study the subjects in which he failed. Because I had to teach physics in Linden, I went to Ypsilanti Normal during the summer of 1913 to study the subject under Professor Gorton, a very good instructor, then finished the examination in August. My average for the nineteen subjects was 93%.

CHAPTER XIII

Financing the Schools

Section 4 of Article 13 of the Constitution of Michigan, adopted in 1836, states:

> The legislature shall, within five years of the adoption of this Constitution, provide for and establish a system of primary schools, whereby a school shall be kept without charge for tuition at least three months in each year in every school district in the state and all instruction in said schools shall be conducted in the English language.

In a footnote to this Section 4, Mr. Oramel Hosford, the superintendent of public instruction in 1869, wrote this comment:

> The legislature of 1869 has at length complied with this requirement. Districts with less than 30 children must have three months of free school; with from 30 to 800 children they must have five months; and with over 800 children, nine months.

This was indeed a giant step forward in education in Michigan.

We have seen the changes made in the laws which provided money to support the public schools. The two most important sources were the two-mill tax levied on all property in the district and the Primary School fund, which was distributed to the schools on a per capita basis. The mill tax, then as now, varied according to the amount of taxable property that could be assessed for school purposes in each district. From the very beginning of our school system this division of our schools into the "have" and "have not" districts has been evident.

When the funds from the mill tax and the Primary School fund were spent, the school board could operate under the Rate Bill or close the school. Under the Rate Bill, the board could charge each parent a definite amount or rate for tuition for each child he sent to school. For many of the districts of the state this meant that the schools were closed after only a month or two of free schooling. At the time, education of the young had not become important to people in many districts. In some districts, if the "rate" money could be collected, a longer term was maintained for those who could or would pay the extra fee. Under this system a property owner with no children paid only the two-mill tax. Children of property owners or people with money could get at least as much schooling as their school could give them. Children of poor families, whose parents could not or would not pay the tuition, grew up without any schooling or, at best, with very little. As there was no compulsory school law, these cases were frequent. The Rate Bill was repealed April 3, 1859, and school boards were given the authority to levy sufficient taxes to operate a school. This was another great step forward, but as late as the 1880s and 1890s there were many elderly persons in Michigan unable to read and to write.

From the annual reports of the superintendents of public instruction some interesting facts may be gleaned. For instance, in Mr. Hosford's report for 1870, he tells how the people were living and thinking and points out the forces that made them react to their environment. To quote:

> In the 1870s in Michigan the population is rapidly increasing. Factories are springing up and the immense lumber interests have by no means reached the limit of their importance. Railroads are multiplying rapidly and pushing boldly into dense forests, those building them knowing that where railroads go, man will follow.
>
> Amid the push to develop material resources, the people have not lost sight of the necessity of securing mental and moral training, hence churches and schoolhouses are among the first buildings to be erected in a village. These buildings are usually the finest and most expensive in the village or city. However, there are some

communities in which the people seem to be more interested in rearing choice flocks and herds than in giving their children the best advantages for education. They build beautiful barns for their cattle and fine dwellings while they continue to use old, open, worthless structures for schoolhouses rather than go to the expense of building new ones.

CHAPTER XIV

Compulsory Education

After the Rate Bill was repealed in 1859 and schools actually became free, the leaders in education began to take notice of the great number of children who were not attending school. Reports going to the state superintendent, Mr. Hosford, who served in that office from 1865 to 1873, pointed out that thousands of children were allowed to run the streets without any occupation, growing up in complete ignorance. Many of the parents recognized the value of the free school law, but in many families parental authority was so low that a significant number of boys became habitual truants. Mr. Hosford recommended that a law be passed requiring an habitual truant to be tried, and if found guilty, to be sentenced to a house of reformation.

It may be relevant to note what European educators who visited the United States observed with regard to our school system. They saw one sad defect in our schools, namely, that not one half of the children of school age in our country attended school with any regularity and that there were thousands upon thousands who never entered a classroom. One of the prominent educators from Europe, after praising many things he had seen in this country, said that in general our system of education was the best in the world, but that it needed one thing to make it perfect— education should be made compulsory. He went on to say:

> I should be uncandid if I did not frankly tell you that North Germany and Switzerland excel you in the thoroughness and universality of their systems and that is entirely owing to the fact that in those two countries the parent has not the right to deprive the

child of the excellent training which the state has provided. . . .
This is chiefly what you need to perfect your educational system.

Also, in Sweden at the time this was written, education was compulsory upon all classes, rich and poor alike, whether living near to or far from a school. The period of school life was not measured by years but by progress made.

In 1846, Massachusetts passed a law calling for compulsory education, which was in principle the same as the policy established more than 200 years earlier. The practical question for Michigan was: Can a similar law be enforced in our state? The thinking was that it would be impossible to enforce such a law if the popular will was against it. Mr. Hosford stressed that *effective* laws are but the expression of the public will.

When our free schools were first established, a compulsory attendance law was not considered necessary. The thinking was that if a parent had the right to send his child to a free school, he had an equal right to keep his child at home. As the years went by, much complaint was registered by educators against the irregular attendance and nonattendance of many children. By 1870 the situation had become so serious that the legislature was prevailed upon to pass the first compulsory school act. This act provided that every parent or guardian of a child or children between the ages of eight and fourteen be required to send such child or children to a public school for a period of twelve weeks in each school year, commencing on the first day of September of 1871. To quote the law:

> Six weeks of these twelve shall be consecutive unless such child or children are excused from such attendance by the board of the school district because bodily or mental conditions are such as to prevent such attendance, or if such child is taught in a private school or at home in such branches as are usually taught in the public schools.
> If a public school is not taught for three months within two miles by the nearest traveled road, he shall not be liable to the provisions of this act.

If a parent or guardian did not send a child to school, the director or president of the district board could bring suit against this parent or guardian who failed to comply with the law. The act provided for a fine of not less than $5 for the first offense and not less than $10 for the second or any subsequent offense. If the director or president failed to bring suit against a parent within ten days after a notice of truancy had been served on him by a taxpayer of a district, he was subject to a fine of not less than $10 or more than $50. This first attempt to require a minimum of attendance was a cumbersome law which was easier to ignore than to enforce.

The 1870 law was amended in 1883 by providing for the appointment of truant officers by the police authorities in the districts of the larger villages and cities. If there had been much truancy in such districts, the boards of education in such districts could open an ungraded school to accommodate the truants who had fallen behind their own age group in their schoolwork.

In December 1876, Daniel Briggs, then state superintendent, at the twenty-sixth annual meeting of the Michigan Teachers Association, complained that the great drawback to the successful working of the schools had been a lack of familiarity with school laws and also a want of disposition to enforce them. He said:

> We have had a law for six years to compel children to attend school and we have yet to learn of a single instance of its enforcement in any locality. Very much good was expected to result from the enactment, but public sentiment evidently is not ready for its enforcement. The attendance of children in our public schools is far short of what it should be.

The law was amended in 1883 to provide that "every parent or other person having control of any children between the ages of eight and fourteen years shall be required to send such children to a public school for at least eight months in any school year." According to the superintendent of public instruction in 1889, Mr. Joseph Estabrook, the force of this provision was lost because no penalty was imposed for its violation. There were other marked defects and inconsistencies in the law which made its enforcement impracticable. Probably the main reason for the failure of these first compulsory attendance laws was the lack of a central authority or county school officer.

That these early compulsory attendance laws had little effect upon the people is shown by W. J. Cocker in his *Civil Government of Michigan,* an 1879 textbook. This book makes no mention of any compulsory attendance law. That the schools should be free and that they should be supported by taxation seemed to be the dominating factors in the minds of the people. The idea that parents should be compelled to send their children to school did not appear to be a vital issue. However, the various superintendents of public instruction were always bemoaning the poor attendance in the schools.

In 1893, the legislature passed the compulsory attendance law that, with a few changes, is in force today. This law provided that all children from eight to fourteen years of age inclusive in all townships and villages without a police force should attend school at least four months a year. In the larger villages and the cities the ages were seven to sixteen inclusive, with attendance required for the length of time the schools were in session. In graded school districts the school board appointed a truant officer. In other districts, the chairman of the township board of school inspectors became the truant officer. This was the first mention of a truant officer and the first attempt to enforce a truancy law.

Compulsory attendance had been for years a most controversial subject. As early as the time when Mr. Cornelius A. Gower served as the second county superintendent of Genesee County, he reported that he had received letters from the teachers blaming those educators who advocated compulsory education, insisting that they were organizing our American schools by copying the Prussian system of education.

The next change in the school laws increased the school year from four months to five. Then came the change which lowered the age for required attendance from eight to seven years. In 1895, the enforcement of the compulsory attedance law was given to the county commissioner of schools, who appointed a county truant officer. The individual teacher was required to notify the commissioner of any truancy in his school.

The annual report of the superintendent of public instruction for 1895 says that the compulsory attendance law was the most helpful bit of school legislation passed in many years. It was enforced with good sense and brought to the classroom thousands of children who had been growing up in ignorance. No child dared to be on the street during school hours unless he had an excuse from the proper authority. The truant officer of Bay City reported a decrease in the number of young boys and girls on the streets at night. Superintendent Hathaway of Flint reported a reduction in the number of petty crimes and much less disturbance of the peace by juveniles.

The James Act, which was passed in 1919 but did not take effect until September 1, 1920, provided for the establishment of continuation or part-time schools. In all school districts of 5,000 or more population such schools were established for minors under eighteen years of age who had left the regular day schools. The law specified that all children under sixteen who were not in day schools and those sixteen or seventeen who left after that date without having completed the equivalent of a high school education should attend a part-time or continuation school at least eight hours per week. Continuation schools under the James Act were aided by state and federal funds under the Smith-Hughes law. The age for a working permit was raised to eighteen years. The subjects taught in continuation schools were intended to contribute to civic and vocational intelligence.

CHAPTER XV

Ypsilanti Normal School

The first laws establishing our Michigan schools system were either incorporated in the constitution adopted in 1836 or written into the laws passed by the first legislature, which met in 1837 after the state was admitted to the Union. In those early laws no mention was made of a normal or teacher-training school. The little training offered was given in teachers' institutes.

In 1849, the legistlature provided for the establishment of a normal school, to be located in Ypsilanti. This was the first normal school founded west of the Allegheny Mountains; the first normal school in the United States was established at Lexington, Massachusetts, in 1838. The State Board of Education was to have general supervision and control of the new normal school, the purpose of which was to give instruction to both males and females in the theory and practice of teaching and in the various subjects taught in the public schools, as well as to give instruction in the mechanical arts, the arts of husbandry, agricultural chemistry, the fundamental laws of the United States and the rights and duties of citizens.

The normal school building, a three-story structure, was completed and dedicated on October 5, 1852. In the 1853 report of the superintendent of public instruction we read, "The site of the building is on an eminence overlooking the village of Ypsilanti and the surrounding country, in a pure and healthy locality and atmosphere." The dedication speech was delivered by John D. Pierce, the first superintendent of public instruction in Michigan.

Because the normal school was founded to train teachers for the primary schools, the legislature gave the school 25,000 acres of salt spring land which was to be sold and the proceeds used to establish a permanent endowment fund. By 1882 all this land had been sold and the endowment fund amounted to $69,000. Other income came from tuition and from appropriations of the state legislature. In 1882, the total budget for the normal school was about $24,000.

It is interesting to note that when the law was passed to establish a normal school, the legislators gave themselves the privilege of appointing two pupils each year who could attend the school without paying tuition. I have been unable to find out when this part of the law became obsolete or was repealed, but it was before 1900.

When the normal school began to train teachers for high schools, the endowment was taken from it and given to the Primary School fund because the initial purpose of the normal school was to train teachers for common or primary schools only.

At the end of the first quarter century, four curricula had evolved. Students were admitted by examination only. The two-year common school curriculum attracted over half the students. It was designed to prepare teachers for the district and graded schools of Michigan by providing instruction "in the various branches pertaining to a good common school education." The three other curricula—the three-year Full English course, the four-year Modern Language course, and the Classical course—were designed to prepare teachers for secondary schools and for positions as principals, supervisors, and superintendents. Only after proving his capacity and zeal for learning by rigid written examinations in a satisfactory number of subjects in what were then considered the basic branches of learning was a student on any of these curricula allowed to begin training in the art of teaching.

Applicants for admission to Ypsilanti Normal had to sign a declaration of their intention to follow the profession of teaching. This declaration was an entrance requirement until about 1930.

From the beginning, the general management of Ypsilanti Normal was entrusted to the State Board of Education. Each year this board appointed persons to visit the school and report to the superintendent of public instruction their opinions in regard to the condition and needs of the school. These visitors were paid $2 per day plus travel expense while engaged in these duties.

From these small beginnings the normal school soon grew to be one of the leading teacher-training colleges in the entire United States. By 1912 the idea of extension courses was developed at the college. This was one of the departments that especially interested me. Although for several years our county normal had been doing good work in training teachers for district schools, there were still many rural teachers who had never attended a normal school of any tiype. During several winters of my term of office we had extension classes conducted by such men as Professors Hoyt and Wilber from Ypsilanti Normal or the University of Michigan. These classes, held on Saturday afternoons, were well attended. Whenever possible, I took advantage of the opportunity to attend these classes.

Although the original purpose for founding the Ypsilanti Normal College was the preparation of teachers for the public schools, and for the first one hundred years this purpose was its main objective, this purpose has always been interpreted broadly. Instruction in the liberal arts and sciences, vital to the background of a well-qualified teacher, was included. The school's capabilities in these areas were formally recognized in 1956 by the change of name to Eastern Michigan College. On June 1, 1959, the college was named Eastern Michigan University. In its 121 years of existence it has had many firsts.

1. It was the first teacher education institution established west of the Allegheny Mountains, the sixth in the United States, 1849.

2. It was the first tax-supported college in Michigan open to men and women alike.

3. It was the first institution of higher learning in Michigan to receive support from the state legislature, 1850.

4. It was the first in Michigan to establish a department of geography, 1890.

5. It was the first in the West to establish a department to train teachers in physical education, 1888.

6. It was the first teachers college in the United States to have a building for religious activities, Startweather Hall, 1896.

7. It was the first teacher education institution in the United States to be raised to a four-year college, 1897.

8. It was the first collegiate institution in Michigan to offer courses in industrial arts, 1901.

9. It was the first state teachers college in the United States to establish training for teachers of handicapped children, 1915.

10. It was the first teachers college in the United States to have a social center building, McKenny Hall, 1931.

11. It was the first teacher training institution to organize a curriculum for library service, 1940.

Until January 1, 1964, the governing body was the State Board of Education. With the adoption of the new state constitution Eastern Michigan University became constitutionally independent and is now governed by an eight-member board of regents, appointed by the governor, subject to the approval of the state senate.

CHAPTER XVI

Teacher Training and Normal Schools

The first teachers institute was held in Lenawee County on September 29, 1845. Twelve such institutes had been held in the state by 1847. In 1852, there was a three-week institute held in Lansing. The day sessions of most institutes were taken up with discussions of the latest methods of teaching. The evening sessions were given over to lectures on educational and popular subjects.

In 1861, the length of the institutes was reduced to five days. Before this, the law had set no time limit. The law, as amended in March of 1861, stated that an institute could be held "whenever reasonable assurance shall be given to the superintendent of public instruction by at least fifty teachers, or twenty-five in counties containing a population of less than 12,000, that they would assemble for the purpose of forming a teachers institute and remain in session for five working days." The state superintendent could appoint a time and place for such an institute and make arrangements and give due notice thereof. The auditor general, upon the certificate of the state superintendent, could draw a warrant on the state treasurer, not to exceed $100, to pay teachers and lecturers for the institute. However, not more than $1,800 could be paid out of state funds for these institutes in any one year. This allocation remained at $1,800 until 1874, at which time the legislature raised the appropriation to $3,000.

The purpose of these institutes was to give instruction in methods of teaching, school discipline, and school management as well as to make those attending profoundly loyal to their calling. Teachers of established reputation in the state were selected to take charge and serve as institute conductors. There were two kinds of institutes, county and state. The superintendent of public instruction was required annually to appoint a time and place for the various county institutes and to conduct them or appoint a suitable person to do so.

In 1852, Francis W. Shearman, then superintendent of public instruction, called a teachers institute to be held in Ypsilanti for four weeks immediately following the dedication of the new Normal School building. The institute opened on the morning following the dedication exercises, which were held on Tuesday, October 5. For some reason it was continued only through the third week. A detailed course of study had been prepared and printed. The subjects studied were English language and grammar, arithmetic, natural science, anatomy and physiology. It is interesting to observe the thinking of the educators who prepared this program. The institute was designed to train teachers to teach in the common schools, in which the subjects taught were reading, orthography, geography, grammar, and arithmetic. In the grammar classes stress was placed on the parts of a sentence, adjuncts or modifiers, connectives, and analysis. For one week the language classes were given over to the study of elocution. Under natural science such items as imponderable agents, caloric, heat, light, electricity, electrical phenomena, and elements of astronomy were studied. In judging these educators, we must remember that free public schools were in their infancy and there were no high schools. It was the duty of the teachers of the common school to give the children as broad an education as possible.

Instructors for this institute came from the University of Michigan and from Boston and New York. Some of the topics for the evening lectures were "The Responsibility of Teachers," "Physical Science," "Female Education," "The Teacher's Mission," "Natural Sciences," "Music," and "The Duties of the Teacher." The superintendents' annual report for 1852 gives the names and addresses of the 150 teachers in attendance at this institute.

Before this 1852 institute adjourned, a meeting of the teachers was held and the Michigan Teachers Association was organized. A. S. Welch, A. M., president of the new Normal School, was elected president; Miss

A. C. Rogers and Mr. A. B. Thair, vice presidents; John Horner, corresponding secretary; and Henry Cheever, treasurer. This organization was to play a very influential part in the development of our school system.

To aid in training teachers for rural schools, many city schools held review classes in the common subjects to prepare their older pupils to take a teachers' examination. In the 1865 report of the state superintendent, the term "union" school was applied to schools with high schools. These union schools were annually training teachers for the district schools. Mr. Hosford, the state superintendent, had sent a questionnaire to the various union schools in the state to ascertain how many were conducting classes for teachers, lasting from six to eight weeks, in some schools in March and April and in others in September and October, to prepare young people to teach the common subjects of district schools. Many of the larger schools were offering these review courses. Ten of the answered questionnaires were published in the superintendent's annual report.

In regard to the teaching of reading, all but two schools said they were using the "word" method, modified by the "object" method. Only one was using the phonics method. (For many years before the 1920s the combination phonics-and-word method was standard procedure; it was the method taught when I was a child in a one-room school and also when I was a teacher in rural schools. About 1920 or 1921 this method was discarded for the "look-say" method, which was adopted without any definite proof or study having been made to insure that it would be successful. After forty years, because of the poor readers it produced, the "look-say" method had been replaced in many schools by the phonics-and-word method.)

For at least sixty years after Michigan became a state, the teachers institutes were the only professional training schools for the great majority of the teachers of rural and small village schools. Usually, these sessions lasted five days. In 1877, to supplement the state funds for teachers institutes, $1 was collected from each male teacher and 50 cents from each female teacher each year, the money being deposited with the county treasurer.

During the first seventy years of our schools these institutes had a great influence in helping teachers do a more efficient job, especially in an inspirational way, but at best they were limited in their achievements. In 1892, Ferris S. Fitch, superintendent of public instruction, sent out a course of study for the institutes, but at the same time he did not consider this a solution to the problem as he saw it. He wrote:

> The faults of the system of teachers institutes are not simply of an administrative character, but are inherent in the system itself. The teachers institute has served a grand purpose, but it has outlived its usefulness. Every year spent in tinkering with this anti-quated machine is a year of golden possibilities lost to the educational advancement of the state. Michigan leads her sister states in the fame of her state university, her state normal school, and her high schools, but *sadly lags in the work of her common district schools.*

Mr. Fitch pointed out some of the glaring defects of teachers institutes as follows: (1) inability of the superintendent of public instruction, in his brief term of office, to gain that intimate knowledge of the many conductors necessary to conduct between sixty and seventy institutes in the short space of six to eight weeks and which would enable him to appoint only suitable men to the needs of the various localities; (2) the small salary paid a conductor, which meant a sacrifice on the part of a man of standing and ability; (3) personal element in the matter of appointments, which should be eliminated or minimized (not every state superintendent would be too high-minded to scorn the spoils system or be indifferent to the claims of friendship, and the present system can never be divorced from this personal element); (4) deplorable lack of unity and of aim and system in the work—the most serious and fundamental defect, and it is inherent in the system, as each institute begins nowhere in particular and leads to no definite stopping point; (5) need for a permanent corps of institute conductors to administer the training of 15,000 teachers of the commonwealth, most of whom never attend a normal school.

As late as 1895 Henry R. Pattengill reported that there were eighty institutes held in seventy-four counties, that attendance had greatly increased with an enrollment of 638 more than in any previous year, and that the contact with the great educators who conducted the institutes gave the teachers a revival of spirit and a grasp of the principals of teaching.

For the first fifty years after the Ypsilanti Normal School was founded nearly all its graduates became teachers in the graded districts in the cities and larger towns. The vast majority of the school children of the state were in the village schools or in the one-room rural schools. If the teachers in these latter schools had any training whatsoever, it was obtained in the teachers institutes. In 1903, there were more than 7,000 school districts in Michigan. Approximately 90% of the teachers had *no normal training* except the little they could get in the teachers institutes or in short review courses in some of the larger high schools.

In the 1880s, to meet the need for more normal training, private normal schools were established in Mount Pleasant, Big Rapids, Petoskey, and Benton Harbor. These private normal schools were schools in which the students could study or review the subjects in which they would be examined for a teacher's certificate; they were not actual training schools. One of the earliest of these private schools was Ferris Institute of Big Rapids, founded by Woodbridge N. Ferris in September of 1884. It offered courses in normal training, college preparatory, elocution, telegraphy, typewriting, and geology. Many of the teachers of our rural schools of that period (from 1885 to 1920) received their training at Ferris. After an existence of sixty-five years, in 1949 this school was given by its trustees to the State of Michigan on condition that the name of its founder, Ferris, would be retained.

In 1895, the legislature voted to accept the building and grounds of the Mount Pleasant Normal School, but failed by one vote to appropriate a sum of $25,000 necessary to support the school. The people of Mount Pleasant gave most liberally of their own money to maintain the school under Professor Bellows, who was then superintendent of the school. Professor Bellows and his assistants labored successfully to start and keep the institution on the course necessary to lay a good foundation for future growth, according to Superintendent Pattengill's report of 1896.

In 1899, the legislature established the Northern State Normal School at Marquette, in the Upper Peninsula, followed soon after by the founding of Western State Normal School at Kalamazoo.

All three of these normal schools, Mount Pleasant, Northern, and Western, established rural departments to train teachers for teaching in one-room or small village schools. At this time, many of these schools were without trained teachers.

To correct this deplorable situation, county normal schools were authorized by an act of legislature in 1903. This act gave a county an option of establishing a one-year course or a two-year course. The first year, eight of these schools were organized in the following counties: Arenac, Clinton, Charlevoix, Kalkaska, Gratiot, Wexford, Oakland, and Antrim. Eighty-six persons were graduated from the eight schools at the end of the first one-year course. The average age of the graduates was twenty years, with eighteen the lower level. In 1904, twelve additional county normal schools were established. That year the number of graduates was 350. Because no two-year schools were contemplated, the section of the law regarding such schools was deleted in 1905.

Three steps were necessary if a school district wanted to start a county normal school. At any annual meeting the district, by a majority vote of those present, could decide to organize such a school. At this time all school meetings were held in a high school session room or in a one-room schoolhouse. The motion would be made and seconded, a hat would be passed, and the written votes collected and counted. If a majority of the votes read "Yes," the motion carried. The second step was a favorable vote by the county board of supervisors. The third step was a request to the superintendent of public instruction for permission to organize such a school. When this permission was granted, a governing board was automatically activated. This county normal board of education consisted of the state superintendent, the superintendent of schools in the city in which the school was to be located, and the county commissioner of schools.

Three requirements were set down for hiring instructors in the county normal schools: (1) teachers hired had to be satisfactory to the state superintendent; (2) special contracts with teachers were to specify time to be given to the school and salary to be paid; (3) to insure the hiring of first-class teachers, no teacher was to be hired who could not command a salary of $700 per year elsewhere. The instructors in the first county normal schools were required to have life certificates. Later this qualification was raised to either an A.B. or B.S. or M.A. degree from an accredited college with teacher-training courses.

The county normals had to be provided with a pedagogical library which included maps of all kinds, a globe, dictionary, and reference books in the subjects taught, manual training supplies, kindergarten tables, sand tables, ordinary schoolroom equipment, and supplies for teaching elementary agriculture.

Classes were to be held for at least thirty-six weeks, with no less than ten students for the first term. A teaching staff of two persons, teaching four full hours a day or eighty hours a month of four weeks, was required.

The superintendent of public instruction gave complete instructions for the operation of the county normal schools and a course of study to be followed. The minimum for practice teaching was one hour per day for ten weeks.

At first the qualifications for admission to county normal schools were: the applicant had to be at least seventeen years of age, had to be a graduate of a ten-grade high school or had to have finished ten grades in any high school, or be the holder of a second grade certificate with two years of successful teaching experience. The applicants also signed a declaration that they would teach in a rural school or in the lower grades of a graded school. Later the qualifications for admission were raised to the requirement of a high school diploma from an approved high school.

The required subjects in the first quarter in addition to the common branches, were psychology and manual training. The extra subjects in the second quarter were psychology and pedagogy. In the third quarter the extras were practice teaching and pedagogy; and in the fourth, school management and elementary agriculture. Music and drawing were to be alternated during the year, and the *Michigan Manual and Course of Study* was to receive special attention.

Counties with county normal schools were supposed to hold county teachers institutes for four weeks, with the normal teachers as instructors. These institutes may have been held in some counties, but I never came in contact with one.

The Genesee county normal was organized in the spring of 1907 when Mr. A. N. Cody was superintendent of the Flint schools. Mr. Fred J. Johnson was the county commissioner of schools and Mr. L. L. Wright was the superintendent of public instruction. The Flint board of education and the county board of supervisors had taken the necessary steps and the school was opened in September with twenty students. Katherine Schoenals was principal and Minnie Oliff was the first critic teacher.

The Genesee County school directory for the 1906-07 school year shows that of the 269 teachers listed as teaching in the 152 school districts outside the city of Flint, nine teachers held state life certificates, nineteen had first grade certificates, three county normal certificates from other counties, 156 second grade and 82 third grade certificates. During the next seven years this picture changed rapidly. When I became commissioner in 1914, there were 79 teachers in the county who were county normal graduates, which was approximately 30% of the teachers outside Flint.

The number of county normal graduates increased each year until World War I began. During the next three years, after 1917, only 33 pupils enrolled in the county normal and the number of graduates fell to 25% of the teachers in the rural schools of the county. As soon as the was was over, the county normal classes were filled to capacity each year. By 1926 there were 122 county normal graduates listed in the school directory or enough to place a graduate in all the primary school districts in Genesee County. However, some of them may have been teaching in the graded schools. By this time, laws governing teacher training had been changed to require at least one year of normal training for every teacher in the state of Michigan.

I have given Genesee County normal school statistics as an example; practically every county in the state had the same experience in raising the standards of teacher training.

CHAPTER XVII

Certification of Teachers

We have seen how certificates for teaching were first granted by a township board of school inspectors, then by county school superintendents, then by the township superintendents who replaced the county superintendents, then by county boards of school examiners and later by the county board of school examiners headed by the county commissioner of schools.

Also, the state superintendent of public instruction was empowered by law in the beginning of our school system to grant certificates in the following statement:

> On such evidence as may be satisfactory to him, he may grant certificates licensing the holders thereof as teachers, duly qualified to teach in any primary or graded school in this state, which certificate shall be valid until duly revoked by the superintendent.

The compiled school laws of 1869 also specify:

> It shall be the duty of the board of school inspectors to examine all persons offering themselves as candidates for teachers of primary schools in their townships in regard to moral character, learning and ability to teach and they shall pass a satisfactory examination in the common branches, reading, orthography, geography, grammar, and arithmetic; and they shall deliver to each person so examined and found qualified a certificate signed by them in such form as shall be prescribed by the superintendent of public instruction.

If a teacher wanted to teach in a higher department of a graded school, he was required to pass an examination in the subjects he intended to teach. In a footnote to the law, the school inspectors were adjured to refuse a certificate to any teacher who was a drunkard or a gambler or who used profane language or indulged in any other gross immorality or indecent habit.

No certificate could be given for less than six months' duration or for more than a two-year period by a board of school inspectors. Certificates could be annulled by the inspectors for incompetence or immorality, but not before the accused was given a public hearing.

From its inception the Ypsilanti Normal School gave certificates to its graduates. Such certificates were good in any county in Michigan. Each of the other three state normal schools was given this authority when it was established.

Another authority which could "inspect and grant" certificates was the several graded school districts which had been given this prerogative by the legislature by special enactment.

Nowhere in the early school laws can be found a list of qualifications for a teacher, other than that the applicant be of good moral character and pass a "satisfactory" examination. In 1893, the minimum age was fixed at seventeen years. In the pioneer days of our school sytsem no minimum age was specified.

When the legislature in 1867 passed a law to establish the office of county superintendent of schools, the authority to conduct teachers' examinations and grant certificates was taken from the township board of school inspectors and given to the county superintendent. His instructions for granting teaching certificates were the same as those previously laid down for the inspectors. He was to hold an examination in each township, after giving the town clerk a notice twenty days before the date of the examination. The town clerk then was to post notices of this examination in three public places in the township. This was a great step forward in the granting of teachers certificates. For the next eight years the various state superintendents had great praise for these county superintendents because they increased the quality of the teaching force by weeding out incompetent teachers and by requiring higher standards in the examinations for certificates.

This step forward, however, was too radical for the times. In 1875, the legislature repealed the act which had established the office of county superintendent and in its place passed an act that created a superintendent for every township. These township officials were given duties in their townships identical to those the county superintendent had had in the county. The mess created by this change was so great that the law was repealed in 1881, at which time the township superintendents were replaced by county boards of school examiners.

This newly created board was given most of the duties formerly carried out by the township board of school inspectors. It was still the duty of the chairman of the board of school inspectors to visit the schools of his township at least once each term, examine carefully the discipline, mode of instruction, and similar matters. It was his duty to consult with the district board in regard to the course of study, discipline, condition of schoolhouse and outbuildings, and if necessary, suggest plans for improvements. Their pay was $2 per day for actual time spent in visiting schools.

The county board of school examiners examined persons desiring to teach and granted certificates. On the day of organization, it elected a secretary, who received $2 daily for as many days as there were school districts in the county, for services and expenses.

After the election of the school examiners, the county board and the chairman of the township board of school inspectors held a joint meeting to coordinate their work and discuss mutual problems. The chairmen of the board of school inspectors received $3 per day when in attendance at this meeting; the examiners were paid $4 per day for each day spent on official duties. The member whose term expired soonest was the chairman.

The law provided for two public examinations each year at the county seat on the last Friday of March and October. Special examinations could be held at any time upon notice by the examiners.

In 1883, because of the agitation of the Temperance Society and the Women's Christian Temperance Union, the legislature passed a law which said:

> All pupils in the state shall be instructed in physiology and hygiene, with special emphasis on the effects of alcoholic drinks, stimulants, and narcotics.

This law required all applicants for a teacher's certificate, beginning February 1, 1884, to pass an examination in physiology and hygiene. These two subjects were considered as one, both in the text studied and in the examination.

In 1895, an act provided that all public schools teach the methods by which dangerous diseases were spread and the best methods of prevention. The State Board of Health sent literature giving this information to all the schools.

There were three grades of certificates issued by the county board of school examiners, as explained earlier. Such certificates were valid only in the county in which they were issued.

County School Commissioners

That the establishment of the county board of school examiners did much to improve the quality of the teaching in the common schools was acknowledged by all the state superintendents in their annual reports to the legislature. However, there remained one defect—there was no executive head in the county school system. To remedy this defect the legislature, by Act 147 of the Public Acts of 1891, provided for the election of a county commissioner. For all practical purposes the title "county commissioner" meant county superintendent. Perhaps the term "commissioner" was adopted because of the odium that may have clung to the title "superintendent" from the period when there were township superintendents. The duties of a school commissioner were practically the same as those provided in the law passed in 1867 for the county superintendents.

Act 147 of the Public Acts of 1891, when Ferris S. Fitch was the superintendent of public instruction, provided for "the election of a county commissioner of schools, for the appointment of school examiners" and defined the duties and fixed the compensation for the same and repealed all existing acts conflicting with the provisions of this act. Although enacted as a new law, it was practically an amendment of Chapter XII of the compiled school laws of 1889. The title of the office was changed from secretary of the county board of school examiners to county commissioner of schools. The term was extended from one year to two, beginning on the first day of July instead of the fourth Tuesday of August.

The law also put the election of the commissioner in the hands of the people; that is, he or she was to be elected at the annual election in April of 1891 and every two years thereafter. Under the old law, the secretary was elected by the county board of school examiners, which in turn was itself appointed by the chairmen of the township boards of school inspectors. The responsibility that filtered down through the two sets of officials was so far diminished as to be almost nil.

No person could be elected commissioner who was not a graduate of the literary department of a reputable college, university or state normal school, or did not hold a state teacher's certificate or who had not held a first grade certificate within two years preceding the time of his or her election. In counties having less than fifty schools, a person holding a second grade certificate was eligible.

The county commissioner was given numerous duties, which included making reports, visiting each school in the county at least once each year, counseling with teachers and school boards, acting as assistant director of teachers' institutes, and being subject to such instructions and rules as the state superintendent of public instruction might prescribe. Also, as secretary of the board of examiners, he was to conduct teachers' examinations and sign teachers' certificates.

The law prohibited the county commissioner from being financially interested in any summer normal training classes in the county in which he held his office.

When the Michigan schools were first organized, the township board of school inspectors was an important part of the organization. It was its duty to organize new school districts, hold examinations, issue teachers' certificates, visit and inspect the schools in the township, advise teachers and school officers, and make annual reports to the superintendent of public instruction from the reports submitted by the various school districts.

In 1881, when the county board of school examiners was established by law, the township boards of school inspectors lost their authority to conduct teacher examinations and issue certificates. Later, they lost to the county commissioner of schools their obligation to visit schools and their duty to elect the examiners. Finally, in 1908, when a new constitution was adopted and only one power was left to them—the power to divide or consolidate school districts after the vote of the people—the office of school inspector was abolished.

The act which provided for the election of a county school commissioner to head the schools of a county retained the board of school examiners, but provided that the commissioner be the chairman of this board and that the examiners be appointed by the county board of supervisors, one each year for a term of two years. These examiners were paid $4 per day for the actual time spent in the performance of their duties. Besides helping to conduct teacher examinations, they helped grade the papers of all the eighth grade graduates from the rural schools and the smaller graded schools. Many of the superintendents of twelve-grade schools, who could pass their own eighth graders, had their eighth graders take the county examination to check the progress of their pupils against the state qualifications for pupils who finish the eighth grade. For the next three decades, this board of school examiners performed a highly important duty, that of examining would-be teachers and granting teaching certificates to a majority of the teachers of Michigan.

The professional qualifications of a county commissioner of schools were determined by the number of schools in his county. In the more populous counties, he had to be a graduate of the literary department of a reputable college or of the University of Michigan or a normal school, unless he possessed a state life certificate or a first grade certificate. In counties with less than fifty schools, to hold a second grade certificate was sufficient.

In 1895, a member of the board of school examiners was required to have had nine months of teaching experience and possess a second grade certificate. The county commissioner was required to have had twelve months of actual teaching experience.

In 1893, the legislature also provided for the renewal of second grade certificates if the applicant had had an average grade of 85% when the original certificate was granted and then had had three years of successful teaching experience. The law also specified that a teacher could have only one special certificate.

In 1895, the law was changed so that no noncitizen over twenty-one years of age could be granted a certificate to teach.

It was not until twenty years later, in 1915, that the next change was made in the qualifications for teaching. Act 7 amended Section 5 of Act 147, under which teachers were examined, by providing that no person could be granted a certificate "who shall not have completed a term of at least six weeks in professional training in a state normal school or in one of the county normal classes in the state or in any school approved by the state superintendent of public instruction; but the completion of one-half year of work in a school maintaining four years of work above high school shall be accepted in lieu of this requirement."

During the summer of 1918 I taught classes in the Mount Pleasant Normal School (now Central Michigan University) in arithmetic and geography to young people who were planning to write their first teachers' examination in August. I tried to show them how to teach these subjects as well as to give them basic knowledge in the subject matter.

Before the advent of county normals, only two percent (2%) of the teachers in rural schols had any normal training. By 1919 the number of teachers with at least one year of teacher training had increased to 20%, with 30% in some counties. World War I had a depressing effect on training, but by 1920 the number of trained teachers in some counties had risen to 47%.

As late as 1906 there were only four normal school graduates listed in the Genesee County school directory as teachers in the county outside of Flint. One of these was Jay Sexton, superintendent of the Fenton school, and one was Belle Jordan, who taught a district school in Atlas township. The two others taught in the school in Clio. There was one teacher, Eleanor Armstrong of Fenton, who had a certificate from the University of Michigan. All the others, a total of 235, had either a first, second, or third grade certificate. Flint had 78 teachers, a quarter of the total of the county. It was not until 1903, when the county normals were started, that the rural and small village schools had many trained teachers.

In 1909, the legislature provided for the certification of teachers in demestic science, art, manual training, and physical education if they had finished a course of at least two years in any of the above-named subjects at the University of Michigan, the four state normal schools, or any college incorporated under the general laws of the state, or any other institution whose course of study was acceptable to the superintendent of public instruction.

Some who read this book may wonder why so much space has been given to the organization of the so-called common schools and to the certification of teachers. The reason is—to use a modern expression—that that is "where the action was." Until the 1920s, three-fourths of the population of Michigan lived on farms or in small villages. The teachers of the pupils of this rural society were the ones who were taking the examinations and receiving the certificates. Even though the normal schools, especially Ypsilanti Normal, were established to train teachers for the common schools, very few graduates taught in a one-room school or a small village school. If any of these normal school graduates did start to teach in a one-room school, they were soon hired away by the larger village or city schools at higher pay.

By 1914, when I became a county commissioner, the educational qualifications picture was changing rapidly. In that year there were in my county twenty-seven teachers holding life certificates; twenty-three with normal school life certificates, two with University of Michigan certificates, one with a college life certificate, and one with a state life certificate. There were seventy-nine with county normal certificates and one hundred and fifty-eight with county certificates.

By 1922-23, my last year in office, in Genesee County there were fifty-three holders of life certificates. Of these fifty-three, thirty-one had normal certificates, seven were from Michigan Agricultural College, five from the University of Michigan, five from other colleges, and five from state examinations. Genesee County was just an average county. All the other counties probably had a similar situation in regard to certificates. (The large increase of M.A.C. graduates was caused by the organization of the three rural agricultural schools in Genesee County and the Smith-Hughes Act. These schools required special teachers in agriculture, manual training, and domestic science and arts.)

OLD-TIME SCHOOLS AND TEACHERS

Just how good were the schools of early Michigan? Judged by present standards, they were very crude. The men elected to the board of school inspectors were the neighbors of those who did the voting. They may have been the best-educated men in the township, but in most cases their education did not go beyond that of a common school, the three "R's" with perhaps a little training in grammar and geography. At first, there was no minimum age for a teacher. That is why an inspector in Richfield township complained in 1865 that, "There are too many little girls teaching." These little girls may have been only fourteen years old. Some of the early teachers may have been wandering schoolteachers, like Ichabod Crane. The law regulating teacher examinations stated only that the applicant for a certificate had to pass a "satisfactory" examination in five subjects. What made up a satisfactory examination was left entirely to the examiners.

An interesting story of how the early settlers came to Michigan and how a daughter of one of these settlers, Eliza Jane Dennis Lee, took an examination before a board of school inspectors is told in some notes written by Mrs. Lee in 1919. (Mrs. Lee was an aunt of my friend John Dennis, mentioned earlier.) To quote:

In 1851, my father moved from Middletown, Pennsylvania, to Michigan. We started the first day of May and arrived in Irving the morning of the 19th, being that length of time on the journey. We went by canal boat to the foot of the Allegheny Mountains and by incline plains to the summit, then descended by the same into Johnstown, Pennsylvania, then on canal boat again. Our boat was taken apart and put on trucks in three pieces to cross the mountains. Then it was put together again at Johnstown and towed to Pittsburgh by horses, where a tug took our boat on the Ohio River to Cleveland where we were taken aboard a Lake Erie steamboat and crossed the lake to Detroit. Then we went on to Battle Creek by railroad, which at that time was finished only as far as Kalamazoo. At Battle Creek, we were met by Mother's brothers with horse teams and we came through mud and rain to Irving.

In 1852, I taught my first school, at nineteen years of age. With many misgivings I went before the board of school inspectors, Dr. Parkhurst and Alphens Hill. The moderator was not there. After being asked to bound Michigan, tell the longest river in the original thirteen states of the Union, tell the rules of the arithmetic as far as square root, parse a short sentence, write a copy in a copying book, and spell Constantinople, I was given a certificate for one year to teach in any school in the Township of Thornapple at $1.25 per week and board. Well, my heart was in my mouth all through that awful examination. You can imagine my surprise when on the first day I had two scholars as tall as myself. But, when I found they had only been in short division, I felt safer.

The school term was three months, May, June, and July. I enjoyed it very much. Indeed, walked home sometimes. Went to school in Hastings that winter. I found it necessary to go to school and learn some things I did not understand, so went to Cordelia Warner, who taught school in Irving No. 1, a red schoolhouse. The summer of 1853 I had school in North Irving, now called the Wood district. Pay was $1.50 per week and board, for a three-month term. I then went back to school at Irving No. 1. We had singing school once a week and a spelling school. Used the little red schoolhouse for all and had (church) meetings every Sunday —the Presbyterian and Methodist, alternate Sundays. I taught in North Irving, new log schoolhouse, in 1853. The summer of 1854 I again taught at Scales Prairie a three-month term. I then went to Hastings school the winter of '54, all of '55 until May, 1856. I engaged for a winter on Scales Prairie for '56, but instead was married to Jefferson Lee in November. That ended my school days.

Many of these early teachers were dedicated men and women. One of these was Miss Mary Lyon, a teacher in Genesee County rural schools for more than sixty years. Born about 1853, she began teaching when she was sixteen and taught until she was nearly eighty years old. When I became county commissioner, she was teaching in the one-room Atlas village school, where she remained for twenty-one years. Mary Lyon was a "no nonsense" teacher. Her pupils usually passed the eighth grade examinations with good marks. She taught on a second grade certificate. Before 1915 she often attended the summer session at Ypsilanti Normal for a week to "observe," that is, to get new ideas of teaching. After 1915, she began attending summer school to get credits toward a life certificate.

Their scholarship may have been of a poor quality, but they knew that each lesson had to be prepared before it was presented to a class of wide-awake pioneer boys and girls. Because his interest would be aroused when preparing the lesson, the teacher could instill his interest in his pupils far better than a teacher who knew the subject from A to Z and had become bored by many repetitions. In my own experience in nine years of classroom teaching, although I had had no training in the common branches beyond the country school and reviews in summer school in the high school subjects, I had no trouble in maintaining a high degree of pupil interest in every class I taught. This may have been because I was learning while I taught.

The superintendents of public instruction were constantly urging that the laws regulating the certification of teachers be strengthened. Some of the reports made by the county commissioners to the state superintendent tell us of the trends of their thinking on the ethics of teaching and on certification.

At one time in Calhoun County each candidate for a teaching certificate was required to fill out the following questionnaire touching on moral character:

> Do you use intoxicating liquors or cider in any form?
> Do you indulge in profane language?
> Are you addicted to the use of tobacco?
> What does the law of this state require of teachers in regard to the effects of alcoholic drinks and tobacco?
> Give the names and addresses of three persons who will recommend you as having a good moral character.

Isabella County Commissioner S. J. Jamison wrote in his 1892 report to the state superintendent:

> The system of examination of teachers is one of the weakest points of our school system. First, we spread ourselves over so much territory that we become exceedingly superficial. There should be fewer subjects and greater thoroughness, especially for third grade certificate requirements.

In 1895 Jennie S. Putnam of Schoolcraft County wrote in her report:

> We have no guarantee of honesty or efficiency in the conducting of county examinations. Certificates can still be granted to teachers (?) whose papers, with good liberal marking, would not

reach an average of 50%. Such people were granted certificates—and in counties were there was no dearth of teachers—by boards of which every member is eligible to election under the new law. We need to make professional training a requirement for certification. Knowledge of the subject to be taught is one prime requirement; knowing how to teach is another and entirely different but equally essential requirement.

In 1929, the legislature made several far-reaching changes in the certification of teachers. From that year on, no city school board could issue a certificate to any person who had not held a certificate previous to September 1, 1929. The superintendent of public instruction was given the authority to issue state second and first grade certificates to persons who had had one year or a year and a third of education beyond a four-year high school in a school approved by the Department of Education. In the same year, the legislature named the regents of the University of Michigan and the State Board of Education as the authorities who could issue teachers' certificates. The issuance of third, second, and first grade certificates by the county boards of school examiners was discontinued. The issuance of certificates of comparative validity was placed in the hands of the state superintendent. Thus, state second and first grade certificates took the place of both city and county certificates.

Those who held a third grade certificate could be granted a second grade by completing a one-year course at an institution accredited by the superintendent of public instruction. A state first grade certificate could be granted to a teacher who had held a second or first grade certificate from a county board and since its issuance had completed four courses of college work of four term hours credit and had taught with success and ability for one year. Renewals could be obtained every three years by earning four credits of college work every three years. County normal certificates could be changed to first grade certificates by the superintendent of public instruction. In these cases, the new certificates were valid in all counties of the state.

In 1928, the law of 1925 for normal school certificates in special fields became effective. This law stipulated that three years of work were required to earn these certificates.

All these changes tended to increase the time spent by teachers in training schools. It also gave many older teachers an incentive to get more professional training or to learn while teaching by attending summer school.

In 1935, an act of the legislature gave to the Board of Education of Michigan the sole authority for issuing certificates to teachers. It also gave this board the power to prescribe the requirements for the preparation of teachers in the different colleges. The kinds of certificates granted were reduced from fifteen to five. Two of these were elementary and secondary provisional and permanent certificates; others were junior college certificates, state limited and renewals, and county limited and renewals. Life certificates were no longer to be granted.

CHAPTER XVIII

Additional Changes in School Laws

Under the Michigan constitution of 1837 the superintendent of public instruction was, and still is, considered to be the chief educational officer of the state. Under this constitution, he was appointed by the governor. However, when the second constitution was adopted in 1850, the office became an elective one for a term of two years only. Although many of the men elected to this office were courageous and farseeing, all of them had to be looking forward to the next election.

For instance, when I first became commissioner of schools of Genesee County, I asked the state superintendent about consolidating some district schools. He outlined the necessary steps to be taken, but his parting word of advice was, "You have to be careful of the afterclap." In spite of the political aspect, most of the progress made in our school system was initiated by the state superintendents.

Under the first Michigan constitution, the Board of Education consisted of three members, elected by the people at the general election in November, for a term of six years. The superintendent of public instruction, by virtue of his office, was a member of the Board and also the secretary. The duties of the Board were to examine teachers for state certificates and to have general supervision of the state normal schools.

Oramel Hosford, the superintendent of public instruction from 1865 to 1873, together with Ira Mayhew, who served from 1845 to 1848 and again from 1855 to 1859, may have been two of the unsung heroes of our public school system. One of Mr. Mayhew's many accomplishments was the organization of the first public school in the Upper Peninsula.

The duties of the state superintendent had been defined in an act approved on April 4, 1851. Section 3 of this act states:

He shall prepare and cause to be printed, with the laws relating to primary schools, all necessary forms, regulations and instruments (instructions) for conducting all proceedings under said laws, and transmit the same with such instructions relative to the organization and government of such schools, and the course of studies to be pursued therein, as he may deem advisable, to the several officers entrusted with their care and management.

Section 4 reads:

School laws, forms, regulations and instructions shall be printed in pamphlet form with a proper index.

An edition of the school laws had been printed in 1854. Between 1864 and 1869 nearly eighty sections of the laws had been added, amended, or repealed. This made it necessary for Mr. Hosford to put out a new edition of Michigan school laws. Following the edict of the law, Mr. Hosford gave samples of every form to be used by a school officer, furnished pictures of furniture suitable for the classroom, as well as pictures of schoolhouses, from one-room buildings to one of four stories. This edition of the school laws gives some interesting advice for choosing the site and for the construction of a new schoolhouse. It advised that a central location be chosen because of its convenience for all the children of the district. It was suggested that the site should contain at least one acre of ground, with the schoolhouse set back at least six rods from the dusty road. The grounds were to be well fenced, with a high board fence from the back of the schoolhouse to the back fence. Then it added:

But there is one consideration that should precede even this of convenience; that is, the health of the children. A house built on low and wet ground will have continually arising from the soil beneath and around it unwholesome exhalations, which, mingling constantly with the air in the school, will seriously affect every child of delicate organization and in the course of years destroy life itself. The schoolhouse should be built on a high and dry piece of ground, well drained if not gravel. Even the vicinity of a malarious swamp or low ground is to be avoided, as we would avoid the presence of a slow but fatal poison in the air.

(Those were the days before Pasteur and Lister and the germ theory.)

If the schoolroom were to be heated by a stove, it was recommended that there be a box tube, from the outside of the building, running under the floor and opening under the stove. The air thus introduced was to be confined for a little while near the stove, and released by an opening at the top of the stove. The chimney was to be provided with two flues, one for the smoke and one to draw foul air out of the room. I doubt that any such ventilating system was ever installed; at least, there was none in any of the schools I visited.

About 1910 the Waterbury Stove Company came out with a jacketed stove, which was placed near the side of the room with a square pipe leading to the outside to bring in fresh air. A Mr. McFadden sold hundreds of these jacketed stoves to the schools of Michigan. For a school to become a "standard school" it had to have such a heating system.

Incidentally, it was fifty years after the 1869 book showing floor plans for a schoolhouse was published that the superintendent of public instruction was given the authority to approve or disapprove plans for new school buildings.

Another recommendation in the 1869 edition was that the pupils should be seated to face north, with no windows in front of them. The light was to come from the south or near south and from both sides.

Another suggestion about the desks and seats to be used gives us a picture of the classroom of pioneer days. It reads:

> The time has been when a board placed on top of two pegs driven in auger holes drilled in the logs that made the sides of the building, and a seat made of a slab or plank with rounded legs driven into auger holes, on which the pupils sat facing the wall, with not a table or chair in the room, constituted the furniture of the ordinary schoolroom.
>
> Good plank walks from the front gates to the doors should never be wanting and good iron scrapers, easily made by nailing a strip of band iron on the edge of the platform or doorsteps, should be provided.

Also shown in the book are diagrams of the North Branch and East Branch schools of Adrian, Michigan, and pictures of model schools in Chicago, Illinois, and Madison, Wisconsin.

One of the duties of the superintendent of public instruction was to compile for publication an annual report to the legislature. As mentioned earlier, it is from these annual reports that I have gleaned much of the information in this book. It is from their timely comments on general conditions of the schools that a clear picture of the history and growth of our schools emerges. For instance, all of these officials complained about the poor attendance in the early schools, the multiplicity of districts, and the poor teachers when the township boards of school inspectors and the township superintendents held examinations and granted teachers' certificates. They were quick in their praise of better teachers and increased interest in the schools when there was a county superintendent and again when the board of school examiners was given the duty of conducting teacher examinations and granting certificates.

At least three times the state superintendent was responsible for bills introduced in the legislature to change from the district system to the township unit system. One of these efforts occurred in 1895. It is evident that until the turn of the century these officials led the forces for improved schools and longer school terms. In these efforts they were aided by the State Teachers Association, now called the Michigan Education Association or M.E.A.

New Ideas in Education

About 1870 there was a growing interest in the Frederick Froebel system of primary education, called the kindergarten system. It was first introduced into the United States twenty years before this in a private school for Germans by a Dr. Douai. The fundamental idea was to "render the first schooling attractive, to connect learning with pleasure, and to make mental food as much conducive to mental growth as bodily food is to bodily growth." Froebel maintained that childhood is developed by associating children together under the guidance of a skillful educator. Another important condition was that the place should be made attractive; it should be a large, airy room adjoining a flower garden that should be planted and cultivated by the children under the direction of the teacher.

The occupations of the children, which Froebel called "plays," were planned around the child's innate desire for activity. Play in the kindergarten was made the means of instruction and children were occupied and amused with games that gave both instruction and discipline instead of games with no aim or point. The proper age to enter kindergarten was thought to be five. No textbooks were to be used.

In 1870, there was a kindergarten in Detroit and one in Lansing. These kindergartens were the beginning of a new era in education and gradually were established in all the larger public schools in the state.

It was in the annual report of 1875 that physical education was first mentioned. Mr. Daniel B. Briggs wrote:

> Complaints are becoming more and more common of the overtasking of pupils by the severe course of study in our grammar and high schools and that many pupils, especially girls, are being prostrated by the mental effort to complete their tasks. The result to be desired in youth is the harmonious development of the mental and physical so as to give greater efficiency to both. The tendencies of the young to physical rather than mental recreation and the necessary demands upon children for active duties out of school have led to the consideration of mental training only in our schools. The error in this direction has engaged the attention of many educators, and in some of our best-appointed schools physical training, with or without some simple apparatus, has been introduced. Physical training is an obvious necessity.

Usually the state superintendents were leaders in presenting new ideas. Perhaps one of the first steps toward grading the schools came with the passage of the uniform textbook law in 1881. Before that year, a pupil was said to be in the "fifth reader" or the "big geography" instead of a certain grade. He studied from any textbook he happened to have; the books used were printed by many different publishers.

The year 1881 also saw another "first" to make education uniform throughout the state. Examination questions for each grade were sent in sealed envelopes to each county to be used in all schools during the last week of the term. This was one of the initial steps in the attempt to get the schools graded.

STATE MANUAL AND COURSE OF STUDY

Another step leading to grading the schools came during the term of State Superintendent Vernum B. Cochran, who, in 1882, prepared and sent to more than 600 teachers in the state a course of study and daily program. This program gave the teachers a guide for their everyday teaching.

In 1889, Joseph Estabrook, then superintendent of public instruction, sent to each district in the state a complete manual and course of study. This was the first serious attempt to organize and grade teaching in the rural schools.

About 1891 the State Association of County Secretaries (the commissioners) appointed a committee of five of its members to prepare a *State Manual and Course of Study* for use in the rural schools of the state. (The county commissioners of schools were first called secretaries, as they served as secretaries of the county boards of school examiners.) This *Manual* reached the schools about 1892, the year I started to school. It was received with much favor and helped to make early progress in getting the schools graded. Three editions were issued during the next six years.

In 1892, Ferris Fitch, who succeeded Joseph Estabrook, sent to each newly elected county commissioner of schools a set of questions for the eighth grade pupils. The county board of school examiners, which consisted of the commissioner and two other persons, was to hold examinations on the first Saturday in May in each township.

These eighth grade examinations were to be followed by formal graduation exercises. According to Mr. Fitch, these exercises were not for mere display, but were to show the work being done, to arouse the ambitions of the pupils and the pride of the parents, thus securing to the teacher the cooperation of both in the effort to reach this first milestone in the path of education. These graduation exercises became very popular. To quote Mr. Fitch:

> They were a rebuke to all who scoffed at the possibility of having a graded system of work in a district school. The diploma conferred opened the door of any high school in the county and thus started him on the road to higher education where his circumstances permitted.

The examinations were usually held in the various village and city high schools where the principal or superintendent could be deputized to assist the examiners.

From 1892 on, these eighth grade examinations were held each year until they were discontinued in 1934, when Paul Voelker was the superintendent of public instruction. In that year, an amendment to the school code transferred the authority to grant eighth grade diplomas from the board of school examiners, of which the county commissioner was chairman, to the county commissioner upon the written recommendation of the teacher or principal.

One of the main results of these eighth grade examinations was that they gave the teachers a greater knowledge of what they were expected to teach in each grade. The manual and course of study gave the teacher guidelines to follow; the examinations gave her a way to check the results.

When the office of county commissioner was established in 1891, the commissioner became the unifying force in getting better schools and more effective teaching. The first results of the eighth grade examinations were meager and disappointing. The reports sent to the state superintendent showed that only a few of the eighth grade pupils took the examinations. Of these only 40 to 50 percent passed. It took several years to get all the schools of the state graded and working along the same lines. Incidentally, I was the first pupil in our district to prepare for and take the eighth grade examination.

One interesting item gleaned from the reports of 1895 was that some counties were adopting the Welch system of reports and records. The forms for these reports and records were published by the William Welch Company of Chicago. The main part of this system was the attendance register. These registers, together with their plan books and class record books, were standard forms used in most Michigan schools for many years. Before 1895 there were no such forms in general use.

For several years after 1893 money was scarce; a financial panic gripped the country. The 1895 legislature listed and set a top price on all items to be purchased for a school, namely: a set of wall maps not to cost over $12; a globe, $8; a dictionary, $5; a bookcase, $10, and other items not priced but which should be provided. These included a mirror, comb, towel, water pail, cup, ash pail, shovel, broom, dustpan, feather duster, washbasin, and soap. A law was passed that every school should have a United States flag and staff or pole, the flag not to be smaller than four feet two inches by eight feet.

A revealing picture of the times is gleaned from Mr. Henry R. Pattengill's report of 1895 in which he pointed out that financial stringency and the low price of agricultural and mining products had a tendency to curtail amounts appropriated for schools. Moreover, the lack of remunerative employment at this time and the rigid enforcement of the new compulsory school law caused a substantial increase in the number of pupils enrolled. He also reported that teachers were giving much more study to the science of teaching and that better methods were constantly coming into use. He thought the ideals of both teachers and patrons were higher. He observed that there were definite improvements, such as more careful supervision of rural schools by the county commissioners, more accurate grading of rural pupils, better-qualified teachers, and an educational revival brought about by teachers' associations which resulted in more regular attendance in the rural schools. In his opinion, the eighth grade diplomas and graduation exercises encouraged pupils to persevere in their studies. Also, the promotion of the pupils showed both child and parent the folly of missing school for trivial reasons, such as picking up chips, making soap or sugar, butchering, or visiting.

In 1894, Mr. Pattengill tried an interesting experiment. He divided the state into twenty-one districts, in each of which a council or meeting of all the commissioners and examiners was held. Superintendents and officers of graded school districts and interested patrons were also invited. Topics discussed were: a more rigorous compulsory attendance law, free textbooks, uniformity of textbooks, necessary apparatus and appendages, the grading of rural schools, school libraries, raising the minimum age for teachers to eighteen years, and many other subjects germane to improvement of the schools. These meetings may have helped put teeth in the compulsory attendance law that was passed in 1895. Soon after 1895 the minimum age for a teacher was raised to eighteen years. The grading of rural schools also received an impetus. I recall that in my early school years in a one-room country school the teachers were beginning to speak of grades instead of "readers."

In 1893, Mr. Pattengill sent out detailed plans for the construction of school toilets, with special emphasis on those for boys. One requirement was that a high board fence be built from the schoolhouse to the back fence to separate the two toilets. One of the duties, specified by law, of the county commissioners was toilet inspection. If one needed repairs, the school director was to be notified. If the director did not have the repairs made, the commissioner could hire it done and charge the work to the school district. Mr. Pattengill devoted three pages of his annual report of 1894 to the condition of school outhouses or toilets, ending with a quotation taken from a report of a county superintendent in Pennsylvania:

> The tumble-down, wooden, sinscratched, hell-sodden sheds that stagger and lear at you from the rear of over fifty percent of the schoolhouses of this state make the heart sick when we think of the injured and blasted minds of the boys and girls therein educated.

(One of my most vivid memories is of a toilet like those described above.)

Mr. Pattengill was quick to give great praise to the work of the newly created commissioners, saying:

> Nothing within recent years has had so beneficial an effect upon our rural schools as the system of county supervision. In every county where the right kind of work has been done by the commissioner the schools have been most wonderfully improved. A good school commissioner needs to have a sufficient education, but besides an education he needs an experience in teaching, a skill to detect defects and note good work, a power to inspire and encourage teachers and pupils, and a love for study and progress. The commissioner should carry cheer and life to every school. His greatest work is not statistical reports, but work with teachers to elevate their ideals and kill off drones. Kind and firm, he should be a noble example to the young and a source of strength to the teachers of the young.

Other items of interest in the 1894 report included the information on district libraries, which had increased 50% over previous years. The county commissioners were warned to keep constant watch over the books bought, to insure that library money wasn't squandered on worthless or injurious books.

In regard to decorating the school grounds, Arbor Day was designated as the day to clean up the school grounds, set out trees and otherwise ornament and beautify the school premises. A Professor Taft of the Michigan State Agricultural College did excellent missionary work by distributing flower seeds free to public schools.

One other interesting item which appeared in the report was that vertical penmanship was being introduced in some schools. Before this time, the Spencerian system had been universally taught.

A recommendation was made in the same report that the United States flag be raised over the schools and that pupils be taught patriotic songs, such as *America, The Star-Spangled Banner* and *The Red, White, and Blue.*

This Henry R. Pattengill, who served as state superintendent from 1893 through 1896, was one of the most dynamic men to hold this office. After he retired, he published a newsletter for teachers called *Timely Topics,* as well as textbooks in orthography, Michigan history and Michigan civil government. He also compiled a book of songs, *The Knapsack,* which was used in nearly every school in the state. When I started teaching in 1905, he was a popular instructor at teachers' institutes. He was the conductor of the first teachers' institute I attended, held in August of 1905, just before I began my first year of teaching.

Surprisingly, the office of superintendent of public instruction was *not* a full-time job until 1909. In Cocker's *Civil Government,* published in 1885, the salary is given as $1,000 a year. The salary of the deputy superintendent was given as $1,800 a year; evidently the job of deputy superintendent was a full-time one. The constitution adopted in 1909 fixed the salary at an amount that would enable the state superintendent to give full time to his duties. Luther Wright was the first full-time superintendent; Walter French was his deputy.

A new manual and course of study was prepared under the supervision of Mr. Pattengill and distributed in 1897. This new edition was made necessary by a law passed by the legislature in 1897, the purpose of which was to bring the State Agricultural College into closer touch with the schools of the state. The law read:

> The superintendent of public instruction shall prepare for district schools comprising the branches now required for a third grade teacher's certificate a course of study which shall be known as the Agricultural College Course and upon the satisfactory completion of this course of study as evidenced by a diploma signed by the county commissioner of schools, a graduate shall be admitted to the freshman class of the college without further examination.

This 1897 course of study became, with a few changes, the basic course of study for rural schools.

A copy of the *Manual* for 1903 presented a program with three divisions: primary or first, second and third grades; intermediate or fourth, fifth, and sixth grades; and advanced or seventh and eighth grades. The subjects for the first grade were reading, spelling, writing, language, and numbers. To these five subjects were added drawing, geography, and nature study for the second year; and to these eight subjects physiology was added for the third year. The only change for the fourth year was that nature study became nature-study-and-science, and numbers was changed to arithmetic. In the fifth year, physiology became physiology-and-hygiene. The sixth year course was the same as the fifth. In the seventh year, nature study combined with hygiene was dropped and United States history and civil government were added. In the eighth year, physiology, geography, and spelling were dropped and bookkeeping was added.

This seems like a very heavy course for all the grades, but in the outline for the program to be carried out, only reading, spelling, writing, numbers, and drawing or copying were listed for the first three grades. In numbers, the class was to begin learning first the combinations, then subtraction with single numbers. By the time a child was through the third grade, he was supposed to know all the combinations, be able to subtract, and divide in short division. The teaching of fractions was to begin in the second grade. Definite instruction outlining what was to be taught and how to teach every subject was carefully presented.

A significant sidelight on the thinking of the educators of the time was the suggestions for teaching morals and manners in the schools. An outline was given to enable the teacher to teach boys and girls how to act in every conceivable situation—at school, at home, in church, at entertainments, in neighbors' homes, in stores, on the street, and when traveling. By inference, some of this teaching was to be by example. One wonders how much time was devoted to the subject of manners and morals. Some teaching may have been done by example; even this is now "old hat."

A complete program of calisthenics was outlined. These must have been in vogue when I attended a rural school, as I remember doing bending and swinging exercises. However, in a crowded school curriculum there was little time for such exercises. Moreover, farm boys and girls usually had chores to do at home and their games at recess were of the active type.

Opening exercises were recommended for every morning. The manual reads, "These should be brief and pleasing and have the elements of moral training, but a teacher should refrain from preaching morals." The outline for these exercises suggested (1) roll call, with each pupil answering with a memory gem or an important current event; (2) singing, led by the teacher, or if the teacher could not sing, a pupil; (3) recitation or reading by some pupil. Bible reading could be a variation to these suggestions, but a note was appended which advised the teacher that if there were objections to this, the matter should not be forced.

The manual also pointed out that behind the teacher's every look, word, and act there should be purity and honesty. A motto coming out of the office of the state superintendent was: "Character in the teacher will develop character in the pupil."

At the back of the manual were given over 200 memory gems or excerpts from English literature covering every human endeavor for the children to choose, read, and memorize. (It amuses my family that I am able almost eighty years later to recite from memory poems by Whittier and other verses learned in a one-room country school.)

Office of State Superintendent

From the beginning of our public school system in Michigan, the state superintendent of public instruction has been the head of the schools, but for many years he was practically a titular head only. Beyond periodically receiving and editing the annual financial and statistical reports of the school districts, which were published in his annual report to the legislature, his authority was limited. From the district reports, he gained information from which he distributed the Primary School fund. As head of the Michigan Board of Education, he conducted examinations, at first for ten-year certificates and later for life certificates. Any improvements in school organization were helped along by his influence. All the many changes brought to him more powers and duties.

By the turn of the century the office of state superintendent had become a full-time job and its prestige and influence had greatly increased. However, in 1913, when I took my examination for a life certificate, the Department of Education consisted only of the superintendent, Mr. Luther L. Wright, one deputy superintendent and three or four secretaries. During the next decade and a half, under Fred L. Keeler and Thomas E. Johnson, the office was given much greater power and many more duties. In W. L. Coffey's report for 1926, he lists the several divisions in the department. These were, in addition to the superintendent, a deputy superintendent, chief clerk, and nine divisions or departments with their duties. These were: rural education, private and parochial schools, vocational schools, vocational rehabilitation, manual arts and special education, child accounting and statistics, physical education, interscholastic athletics, and educational supervision.

There were still many defects in our educational system. Mr. Coffey's list of objectives, some of which are still controversial, have not all been carried out. These objectives were: a wider extension of special classes for the physically handicapped, a definite plan for character education, public support of religious education or parochial school aid, increased opportunities for rural children, more effective health education, improved curricula for all schools, improved library facilities, equalization of taxes, consolidation of rural schools, and a better way to select county commissioners of schools. Three of these objectives, parochial school aid, increased opportunities for rural children through more consolidations, and equalization of taxes are in Governor Milliken's reorganization plans for 1970.

In 1924, a uniform child-accounting system was adopted by the state. In 1922, Dean A. S. Whitney, president of the M.E.A., had appointed a committee with W. L. Coffey, then deputy superintendent of public instruction, as chairman, to outline such a system. In 1924, this committee published its first report, a report which, with a few changes, set up a system that provided for a complete record of the health, scholarship, and transfers of every child in the state. Standard forms for all facets of child accounting were made by the committee and copies printed by the state printer. A sample set of these forms was then sent to every county commissioner of schools and every city superintendent. (It was this set of forms that Mr. William E. Hamilton, then the county commissioner of Genesee County, brought to my printing shop in the fall of 1927. His order for these forms put The Riegle Press into the form printing business.)

Another act passed in 1927 fixed the time for taking the school census as the last twenty days in May. This census report was to be filed with the county commissioner from all districts of less than 3,000 population before the third Monday of June; he was to file this report with the superintendent of public instruction before the second Monday of September.

Another act raised the state aid for county normal schools from $2,000 per year to $3,000. It was at this time that the names of the four normal schools were changed to State Teachers College. The same act also provided that school districts with a population of 18,000 could establish junior colleges. All these changes took place in 1927.

In 1924, a comprehensive plan of supervision was set up in Oakland County. Three persons especially trained were employed to devote their entire time to supervision. At the end of the year, competitive tests were made in the schools under this supervision and in neighboring schools in Macomb County, where there was no special supervision. The supervised schools showed 75% greater achievement than the unsupervised. Perhaps because of this experiment, an act was passed in 1927 to allow county boards of supervisors to authorize county commissioners to appoint deputy commissioners and supervisors of education.

The first teacher tenure act was passed in 1934. This was an optional law; that is, any district could adopt tenure by a majority vote at an annual meeting. Operation of the law was placed under the supervision of a tenure committee to be appointed by the governor.

CHAPTER XIX

High Schools

The laws setting up primary school districts, passed under the Michigan constitution of 1837, made no mention of high schools or of appropriating money for their support. The district schools were to educate children in the primary subjects only, which were the three R's, with some attention to grammar, geography, orthography, and physiology.

In 1844, the first high school in Michigan was established in Detroit, at which time the local board of education appropriated $150, together with money for fuel, to support such a school. Only twenty-five pupils, all boys, were to be admtited, from age eleven up, who had attended school for three months and had passed an examination before a committee of teachers. Unfortunately, the school did not last long.

During the next two decades several cities toyed with the idea of forming high schools. Perhaps a graded school district would add a ninth grade, then a tenth, and so on. However, these schools were not free but were tuition schools, although some public money may have been used for maintenance. There was great opposition to using tax money for this purpose. Nowhere in any school law was it specifically mentioned that a district could use taxes to support a high school.

Finally, in 1873, a suit was brought in the ninth judicial district against the village of Kalamazoo. The complainant charged that money used to support a high school was used illegally under the law of 1859, which gave a district the right to organize a graded school. After hearing arguments for and against, Judge Charles R. Brown ruled that under this statute, which gave a district or two adjacent districts the right to organize a graded school, the right to establish and maintain a high school was implied, and thus legal.

From the time of this 1873 decision, high schools began to proliferate, but only the high schools in the larger villages and cities had twelve grades. As late as 1900—about half the length of time between the year Michigan became a state and today—many high schools had only nine or ten grades. Genesee County had only two twelve-grade high schools, Flint and Fenton. Davison, Flushing, and Clio had eleven grades.

The published records of high schools in the year 1881, found in the state superintendent's annual report, are enlightening. They show the existence of 65 high schools, with a total enrollment of 5,002, 2,000 of whom were boys and 3,002 girls. During the five years preceding, beginning with the classes of 1876, 417 males and 1,214 females had been graduated from five high schools. These statistics show the growth of the idea of schooling beyond the eighth or ninth grade. In fact, the superintendent comments on the fact that high schools were beginning to occupy an important field of educational labor.

When the academies, described earlier, were discontinued or taken over by graded school districts, many private seminaries and academies were founded. These were tuition schools and only the well-to-do families could send their children to them. At one time it was suggested that these private schools be endowed; perhaps some of them were but as a rule this did not happen. The life of most of these seminaries was of short duration; when public high schools were established there was no need for very many private schools.

For many years the children of the rural areas grew up without the advantages of high schools. It was not until the Rural Agricultural School Act, which was finally enacted in 1919, began to operate that the system —which could even be called segregation of rural children—gave way. It was only about ten years ago, when the K-12 Act was passed, that this segregation or discrimination ended.

For several years, until twelve-grade schools became common, the University of Michigan had preparatory classes equivalent to the eleventh and twelfth grades for graduates of schools having only ten grades. Admission to the University was by examination only. In 1869, Professor

Henry Simmons Frieze became president of the University. He served only two years but in that time he initiated a practice that had a profound effect on the high schools of Michigan. He proposed that graduates of approved high schools be admitted to the University without examination. His idea was accepted by the faculty and the board of regents. He then began the practice of sending a committee of professors to visit high schools and report on what they found. If this committee found the work in the high schools they visited to be satisfactory, the schools were placed on an accredited list and their graduates were admitted to the University without examination. The first accredited list carried the names of Adrian, Ann Arbor, Flint, Detroit Central, and Jackson high schools. Between 1870 and 1880 the high schools of Battle Creek, Coldwater, Fenton, Grand Rapids Central, Monroe, Kalamazoo, Niles, Pontiac, Saginaw Eastside, Saginaw Arthur Hill, and Ypsilanti were added to the list. This new policy made for closer ties between the University and the high schools and tended to improve the educational standards of teachers and the physical equipment of the schools such as laboratories and libraries.

By 1893 there were so many high schools to inspect that a standing committee of faculty members of the University was appointed to pass on all questions relating to secondary schools. This committee was called the "Committee on Diploma Schools" and the president of the University served as chairman.

In 1899, the University created a special office to take charge of accrediting high schools, with Professor A. S. Whitney, then superintendent of Saginaw Eastside schools, in charge. By 1918 nearly all high schools having a staff of three teachers were accredited.

To be on the accredited list became a status symbol for a high school. Most of the effects of this relationship of the high schools to the University were good but there was one bad effect which had not been foreseen. The courses of study for the secondary schools were designed to train pupils for admittance to the University or one of the many sectarian colleges in the state. Many of the boys and girls who could not or would not attend a college or university were not prepared for the life ahead of them. A few vocational schools were established, and some high schools added commerical courses, but to this day this defect in the curriculum of Michigan high schools has not been corrected in many areas.

Before 1909 the many high schools that were being organized in every village and city had never been recognized as high schools by the state legislature. In that year, the first law defining a high school was enacted; it was an amendment to the free tuition law of 1909. Under this amendment, a high school "shall be a graded school maintaining twelve grades of work, with at least three teachers devoting their entire teaching time to the work of the seventh, eighth, ninth, tenth, eleventh, and twelfth grades or two teachers devoting their entire teaching time to the work of the eighth, ninth, tenth, eleventh, and twelfth grades." It further provided that any graded school with one teacher devoting his entire teaching time to the eighth, ninth, and tenth grades need not pay tuition to a twelve-grade school "until such pupils have finished ten grades of work." It also specified that these ten-grade schools were tuition schools for the ninth and tenth grades, with the rural district paying the tuition for their eighth grade graduates who wished to continue their schooling.

This same act provided for the discontinuance of a rural or township high school by a vote of two thirds of the vote cast at a meeting of the district. The law giving a township the right to organize such schools had been in effect only a few years. Munday township, Genesee County, had a high school of sorts for a short time. It was poorly set-up, badly equipped and sadly neglected. Soon after the enactment of the law giving a township the right to discontinue a high school it was closed. The Munday high school was never given a chance to succeed, as it was held in an old house with no facilities to give it the appearance of a school and its last teacher had only a third grade certificate.

Junior High Schools

As early as 1915 the superintendent of public instruction recommended that Michigan school districts adopt the junior high school system. Soon after that, a few districts began to experiment with such schools. By 1918 approximately one-fourth of Michigan schools accredited by the University claimed to have taken positive action in the movement. In State Superintendent Fred Keeler's report of 1920 for the years 1918 and 1919 he writes that certain principles were seen to be operating for junior high schools. These were: (1) a special building or part of an old building should be furnished; (2) a program of studies richer in content for regular eighth and ninth grades; (3) provisions for testing individual aptitudes; (4) some recognition of peculiar needs of retarded children, as well as special consideration of supernormal children; (5) some choice of subjects; (6) departmental teaching; and (7) promotion by subjects.

TUITION SCHOOLS

The law defining tuition schools was amended in 1917 to require that schools, in order to get tuition from rural districts, had to be approved by the state superintendent. Tuition was increased to $25 and primary schools could vote to pay transportation to high school. Districts could also vote to pay more than $25 per pupil per year. To approve high schools for tuition the state had to organize an inspection department. To avoid duplicating efforts, an arrangement was made by the state with the University accrediting group whereby the two committees met each month to exchange reports. The state accepted the University accredited list for tuition schools. If the University inspectors found a school that was not acceptable for accreditation but fulfilled the conditions for a tuition school, the school was so listed. In 1918, there were 598 schools that could be called high schools, with 318 accredited by the University and 280 not accredited.

In tuition schools it was expected that no teacher would be hired who did not have two years of professional training above high school and that no teacher would have more than seven class periods a day of forty to forty-five minutes each. For several years the rule about advanced work could not be enforced because there were not enough teachers with two years professional training beyond high school to fill the positions. In 1919, our Genesee County village school superintendents association made a ruling that no teacher be hired unless he had at least one year of professional training beyond high school.

All twelve-grade tuition schools in the state were to give four units of work each year. To graduate, a pupil was required to have completed at least three English units, two mathematic units, one of American history and civics, and one in a laboratory science. Other requirements of a tuition school were a dictionary, a set of encyclopedias, a library of carefully selected books, and a permanent student record system.

In a high school to be accredited by the University, no teacher was to have more than six periods a day. To graduate, a student had to have three English units, two of a foreign language, one of algebra, one of geometry, and one of a laboratory science, plus three electives. For admission to the University, a high school graduate needed fifteen units, twelve from the list given above plus three elective from agriculture, domestic science or art, and manual training. The foreign language could be Greek, Latin, French, Spanish, or German. In the smaller high schools Latin was the only language offered. The science course could be physics, chemistry, zoology, or botany. Smaller high schools usually alternated physics and chemistry in the eleventh and twelfth grades to make the classes large enough to be interesting.

Professor Gorton of the Ypsilanti Normal School published a physics laboratory manual which described plans for making instruments to be used in a physics laboratory. In 1913, I took a review course in physics in his class at Ypsilanti. When school began that fall, I used his manual; my junior and senior classes became intensely interested in making much of the apparatus we needed. The following year the incoming junior class joined the senior class to study chemistry. The boys in the class made the workbenches and other accessories needed for chemistry experiments, as was probably done in many schools when chemistry was added to the curriculum.

It was not until 1929 that a High School Department was added to the Department of Education. In addition to all public high schools, which had been placed under the supervision of the superintendent of public instruction by a law of 1921, the private and parochial high schools were placed under state supervision. This meant that the Department of Education took over the duties of accrediting high schools and of approving tuition schools.

The definition of a high school for approval as a tuition school was changed September 1, 1928, to require twelve grades of work with three teachers giving their teaching time to the seventh, eighth, ninth, tenth, eleventh, and twelfth grades or two teachers with the tenth, eleventh, and twelfth grades and one teacher for the seventh, eighth, and ninth grades.

In 1928, a change was made in the rules for accrediting high schools. Before this date, schools had been approved for accrediting or approval for one year; after 1928 they were accredited or approved for two. If an inspected high school did not meet all the requirements of a two-year accredited school it was placed on probation for one year. At the end of one year, if the school had not met these requirements it was removed from the accredited list.

In 1926, Michigan had 515 accredited high schools and 221 tuition schools out of a total of 1,142 offering high school work.

The Michigan High School Interscholastic Athletic Association, a voluntary organization, was replaced in 1924 by the Michigan High School Athletic Association to comply with a state law giving general supervision and control of high school athletic programs, both public and private, to the superintendent of public instruction.

When the definition of tuition schools was amended in 1917, the rules for admission to the state normal schools were established. Graduates could be admitted from any high school having twelve grades and thirty-six weeks of school annually, if the school had two teachers devoting their full time to teaching.

FEDERAL AID TO EDUCATION

The first federal aid to education was the Morrell Act of 1862, which gave land for the establishment of agricultural schools. The second act was the Smith-Hughes Act of 1917, which provided federal aid to schools under college grade which were under public control. To receive this aid, a state had to appropriate a sum equal to the amount from the federal government. These funds were to be used to pay salaries of teachers of trade, industrial, agricultural, and home economics subjects and of the "instructors who shall direct the training of these teachers." The Michigan legislature of 1917 immediately made this law effective by providing for a Board of Control for vocational education. The state treasurer was made custodian of both the federal and state funds. The superintendent of public instruction was made the executive officer of the new Board of Control. The other officers were the president of the University of Michigan, the president of Michigan Agricultural College, and the president of the state Board of Education.

Districts wishing to cooperate were to furnish suitable buildings, employ teachers approved by the Board of Control, and appropriate for instructional purposes a sum of at least one-half as much as received from the federal government. The State Board issued a bulletin giving explicit rules governing the formation of such a course in a high school.

In 1917, Michigan received approximately $45,750, which was about equally divided for agriculture, trade, and home economics courses and teacher training. Much of the money for "trade" was used to maintain courses in manual training in the newly organized rural agricultural schools. Federal aid increased each year thereafter. In 1926 it amounted to $214,960.

In 1908, the Michigan Agricultural College had created a department of agricultural education and had begun the work of introducing courses of agriculture in the public high schools. Instruction in manual training was also being given in several high schools. By 1917 there were 67 high schools ready for implementing the Smith-Hughes program but there were funds for only 43 of them to participate. Mr. W. H. French was placed in charge of the work in Michigan. On July 1, 1918, Mr. E. E. Gallup became the state supervisor of Smith-Hughes schools. Flint and Flushing were the first of these schools in Genesee County.

After the organization of the three rural agricultural schools in Gaines, Grand Blanc, and Goodrich during my term as county commissioner, all three became Smith-Hughes schools. Because of my work in consolidating these three schools, Mr. Gallup promised me that Genesee County could have a Smith-Hughes school whenever I asked for it.

CHAPTER XX

Defects in the System

The basic defect in our Michigan school organization has always been the district system, which was incorporated in the first state constitution, adopted in 1836. One sentence provided that no schoolhouse could be built that would require a child to walk more than two miles to school by the nearest traveled road. This disrict system was patterned after the Massachusetts system. Fortunately for Massachusetts, that state changed to a township unit plan in 1850. Our district plan led to a proliferation of districts; at one time there were more than 7,000 in the state.

The first attempt to consolidate or eliminate some of these districts was initiated by the enactment of Section 152 of the general school laws. This law stated that any two contiguous districts having together more than 200 children between the ages of five and twenty years could, by a vote of two-thirds of the voters attending the annual meetings in said districts, determine to unite for the purpose of establishing a graded or high school. Such schools were usually called union schools. The union school district of Flint was made up originally of five district schools.

Time after time the various superintendents of public instruction urged that the district system be changed to a township unit system. At least three attempts to change to a township unit system were made, but it wasn't until 1891 that an optional bill, Act No. 176, was passed by the legislature for the organization of township distiricts in the Upper Peninsula. By 1900, in the Upper Peninsula, twenty-three township unit schools had been established. Soon after that, other township unit schools were organized, much to the advantage of the children of the Upper Peninsula.

By the turn of the century the "machines of plenty" had greatly reduced the number of laborers needed on the farms. These workers had emigrated to the cities to work in the factories that produced these machines. This emigration greatly affected the rural schools. In 1901, Delos Fall, then superintendent of public instruction, reported that there were 1,000 district schools with fewer than fifteen pupils enrolled. Before that, Jason Hammond, superintendent of public instruction in 1900, railed against the system which permitted too many small districts and too many school officers. At that time Genesee County, for instance, had 160 districts with 1,443 school officers. Mr. Hammond called the little red schoolhouses "the sweetheart" of the people and urged the adoption of a township unit system. A committee was sent to Ohio to investigate their consolidated or centralized schools. This committee, after a thorough investigation, made a report most favorable to consolidation. It found that at first there had been much opposition in Ohio to consolidation but that, as the new schools proved their superiority over the one-room schools, the opposition disappeared.

In 1903, Mr. Fall, who succeeded Mr. Hammond, strongly urged the centralization of Michigan schools. He called the attention of the people to the advantages to be had by consolidating small districts and small schools into larger districts and schools. Already the movement had begun in Michigan. In Isabella County several districts were combined, a two-room schoolhouse built and a ten-grade school established. In Clare, Kent, Berrien, Genesee, and Mecosta counties the people had taken steps by 1902 toward uniting several districts. The plan of transporting pupils had been in operation in Menominee County for several years with entire satisfaction.

The legislature of 1902 amended the school laws so that districts could levy taxes for the transportation of pupils to and from schools and also pay the tuition to other schools for pupils who had completed the eighth grade in their home school. Legal machinery left the entire matter completely in the hands of the voters themselves.

In Mr. Fall's report of 1902 he listed the results of consolidation as follows:

1. The health of the children is better. (No sitting in damp clothes.)

2. Attendance is from 50% to 150% greater. (No truancy or tardiness.)

3. Fewer teachers required. Better teachers secured. Higher wages.

4. Schools are under closer supervision.

5. Pupils are in better buildings, with better heating and ventilation.

6. Greater opportunity for special work in music, drawing, and so on.

7. Cost is reduced in nearly all cases.

8. School year is often longer.

9. Pupils benefit by wider circle of acquaintances.

10. The whole community is drawn together.

11. Public wagons used to convey children in the daytime may be used to transport parents to evening meetings and lecture courses.

12. Finally, by transportation of children, the farm again becomes the ideal place in which to bring up children. There is no loafing about town after school hours.

Incidentally, these arguments are much the same as those I stressed eighteen years later when I was working for consolidation, although I had not seen Mr. Fall's report.

Within the next few years a number of small schools consolidated. In Genesee County the Cook district joined the Grand Blanc village district and the school was then listed in the school directory of the county as the Grand Blanc Centralized School. In 1906, another district was added to Grand Blanc. In 1919, it became one of the first six rural agricultural schools in Michigan and in 1921 Grand Blanc township schools reorganized as a township unit. From the turn of the century on, Grand Blanc has been a leader in the movement for better educational advantages for its children.

During this first campaign (in the early 1900s) the centralized schools of Gladwin County in the lower peninsula became the first county to change to the township unit system.

This zeal for consolidated schools shown by the superintendents of public instruction was only temporary, however. In fact, it was even played down by later superintendents. In 1915 or 1916, I asked the current superintendent how to organize a consolidated school. He outlined the procedure, but his closing remark was, "You want to be careful of the afterclap."

In 1913, the "Standard School" concept came to Michigan and the various superintendents of public instruction gave great emphasis to this idea. However, in my opinion it was always a step backward. After twenty to twenty-five years it was practically abandoned. In the interim it had a bad effect on the reorganization of our schools under the Rural Agricultural Act. Key schools in plans for reorganizing were often standard schools, and being "Standard," they were considered perfect by the voters of the district.

By 1900 the pieces of the pattern that was the Michigan school system in my time had fallen into place. In the sixty-eight years from the time Michigan became a state until I began to teach school, many changes had been made in our schools but the one great *defect,* the district system, had not been changed. It was, and still remains, with its inequality of education and taxes, the cancer in our educational system.

In 1887, the law regarding apportioning of the one-mill tax was changed. In 1841 the legislature had provided for the levying of a one-mill tax, then changed in 1858 to two-mills, for the maintenance of schools. In 1881 this tax was reduced to one mill. At first, this money was apportioned according to need, that is, on a per pupil basis. In 1887, this method was changed to require all moneys raised from the mill tax to be apportioned to the district in which it was raised. Unwittingly, the legislature, by this law, divided school districts into two classes—the rich and the poor. For years wealthy districts with proportionally few pupils needed no other tax, of if any, just a mill or two. Other districts, with many children but with low property values to tax, had to levy special taxes or have inferior schools. Even to this day, this has been the big evil in our school system. Until the 15-mill limitation tax law was passed in 1933, any district at its annual meeting could vote the amount of money needed to run its schools for the ensuing year. Because of the vast differences in the amount of taxable property in the different districts compared to the number of children of school age, an intolerable taxation problem was created. Many thoughtful people became interested in school problems and in possible ways to secure better schools. The one-mill tax was abolished when the 15-mill tax limitation was adopted.

RURAL AGRICULTURAL SCHOOLS

In 1917, the State Grange passed a resolution calling for the appointment of a committee of seven members to investigate the problems of rural education. The duties of this committee were to ascertain the adequacy of the primary school district system to meet rural needs from several standpoints, namely (a) training rural children, (b) service to the community, (c) supervision and economical administration, and (d) ways and means to improve rural schools. At this time Dora Stockman was the lecturer of the State Grange. It must have been from the studies of this committee under her guidance that the Rural Agricultural Act was written and passed by the legislature. Unfortunately, at this time the Department of Public Instruction was enamored with the idea of the "standard school." They paid no attention to the bill and it was passed without providing officers for the new districts when they were formed. The attorney general ruled that the law could not be put into effect until the legislature could amend it, which it did in 1919.

I have always thought that if the law had been operative when passed I could have consolidated all the rural schools of Genesee County. (As it turned out, this was not accomplished until June 16th, 1965, when the Beebe school in Gaines Township was annexed to the Linden district in Fenton Township.)

In 1919, our boys were coming home from World War I. There was an aura of change in the air; many people wanted better schools. As I have mentioned before, six of the rural agricultural schools in Michigan were organized in 1919, with three of them in Genesee County.

By 1920 the postwar depression had set in. Farmers' prices plunged downward. The great opportunity to improve rural schools was lost by the delay of two years in putting the Rural Agricultural Act in force.

The law establishing rural agricultural schools provided for two classes of schools, A and B. Class A schools were to receive $200 for each bus and $600 to help pay the salary of the teacher of agriculture. They had to have at least nine months of school. Class B schools were required to have twenty acres for an experimental farm for demonstration work and to hire a principal for twelve months, with two or more teachers for a ten-month school year. State aid was $900 to help pay the salary of the principal. Aid for buses was the same as for Class A schools.

The six rural agricultural schools organized in the lower peninsula in 1919 were: Napoleon in Jackson County under Commissioner Townsend; Hanover and Hoxeyville in Wexford County under Roy Noteware; Gaines, Goodrich, and Grand Blanc in Genesee County under my administration. The 1920 report of the state superintendent lists two others, Bennington in Shiawassee County and Albion in Calhoun County, as having been voted but for some reason they did not organize as rural agricultural schools, because they are not mentioned in the superintendent's report of 1925 when Wilford Coffey was the state superintendent. His report lists 52 rural agricultural schools, with 35 of them receiving Smith-Hughes money. Eleven others were eligible and had applied for aid under the Smith-Hughes Act.

By 1925 state aid had been increased to $1,000 for payment to teachers and $400 annually per bus. All rural agricultural school buildings, if to be built or remodeled, had to be constructed to plans approved by the state superintendent of public instruction. These buildings were to serve as community centers, available for public meetings when school was not in session. This was the beginning of the community school concept in Michigan, although this term didn't come into use at the time. The law specified that the building should have a combination gymnasium-and-assembly room so that it would become the community center for the neighborhood. Several of these schools also had evening schools for farmers, with extension courses conducted by teachers from Michigan State College. As these rural agricultural schools grew in number, they made it possible for the farm boys and girls to study agriculture, manual training, and domestic science. In reality, they gave the advantages of vocational training, a privilege still denied many city children. Most of these schools became accredited high schools as well, which put them on a par with city schools in that respect. These consolidated schools also brought other side effects, such as improved roads.

Motor buses were used by all the rural agricultural schools, with Goodrich rural agricultural school leading the way. With district-owned buses came the necessity of a central garage for storage and minor repairs, under the supervision of a superintendent of transportation in each school.

All kinds of subterfuges were used when a district did not want to be incorporated into a proposed township unit or join a village to form a rural agricultural school. In 1920, three districts in Fenton Township of Genesee County, with Long Lake school as the center, voted to form a rural agricultural school. The organization did not get beyond the election of five board members. However, it reduced the number of districts in the county by two. In 1953, thirty-three years after it was first organized, the voters organized a high school, with Russell Hadden as superintendent. By this time the population of the district had grown considerably because of its proximity to Flint. In 1954, after two districts from the adjoining township of Mundy joined the district, they completed the organization of a rural agricultural school. This maneuvering left three districts in one township, Fenton, Linden, and Long Lake, and all three can be considered poor districts under present conditions. Had they had the foresight to form a township unit school in the 1920s, they would be in a much better financial condition today.

The Rural Agricultural School Act was the first serious attempt to alleviate the evils inherent in the district system of schools. The two greatest evils were the inequality of taxation and of scholastic opportunity. Until this law was put into effect the rural children lived under *de facto* segregation. In other words, the poor and rich districts translated as the poor and good schools.

School Taxes

The new constitution of Michigan, adopted in 1908, had made an attempt to equalize taxes by providing that any district which had enough money on hand at the close of the school year to pay teachers' salaries and tuition for eighth grade graduates for two years would be deprived of its share of the Primary School fund. In many wealthy districts with few children, mill tax brought in more money than could be spent.

The Primary School fund had been enriched by a Supreme Court decision in 1907, at which time the Court ruled that *ad valorem* taxes assessed against railroads were legal. Thus the railroads were forced to pay large sums into the Primary School fund.

In 1920, State Superintendent T. E. Johnson began to discuss plans to correct the great difference in the amount of taxes necessary to be raised in the various districts in order to run the schools. He wanted suggestions for remedies to correct this evil. In that year a study was made of the tax rates in eight districts. The highest tax rate was $54 per thousand and the lowest, $1.54. The average assessed value back of each child in the state was $7,530. If the state had been the unit for taxation, $8 per thousand on all property would have been sufficient to cover school expenses. In 1907 the per capita cost of education was $15.61; by 1920 this cost had risen to $55.95, an increase of nearly 400%.

The next attempt to equalize taxation came in 1927 with the passage of the Turner Bill. This bill appropriated $1,000,000 to be distributed to districts having a tax rate of ten mills or more. That the schools were in a desperate situation is shown by a survey made in 1927 which shows the lowest tax rate to have been 12c per thousand and the highest $63.52 per thousand. In 1927 the Turner Bill was amended to raise the amount of state aid to $2,000,000 per year.

From 1930 on, the legislature passed many laws affecting schools, most of them of a financial nature. In 1932, a depression year, it reduced state aid for transportation to $300 per bus. In 1933 the rural agricultural school law was changed to require a minimum valuation of $700,000 for any new consolidation. To receive state aid a district was required to levy at least 2¾ mills.

From 1930 to 1934 there was a general breakdown in the collection of school taxes. The amount collected was reduced from aproximately $267,000,000 to $159,000,000. The average tax rate in the 1930-31 school years was $31.64; for the 1933-34 year it was $27.30. The primary school interest money decreased from $17.92 per child in 1931 to $10.41 in 1934. One cause of this decrease was that the 15 mill limitation, which was adopted November 8, 1932, drastically reduced the tax money received from the railroads and other public utilities. All of this resulted in a decrease of 45% in the amount of money received from all sources for the pubilc schools.

In 1933, the legislature passed the Thatcher Act, which provided for the disbursement of $15,000,000 annually to the schools. Two-thirds of this sum was to be distributed on a per capita membership basis and one-third as a tax equalization fund. The revenue act which earmarked sums from the 3% retail sales tax and the liquor tax provided $4,609,000 of the $15,000,000 Thatcher Act money. In the 1933-34 school year the money from this law gave the schools only 50% of the money due them. As a result, many schools were forced to reduce the length of the school year and eliminate many worthwhile programs.

Under the fifteen mill amendment, an allocation board was set up in every county. These boards as first organized consisted of three to five members, according to the size of the counties. The members represented different governmental units in the county. It was the duty of these boards to allocate to the various units their proportional share of the fifteen-mill property tax that could be raised each year. In most counties the schools were given eight or nine mills, approximately 60% of the taxes raised. In 1937 the number of members on these boards was raised from five to six and the commissioner of schools was made a member. In 1964 a seventh member was added. Under this tax limitation act, school districts or any other political division could raise taxes above the fifteen mills by a two-thirds vote. At the same time an amendment to the election laws was passed to provide that electors, to qualify to vote on a bond issue or direct expenditures of public money, must be owners of property which is assessed for taxes in the governmental unit affected or be the husband or wife of a person thus qualified.

Because so many property owners could not pay their current taxes and had been unable to pay their taxes for one or two previous years, a tax moratorium on all taxes unpaid back to 1931 was declared. These conditions were the result of the Great Depression. Beginning September 1, 1935, these back taxes could be paid in ten annual installments.

When the $15,000,000 appropriated in 1933 failed to meet the needs of the schools, the Thatcher-Sour Act of 1935 appropriated $36,-000,000 from the general fund of the state. For 1938 state aid was raised to $38,000,000 which sum included the interest from the Primary School fund.

In 1937, the approval of all plans for new school buildings and the remodeling of old buildings was given to the superintendent of public instruction. During a four-year interval, between 1933 and 1937, there had been no law governing the buildings for schools except federal regulations.

In 1939, state aid was fixed at $45,000,000. The equalization fund was increased to $15,000,000, with the millage increased to three. Trailer camps were springing up all over the state. To help take care of the cost of education of the children from these camps, a license fee was established, to be distributed between the township and the school district where the camp was located.

In 1942, a commission was appointed by State Superintendent Eugene Elliott to make recommendations for the improvement of the public schools. This commission complained that there were *too many districts*. At that time there were over six thousand districts in Michigan. In 1970 this complaint is still valid. The commission proposed that a committee of nine be appointed to prepare a plan for the reorganization of the school districts in the counties of Michigan. This was fifty years after the M.E.A. legislative committee, led by school commissioner Alan Freeland, introduced an optional county unit bill in the legislature which did not pass.

In 1935, the state assumed the duty of paying the tuition of all non-resident pupils attending the ninth to twelfth grades inclusive of a tuition high school, at the rate of $65 per pupil. During the same year the federal government gave further much needed aid of $41,829.83 for vocational agriculture, trade, and industrial education and $46,670 for home economics education. This aid was on a biennium basis.

By 1929 the number of rural agricultural or consolidated schools in Michigan had increased to sixty-one, which meant that 380 one-room schools had been displaced. In the new schools there were 12,923 pupils in the first eight grades and 4,343 in the high schools. These figures do not mean that all these pupils came from one-room rural schools, because many of the rural agricultural schools were organized around small village schools, as where the schools in Grand Blanc, Gaines, and Goodrich in Genesee County. Forty-two of the new schools had four-year courses in agriculture and forty-nine of them were accredited by the University of Michigan.

During the next fifteen years, because of the Great Depression and World War II, reorganization of our rural school districts practically stopped, although there were a few new rural agricultural schools organized. Among these was the Kearsley rural agricultural school in Genesee County, organized in 1940 under the wise leadership of Mr. George Daly. Two schools, the Tanner and the Wentworth, joined with Kearsley to form the new school. At that time, Mr. Daly was the superintendent of the Kearsley school. He is a native of Genesee County who attended the Pine Run elementary school and the Clio high school. He received his Bachelor's degree at Central Michigan University and his Master's at Wayne State University. He began teaching in the Kearsley school when it was a two or three-room school; during the ensuing years many of the farms in his district were subdivided and hundreds of new houses built.

Soon after the end of World War II, the tempo of reorganization accelerated. By 1946 the number of districts in the state had been reduced to 5,671. Changing economic conditions, movements of population, and improvements of roads tended to increase the size of new districts. From 1920 to 1933 the average number of districts in a reorganization was 5.6; in 1946 it was 13. This was all to the good.

The state laid down seven principles as guidelines for reorganization, which included size and financial conditions, but in many cases the new districts were formed without a master plan for the county. In 1920 we made such a plan for Genesee County but it was never carried out. The result of this haphazard way is that Genesee County still has three townships with three poor districts each, instead of one fairly well-to-do district in each township. By 1960 the number of school districts in Michigan had been reduced to 2,145.

OFFICE OF COUNTY SUPERINTENDENT

In 1935, the powers and duties of the county school commissioners had been so diminished that many people thought the office should be abolished. When the office was created in 1891 it was indeed a necessary and useful office. The county commissioner, with the board of school examiners, examined and issued teachers' certificates to from 80% to 90% of all the teachers in most counties. They visited the schools and supervised the primary school districts. They conducted eighth grade examinations and issued diplomas to all eighth grade graduates except those in graded districts which had twelve grades and a superintendent. We have seen how these powers and duties were gradually taken from the commissioners and given to other authorities. Besides the supervision of the one-room or primary schools, there was left to them the enforcement of compulsory attendance laws and the keeping of child accounting records for the county schools. In some of the larger counties the commissioners made themselves useful in different ways. Several had "helping teachers" to aid schools with special problems, such as reading.

Consolidation was rapidly lessening the scope of the duties of the county commissioner. To save their official office (there was one in each of the 83 counties) they pressured the legislature until it passed a law to establish a county school district with a county school board. This board had its beginning in 1935 with the passage of Act 117 of that year. The office of county commissioner was retained, but the name was changed to county school superintendent.

Act 117 was amended by Act 269 of 1947 which called for the election of a county board of education by representatives of each district in the county. In Genesee County, notices were sent to all directors of the primary districts, to secretaries of graded school districts, and to the president of the Flint board of education. These officials met on August 4, 1949, and elected a county board of education of five members. This new board of five met in the office of the county superintendent, Mrs. Daisy Howard, on Monday, August 18, to organize as a county board of education. Dr. E. C. Mosier was elected president and Mr. James J. Hill, vice-president. The board then appointed Mrs. Howard, the last county commissioner and the first county superintendent since 1875, when the office was first abolished, to the office of county superintendent of schools.

This same procedure was followed in all the counties of the state. Just eighty years before this date, the legislature had provided by law for the election of a county superintendent of schools. This office was discontinued in 1875, when the office of township superintendent was established, only to be abolished as a failure in 1881. From 1881 to 1891 the chairman of the county board of school examiners performed the duties of county superintendent. The law was changed in 1891 to provide for the election of a county school commissioner.

Besides adding a few duties to the office, the 1947 law changed the method of selecting a superintendent from the election by a direct vote of the people to appointment by a county board of education. This was just one of the many ineffective attempts to change our school system that have been made since it was organized in 1836. The school system has always been burdened by too many school districts and by unjust and unequal tax burdens.

Because no real reorganization had been accomplished by creating a county school district, in many districts the results were not good. In 1962 the legislature passed the Intermediate School District Act, which provided for the consolidation of one or more county school districts in the interests of economy and increased efficiency and gave the county board of education some control over its finances. It also provided for the addition of several special functions, such as the operation of specialized clinics not available to local districts, services of helping teachers, special education programs, operation of day care centers for the mentally handicapped and for wards of the court.

The county school districts and their succesors, the intermediate districts, had advisory control over consolidation. The rural agricultural school law and the K-12 act have radically reduced the number of school districts in Michigan to 520. The K-12 act, which was passed in 1964, provides that all districts either provide educational opportunity for all children from kindergarten through the twelfth grade or join a district which does maintain such a school. This law gives every child in the state the opportunity to have a twelve-grade high school in his home district.

Because of the haphazard way many consolidated districts have been organized and because there are still two or three hundred too many districts, our schools have suffered. Many of the districts are too small; some have no more territory than when established more than over one hundred years ago. Bendle School in Genesee County is one of these. Many have no tax base other than small homes and farms. Some have much wealth but few children. Because the districts, like Topsy, "just growed," many children are transported several miles to school. If district lines were abolished, in many instances these children could attend a school less than half the distance from their homes.

All the laws now on the books are just mustard plasters on a deep infection. Only a complete operation (reorganization) will cure the illness. To begin, the slate should be washed clean. For taxation purposes, all district lines should be abolished. A general tax of from ten to sixteen mills should be levied against all taxable property in the state. This money, together with the sums received from the Primary School fund, the sales tax, and other sources such as the income tax, should be distributed to the schools on a per capita basis. New school buildings should be financed by bond issues in each district. However, special state aid might have to be given to districts with low valuations.

For administrative purposes, the state should be divided into not more than 100 districts. In some cases, county lines could serve as district lines, but should not be sacrosanct.

By reducing the number of districts, much duplication of effort could be abolished from the work of superintendents down to local bus superintendents and board members. At present, on a given day, 520 superintendents and other officials could be performing the same identical duties. By eliminating 60 to 70% of the present districts millions of dollars would be save annually. Opposition to this plan would come from the people who love the "little red schoolhouse." In many cases this opposition would be led by the army of bureaucrats who now hold school offices.

The three fatal defects in our school system as enumerated earlier are still most evident. In 1969 Governor Milliken appointed a committee to make a complete evaluation of our school system. This committee met and submitted to the governor a complete plan for the reorganization of our public schools.

From my research for this book and from my experience in school administration I came to the conclusion long ago that a radical reorganization of our public school system is absolutely necessary if the system is to survive. In 1969, before Governor Milliken announced his plan, I wrote him a letter outlining my ideas for reorganization of the Michigan school system as stated above.

Michigan is one of the few states continuing to operate under the district system. For instance, Florida's schools have always operated under a county unit system and Florida is now considering the uniting of the smaller counties in the interests of economy and efficiency.

Governor Milliken's latest proposal is to abolish all property taxes for schools and raise the moneys for this purpose by an income tax. It would allow the districts to raise five or six mills for special educational purposes by a vote of the people.

CHAPTER XXI

Vocational Education

Vocational education as a facet of our total educational system is not a new idea but it is one that has been neglected far too long. When Father Richard purchased some spinning wheels, a spinning jenny, and a carding machine for his Academy for Young Ladies and proposed that carpenters, shoemakers, and other craftsmen be invited to his boys' school, he initiated the first vocational training in Michigan. The agricultural departments planned for the branches of Michigan University in the early 1840s showed that teaching for vocations was a live question. In the report from the Ypsilanti Union School for 1852, one of the subjects mentioned for the third year of the upper department is agricultural chemistry. This subject is also mentioned in the courses to be studied in the Ypsilanti Normal, which was in fact a vocational training school.

Ira Mayhew, superintendent of public instruction from 1845 to 1849, was one of the first educators to lament the lack of vocational training in Michigan. The rapid development of the commercial and industrial life after the close of the Civil War made the need for skilled workers more urgent. Schools began slowly to respond to the call for trained personnel. By 1880 definite courses to prepare students for business life, such as commercial arithmetic and bookkeeping, were becoming common. Private schools to teach trades and business colleges to train students for office work were opened in several Michigan cities. One of these was Ferris Institute at Big Rapids, which was opened September 1, 1884. Six courses were offered: teacher training, college preparatory, elocution, telegraphy, typewriting, and geology.

In 1900, Jason Hammond, superintendent of public instruction, devoted almost all of his annual report to the subject of teaching manual training. He concludes:

> The high school gives training to the intellectual powers of the student, thus imparting facility for further intellectual preparation. Why should not the same school give facility to those faculties or powers that the masses need in their calling?

By the turn of the century many of the schools in the larger cities had programs in vocational education. Bay City had classes in business, sewing, cooking, carpentry, and turning (running a lathe). By 1896 Muskegon and Ishpeming offered shopwork, foundry, cooking, sewing, and mechanical drawing. By 1900 Ann Arbor, Calumet, Detroit, Flint, Grand Rapids, Menominee, and Saginaw offered a variety of vocational courses—from forging machine shop and business courses to cooking and sewing.

In 1900, Mr. Hammond, state superintendent, asked for and secured funds from the state to investigate this phase of education. This was the first time a Michigan legislature appropriated funds to study the various phases of training "the hand, eye, and ear."

The course of study for rural schools, published in 1903, stressed the study of agriculture and tried to bring about closer cooperation between the Michigan Agricultural College and the common schools. In 1907, the legislature voted to allow counties to establish county agricultural schools but no action was taken under this law, although it may have laid the foundation for the later Rural Agricultural Act.

The 1903 course of study for rural schools, in addition to stressing the study of agriculture, also outlined a course for the ninth and tenth grades of small village schools. This manual and course of study was to comprise branches required for third grade teachers' certificates and was to be known as the Agricultural College course. The diploma granted on completion of this course by the county commissioner of schools was the official requirement for admission to the freshman class of the College. This procedure was initiated to bring about closer cooperation between the Agricultural College and the schools.

In 1908, under the direction of the Agricultural College, the teaching of agriculture was introduced into some high schools of Michigan.

The same year the College established a department of agricultural education. The work of this department was twofold; first, to assist the boards of education and superintendents to organize classes in agriculture, and secondly, to train men to be instructors in these high school classes. As I remember, the first class in this subject in Montrose high school was organized in 1910 when I went there to teach. By the time the Smith-Hughes law was enacted, 67 high schools were providing regular courses in agriculture. In many of them the instruction was given by graduates of agricultural colleges.

On February 17, 1917, the Congress enacted the Smith-Hughes law, which provided for the appropriation of federal funds for developing practical vocational education programs throughout the United States in institutions of less than college rank. To receive this aid, it was necessary for the state to furnish matching funds. When this act was passed, the Michigan legislature, which was in session, immediately passed the Tuft Act to meet the requirement of the federal law. This act established a state board of control for vocational education. The state Treasurer was made custodian of the funds. The board of control consisted of the superintendent of public instruction as executive officer, with the president of the state Board of Education, the president of the University of Michigan, and the president of Michigan Agricultural College as members. W. H. French was appointed acting state supervisor for agriculture. In May of 1918, E. E. Gallup, then superintendent of schools in Monroe, Michigan, was appointed state supervisor. His service began July 1, 1918.

In 1917, the Michigan legislature also passed the Rural Agricultural School act, which has been explained in another chapter. In 1920 Congress passed an act known as the Vocational Rehabilitation of Physically Disabled Civilians. To qualify for funds from this act, a state had to appropriate an amount equal to the federal funds to be received, such sum not to be less than $5,000. The Tuft Act was amended to accept conditions of this act, and placed its operations under the board of control for vocational education. These funds and the funds of the Smith-Hughes act increased each year. By 1927, $69,693.28 were available for promotion of vocational rehabilitation in our state. This very worthwhile project accomplished the rehabilitation of 34 persons the first year. By 1925 the number had increased to 321.

The national act appropriating these funds contained important provisions for the training of vocational teachers. The state also received special funds which were matched by our legislature for the training of teachers, supervisors, and directors of agricultural, industrial, and home economics subjects. This program also came under the supervision of the board of control mentioned above.

The Deen Act of 1936 provided for training in the distributive occupations and the public service field. In 1939, the state board of control extended the scope of vocational education by creating an occupational and guidance service.

As agricultural classes grew, other related organizations came into existence. In 1928, a club called Future Farmers of America was organized. This organization is now considered an integral part of agricultural education. Its aim is to complement classroom instruction with outside activities.

Perhaps an account of evening or night schools should be included in this chapter. They may well be considered as vocational schools, since their purpose is to impart knowledge in reading, arithmetic, and history in order to enable their students to earn a living and become self-supporting citizens. One of the first accounts of an evening school is in the report of S. Wright, clerk of the district board of the Battle Creek Union School, dated November 25, 1852. He reported, "The evening schools are superintended by the principal, who is assisted by his advanced class of students." Before 1900, evening high schools had been established in Detroit and Kalamazoo. Slowly thereafter public schools in other larger cities organized programs for the foreign born, for native illiterates and for adults wishing to complete studies required for an eighth grade or a high school diploma.

Beginning in 1917, with state and federally subsidized vocational education, the public schools expanded their courses to provide organized classes for adults in job training. During and after World War I hundreds of immigrants from southern Europe came to work in the automobile factories in Detroit and Flint. Miss Elizabeth Welch, principal of the Fairview school of Flint, gained national recognition for the work she did in organizing night classes to teach these newcomers the English language and United States history that would enable them to become good citizens. The second generation of some of these immigrants have become promintent in law, medicine, business, and politics. Other night schools in many northern cities were opened to teach the illiterate black people who came north to work in the factories, which migration increased later during and following World War II.

Notwithstanding the many programs for vocational education which have been introduced, vocational training has always been and still remains the foster child of our Michigan educational system. However, some light is beginning to show through the darkness. Under the plan chosen by the court for reorganization of the schools of the city of Detroit, five regional vocational schools are to be built. The Lansing board of education also has an outstanding plan of vocational training in successful operation. Lansing's program has been published in many magazines over the years. In 1958 the United States Office of Education invited Lansing to present its program on employing handicapped at its national conference in Columbus, Ohio. Another of the new vocational training programs is the Skills Center in the Flint area.

GENESEE AREA SKILLS CENTER

The Genesee Area Skills Center, first of its kind to be built in Michigan, offers a practical solution to the increasing need for vocational training for young people. The $2.5 million structure is located in Mundy township between Torrey Road and the U. S. 23 freeway. Operation is by the Flint Board of Education in accordance with a contract between the Board and the Genesee Intermediate District Board of Education.

Its brief history included the acquisition of a site of 49 acres on May 8, 1967, after plans were made in 1966. A first principal, Richard G. Loomis, was named May 23, 1968, and a deputy principal, Donald B. Bentley on June 26, 1968. The original site was enlarged by the purchase of an additional twelve acres on September 4, 1968.

The building, which consists of two wings separated by a courtyard, covers 104,886 sq. ft. It serves some 1300 students of the 11th and 12th grades from both public and parochial schools throughout the county, who attend classes for 2½ hours each day in addition to attending regular classes in their own high schools. These students are transported by buses owned by the several school districts in the Intermediate District.

Tuition-free instruction in a wide range of vocational courses supplements the vocational offerings in established school systems. The curriculum covers courses in four subjects in graphic communications, seven courses in mechanical occupations, three in business occupations, four in electrical occupations, and seven in diversified trades and industry which include such subjects as house construction, floriculture, domestic appliance service and beauty culture. In addition, the building is used for adult education courses.

The participating schools include all districts comprising the Genesee Intermediate School District (Atherton, Beecher, Bendle, Bentley, Carman, Clio, Davison, Fenton, Flushing, Genesee, Goodrich, Grand Blanc, Kearsley, Lake Fenton, Lakeville, Linden, Montrose, Mt. Morris, Swartz Creek, and Westwood Heights) and the city of Flint plus the non-public high schools of Genesee County.

The Skills Center is financed by a tax levied by the Intermediate School District, which may be as much as one-half mill. The Flint Board of Education furnishes a proportionate amount for its share of the maintenance costs.

INTERMEDIATE SCHOOL DISTRICTS

Intermediate school districts are a new and interesting experiment in our Michigan school system. The eighty-three counties of the state have been reorganized into 60 intermediate districts, all doing specialized work for the districts within their boundaries—work that single districts alone cannot do. Two of the outstanding leaders in this field are William J. Emerson in Oakland and Erwin L. Davis in Genesee County. Although space does not permit me to go into this new concept in detail, these intermediate districts could very well be an important cog in our school system, especially if the number of districts is reduced to a level that is compatible with efficiency in education and finance.

CHAPTER XXII

Community Schools

The community school concept may have had its beginning as a part of the Rural Agricultural School law which gave the superintendent of public instruction the authority to approve the plans of any new school building to be erected in any district organized under the act. It specified that a room be provided for the use of the people of the district for extension classes or any allied purpose. These early consolidations were made up of one-room district schools or centered by small villages like those of Gaines, Grand Blanc, and Goodrich of Genesee County, where the economy was nearly all of a rural interest. As the idea grew, many consolidations were organized around large villages and even cities where the word "rural" did not always apply. These districts then began to call their schools community schools to show that they were part of a rural and urban community. Thus the term "rural agricultural school" gradually disappeared as the new schools became the center of community activities.

THE MOTT FOUNDATION

The community school idea may have reached its greatest development in Flint. In 1926, the Charles Stewart Mott Foundation was established, with its primary objective the development of the human resources of the city to such a degree that Flint should become a model community. The Foundation has worked in close cooperation with the public schools in the development of a broadly based and defined community education system.

In October, 1935, a committee was appointed in Flint "for the promotion of recreational and athletic activities in our schools." It began by having two supervisors for each of five schools to enlist all the children possible in activities during the evening hours. The first appropriation by by the Mott Foundation to finance this project was $6,000. Frank J. Manley is considered the father of this community school concept, which is now established in 51 other schools in Flint. Frank F. Minardo, a physical education instructor who became Flint's community school director, and Dr. Myrtle Black, who became director of adult education for the Mott program, took part in the first activities of the program. These activities were primarily to keep the children off the streets, to cut down accidents, and to combat juvenile delinquency. However, Mr. Manley's hopes for preventing juvenile delinquency did not come true. To find out what made children become delinquent, a visiting teacher program was initiated by the Mott Foundation, hiring social workers to visit the homes of delinquent children to study the home situations of such children. Many other groups were asked to cooperate or were organized to get at the problems of the child under stress. The local Girl Scouts volunteered to supervise backyard safety playgrounds; Golden Gloves training centers for boys were organized; story hours were introduced at playgrounds; tot lots for small children were started at summer playgrounds; and the Stepping Stone Club for junior and senior high school girls was established. The latter was founded by Mrs. Elizabeth Pollock and now owns a large home donated by Michael Hamady as a laboratory for the members to get practical experience in homemaking.

As the years went by, other facets of community activities such as a college division of adult education, a veterans' counseling service, an evening high school, a youth bureau, an interracial community center, a University of Michigan extension center, and a Flint recreation commission were established.

A PILOT PROJECT

In 1947, Mr. Mott suggested that a pilot project be set up "to get the bugs out of the product." The Fairview school was selected as the pilot school to try out many educational experiments. One key result was the conversion of all the Flint schools to community education. Funds for two new schools were voted, the buildings to be specially designed to provide facilities for everyone in the neighborhood. The Ralph M. Freeman school became the first building designed for this purpose. Thus the Flint "community school concept" has developed under the Mott Foundation, which has channeled more than forty million ($40,000,000) through the school board to underwrite programs in recreation, adult education, juvenile assistance, curriculum experimentation, and enrichment of social services and health services. The school buildings are now used as meeting places where community needs are served by community resources. The schools are now open from 4 p.m. until 10 p.m. from September to June for classes for adults in every phase of legitimate endeavor. Over 1,000 classes are offered, ranging from public speaking or furniture making to sewing, flower arranging, or cooking for guests. The schools of Flint have become community schools in the true sense of the term.

Educators and recrceational directors from all over the nation and from foreign countries as well have visited Flint to study the program and the community school idea has been adopted in other places as their finances permit.

The philosophy of the Mott Foundation is "to increase the strength and stature of character in individuals and thereby also strengthen our free enterprise system of society. The goals should be first to produce citizens of strength and quality each of whom accepts his full responsibility as a citizen."

CHAPTER XXIII

Special Schools and Wards of the State

BOYS' REFORM SCHOOL

The Michigan Reform School, founded on September 2, 1850, was located on a farm of 134 acres, east of Lansing. In 1858, the school was placed under the supervision of the superintendent of public instruction. The report of Superintendent Oramel Hosford for the year 1865 has a most revealing account of the Reform School. The 1865 budget for maintenance of the school was $30,524.94, of which the state treasury furnished $22,000. Other receipts were from such items as boys' labor, $4,033.04; old iron, $5.15; ashes $6; old rags $47.62; sale of pigs and miscellaneous farm crops $74.50. Much of the food eaten by the boys was raised on the farm.

In 1865, ninety-five boys ranging in age from seven to sixteen, the average age being thirteen years, two months and twenty-seven days, were received at the school. By present standards, these boys were from under-privileged homes. Eighty-five of the ninety-five were sent to the school because of petty larceny. All of them were from homes where either the father or the mother or both parents were dead or missing.

At the school the boys were kept busy at various tasks, such as working in the tailor shop where they made their clothing or in the shoe shop where they made their shoes. There was also a chair shop where woven chair seats, matted chair seats, and chair seat frames were made to be sold. The total output was seats or frames for more than 5,500 chairs annually.

Of the ninety-five boys entering the school in 1865, sixteen did not know the alphabet; only thirteen could read in the primer, thirteen in the first reader, twenty-two in the second reader, twenty-three in the third reader, and four in the fourth reader. Of the ninety-five boys, only twenty had had any instruction in arithmetic. In addition to working in the shops and in the fields, the boys attended regular classes taught by four teachers. When the boys were discharged from the school, the teachers made a report on their accomplishments which said their progress was slow but they added, "We find in point of scholarship the school stands higher than it did a year ago."

When the boys were released at the end of their term, they were encouraged to write back. Eighteen letters that came back to the school were sent to the superintendent of public instruction and printed in his report of 1865. All of these letters praised the school and the people in charge for the benefits the boys derived from living in the school for two or three years. All the letters were well-written and fairly correct as to grammar. (One wonders if they were corrected or changed before being printed.) The thought also comes to mind that the publishing of these letters was a subtle request to the legislature to appropriate more money so that the Reform School could do an even better job.

When the Reform School was first organized, it was set up to accommodate boys and girls together, but this idea was soon abandoned. At first, eight girls were sent to this school, but they were soon removed. What became of the eight girls who needed correctional training the reports do not show.

GIRLS' REFORM SCHOOL

The Michigan Reform School for Girls was established in 1881, and located on forty acres of land one-half mile north of the city limits of Adrian. On July 1 the superintendent of public instruction took posession of the farmhouse on the grounds and began at once to furnish it for a temporary administration building. The first cottage residence was built, officers for this cottage appointed, and the first two inmates received on August 3. For the next two months an average of two girls per week entered the school. Before the year ended, a second cottage was completed. The two cottages were built to house sixty-four girls. The engine room and a chapel were also completed soon after and two additional cottages were built before the end of the year.

The first superintendent of the school was Miss Emma A. Hall. The first assistant superintendent was Mrs. F. S. Hillier, who also served as the school physician. The report made to state Superintendent Varnum B. Cochran says that the faculty was working on a course of study that would embrace five classes. The list of textbooks given would indicate that the course of study was that which was later included in the first eight grades. Of the first eighteen girls received in the school seven could not read, three could read in the second reader, five in the third, and three in the fourth.

Home for Dependent Children

Even in these early days, Michigan did not neglect dependent children. In the annual report of 1876 of the superintendent of public instruction we read:

> In 1871 the legislature established a state public school for dependent children. This step was without precedent in any other government, a new departure in social and educational reform, by the establishment of a home and school that would carry school privileges to the poorest classes under a system unconnected with the penal administration of the state.

This temporary home was established and opened May 21, 1874, to take care of orphans or dependent children until a permanent home could be found for those children who without it would have to be placed in county poorhouses. The Home was located in Coldwater on a farm of fifty-one acres, where it is still maintained. The children were housed in cottages with twenty-five to thirty children in each. The care was supposed to be the same as it would be in a home with a mother, as each cottage had its own "mother." The children admitted ranged in age from four to sixteen years.

Dependent children lived in this Home until they could be placed in permanent homes by adoption or by indenture. If adopted, the usual laws of adoption were observed. If indentured, the family who took a child signed a contract to treat the child as they would treat one of their own, by sending him to school the usual required length of time or by teaching him a trade, if possible.

The reports of the first several years after the school was founded show that it was progressing favorably but because the children were constantly being placed in homes and new children admitted, it was difficult to measure progress. Regular classes were provided to teach the usual studies of primary schools.

To supervise the children after they were indentured, the State Board of Charities had agents to supervise the indentured children in twenty-eight counties. Mr. Cornelius A. Gower, the superintendent of public instruction (1878-1881), recommended that an agent of the Board be appointed whose duty would be to visit the homes in which children had been placed to see that they were treated well. Another duty of this officer would be to seek out proper homes for the children so that more children could be removed from the poorhouses and sent to the state school.

SCHOOLS FOR THE DEAF AND BLIND

History doesn't tell us much about the children who were so unfortunate as to be born deaf or blind before the dawn of the nineteenth century. Those who were born deaf were called "dumb" because they were unable to speak. The first institute to educate deaf and dumb children in the United States was founded in Connecticut in 1817. A Mr. Thomas H. Gallandet became interested in a neighbor's child who was deaf and dumb. Through his efforts, a survey was made and it was found that there were eighty children so afflicted in Connecticut. Institutes for the training of such children had been established in Paris, London, and Edinburgh. Mr. Gallendet was selected to travel to London to study the methods used there to teach deaf children. However, he was not allowed to enter either the London or the Edinburgh school. M. Secord, then head of the Royal Institute in Paris where the deaf children were being taught, invited him to visit his school. Laurent Clerc, a deaf mute in the Paris school and one of M. Secord's best pupils, was persuaded to come to the United States to teach in the first institute for the deaf, founded in Hartford in 1817. M. Clerc remained in the Hartford school for many years.

The first institue for the blind was opened in Paris by Abbe Hany, who had invented a method of printing books for the blind by using embossed letters. In the United States the first school for the blind was opened in Boston about 1830. In 1848, Congress appropriated eight sections of salt spring land (swamp land) in Michigan to be sold to raise funds for the erection of a building suitable for a school for the deaf and dumb and blind. The Michigan legislature provided for a board of five members to take charge of the asylum. Congress increased the site of eight sections to fifteen in 1850. That year Charles C. Hascell, Charles E. Stuart, John B. Cook, C. H. Taylor, and Elon Farnsworth were appointed to the board of trustees. The village of Flint was chosen as the site for the asylum. The citizens of Flint had donated $3,000 and ten acres of land for the site. Because Governor Barry thought that the sale of the fifteen sections given by Congress would not bring in sufficient money to build the necessary buildings, he persuaded the state legislature to appropriate ten additional sections of salt land and $5,000 from the state's general fund. Only $1,000 could be drawn within one year of the act and $3,000 the next year, after which according to law the state was to be reimbursed, when the salt lands were sold, for the total sum drawn.

To clear, fence, and seed the site, $2,000 of the money donated by the citizens of Flint were used. Before the first building could be built, a suitable temporary building, the old Dewey place on the corner of Fifth Street and Church Street, was rented and the first pupil was admitted on February 6, 1854. By April 18 there were eleven deaf mutes and one blind pupil in the school. After several months the school was moved to the Hazelton homestead, where it remained until the first building was completed in 1856.

The legislature of 1855 made board and tuition free to all pupils in the asylum and appropriated $33,000 to furnish the building which had been built the year before and to defray the expenses of the institution for the years 1855 and 1856. The cost of the first building was about $30,500. At the time of its completion there were 77 pupils. In 1856 the site was increased to 90 acres by the legislature. The cornerstone of the main building was laid July 15, 1857.

Upon the appointment of the first board of trustees, two of its members were sent to visit schools for the deaf and blind in other states. In their visit to the Indiana Institute for the Blind they were greatly impressed with the Rev. Barnabas Maynard Fay, an instructor in that school. When the Michigan school was opened, they invited the Reverend Fay to become its first superintendent. He accepted the appointment and remained in charge of the school for ten years.

Until 1856 the school in Flint and the Asylum for the Insane were under the same board of trustees. That year, the legislature by legislative act provided for a separate board for the school for the deaf and blind. James B. Walker, Benjamin Pierson, and John F. Leroy were appointed to the newly created board. The first two teachers in the school were W. L. Bregand and James Denison. In 1858 the first two women teachers were hired, Belle H. Ransom and Harriet L. Seymour.

In 1880, the blind children were removed from the Flint school and placed in a new building in Lansing under the jurisdiction of a separate board of trustees.

In 1891, the management of the School for the Deaf was placed in a central board of control of state institutions. In 1893, it was again placed under the control of its own board of trustees. It seems that these changes were made in the interests of economy. Under the new board, the emphasis was placed on those things that tended to promote the best interests of the pupils. From this time on it became a leader in education of the deaf.

In August of 1872, an interesting event occurred during a conference of superintendents and principals of the American Institutions for the Deaf being held at the Michigan school. This meeting was addressed by Alexander Graham Bell Jr., son of the inventor of the telephone. Mr. Bell urged the adoption of his father's "visible speech" but this method was not adopted.

Special Classes for the Handicapped Children

In order to offer education locally to physically handicapped children the Michigan legislature in 1923 provided that the board of education of any school district could establish and maintain special schools or classes for the blind or partially blind, the deaf and hard of hearing, and crippled children. A special class could be started if there were five or more resident children between the ages of five and twenty who could not be profitably or safely educated in regular classes. The board of education maintaining such classes was to make a detailed annual report to the superintendent of public instruction. The state was to reimburse a local school district the difference between the average cost of instruction of other children in the first eight grades and the average cost of educating the children in the special classes for the handicapped. In no case could the state aid exceed $200 per child per year. The superintendent of public instruction was given general supervision over the operation of this act and the work of training teachers for this work was centralized in the Ypsilanti Normal College.

LAPEER HOME AND TRAINING SCHOOL

Michigan has always been foremost in caring for its unfortunate children. Public Act 209 of the public acts of 1893 provided for the organization of a home and training school to be located in Lapeer "to train those unfortunate children who have been born or by disease have become imbecile or feeble-minded or epileptic, by a judicious and well-adjusted course of training and management to ameliorate their condition and to develop as much as possible their intellectual faculties and to reclaim their unhappy condition and fit them as far as possible for future usefulness in society."

As soon as the law went into effect, contracts were let for four buildings. The Home was built on the cottage plan and opened on January 2, 1895, with a bed capacity of 200. In 1968, the total number of residents was 3,347. There are now 39 buildings, with 1,250 employees.

In a 1968 publication of the school there is an apt quotation from Pearl S. Buck:

> These are the times in the generation of human life when a dawn rises over the hills of the past. I perceive another dawn rising over the mountains of ignorance and cruelty, and this time the sun is to shine upon children who never grew up, because somewhere along the way an unknown cause has stopped the normal growth of their minds . . . Of all God's children, these are the most innocent . . . retarded children are only hopeless when they are neglected.

This expresses very well the philosophy of the Lapeer State Home and Training School, based upon the concept of conservation and development of human abilities with recognition of the basic dignity and integrity of the individual, regardles of ability or status.

CHAPTER XXIV

Michigan Universities

THE UNIVERSITY OF MICHIGAN

By a congressional enactment of January 11, 1804, Michigan was cut off from the Northwest Territory and given a definite boundary. The act which designated that Section 16 of each township should be reserved for school purposes also set aside two entire townships to be reserved for a seminary of learning. When and how this seminary or university was planned and organized and how it was operated until it was moved to Ann Arbor is told in Chapter I of this book.

When the legislature moved the University of Michigan to Ann Arbor in 1837 it placed the school under a board of regents and a chancellor. The board of regents was to be nominated by the governor and approved by the senate.

The site in Ann Arbor was a 40-acre plot which had been donated for that purpose. By 1841 five buildings had been completed, one of which was Mason Hall. The first class of six students was admitted in 1841. The faculty consisted of two members, the Rev. Palmer Williams, an Episcopalian minister who taught mathematics and the Rev. Joseph Whiting, a Presbyterian who taught Latin and Greek. For the first ten years of its existence, the University was without a president appointed by the regents. Each member of the faculty served in turn for one year as president. The curriculum followed in the literary department was the traditional one of the classics, logic, rhetoric, and religious philosophy. However, there were some innovations in 1846, when courses in science and modern languages were added.

In 1850, the new state constitution, which had just been adopted, provided for direct election of the regents of the University by the people and gave these regents entire control of the affairs of the University. The first man they chose for president was Philip Henry Tappen, who was inaugurated on December 28, 1852. The medical department was also opened in 1850, with 91 would-be doctors in attendance. This brought the enrollment to 159.

The act of March 18, 1837, which organized the University of Michigan, was amended on June 21 to give the University the power to establish branches or preparatory schools without further legislative sanction. This was to implement that part of the general plan outlined by John D. Pierce which called for the cooperation of the University and the counties. This part of the general plan did not become operative, perhaps because of lack of cooperation by the counties, or because the necessary laws were not enacted by the legislature. However, seven of these preparatory schools or academies were organized by the University, one each in Pontiac, Monroe, Kalamazoo, Niles, White Pigeon, Tecumseh, and Romeo. Because agriculture was the principal industry of Michigan, each school was to have a department of agriculture which was to include courses in vegetable physiology, agricultural chemistry, and experimental and practical farming. Another department was designed to educate students to become teachers. The main purpose of these schools, however, was to prepare students for the University. An institution for the higher education of females was to be set up in connection with each academy whenever a suitable building could be provided, probably by the county.

When the appropriations by the legislature were not sufficient to support both the University and the branches, these branches were closed. No reports concerning them appear in the state superintendents' reports after 1853.

Superintendent Oramel Hosford's annual report for 1865 records that there were 944 students attending the University; 270 in the department of science, literature and arts; 414 in medicine and surgery; and 260 in law. From all departments there were 218 graduates, including five civil engineers, six with B.S. degrees, 28 with M.A. degrees, 21 with B.A. degrees, seven with M.S. degrees, 71 with M.D. degrees, and 80 with Bachelor of Law degrees.

The faculty consisted of 20 professors with salaries of $1,000 and $1,500, one librarian, one demonstrator of anatomy, five assistants and one instructor. Their salaries ranged from $100 to $1,000 a year. There were also four janitors, with salaries of $175, $350, and $400 annually.

The Reverend Erastus C. Haven, D.D., L.L.D., was president and professor of rhetoric and English literature. His salary was $2,000.

The estimated receipts for the year ending June 30, 1867, were $70,422.73. The estimated expenditures were $68,681.86. The report listed items that had been presented to the University museum. Among these was a vial of crude petroleum from a flowing well in West Virginia. Another was a section of a tree trunk knawed in two by beavers.

A significant part of this report was the Honor Roll, which listed the graduates and students who were then serving or had served in the United States military or naval service. The classes of 1846 and 1847 showed two names on this list. The number increased each year until there were 301 in the class of 1867. Besides giving the names of those who served in the armed forces, it gave a list of the 81 who died that this country might live. Of the enlistees, 400 were of the classes of 1865, 1866 and 1867, who re-entered the University after the war was ended. Of the 416 of prior classes, 61 died in service or were killed in battle. Of the enlistees, 170 were surgeons or assistant surgeons; 8 of their number died in service. Of the 246 others of prior classes, most of whom were commissioned officers, 52 died in service or were killed in battle.

When the War between the States ended, attendance increased rapidly. In 1869, Professor Henry Simons Frieze became president. He served only two years but in that time he initiated the accredited school admission plan which, in substance, dictated the curriculum that the many high schools which were being organized were to offer.

He was followed in 1871 by James Burrell Angell, who served the University with distinction for nearly forty years. During his tenure, the attendance rose from 1207 to 5223 and several new courses of study were added. The School of Dentistry was founded in 1871; the College of Pharmacy in 1876; the School of Nursing in 1891; and the Graduate School in 1892. Summer sessions began in 1894. When President Angell retired in 1909, he was succeeded by Henry B. Hutchins.

Many firsts in education may be attributed to our great University of Michigan. It was the first to be governed by a board of regents elected by the people and the first to admit women. After much discussion pro and con, Miss Madelon Stockwell was admitted in 1870. It was also at this time that the University became the first to admit pupils on presentation of high school diplomas. It was the first university west of the Allegheny Mountains to offer professional education, with the establishment of the medical school in 1850. In 1879, the first professor of the science and art of teaching was appointed to the first full-time professorship in education in an American university. In 1895, the College of Engineering was established. Previously the course in engineering had been part of the College of Science and Arts.

Dr. Alexander G. Ruthven followed Dr. Hutchins in 1929 and he, in turn, was followed by Dr. Harlan Hatcher in 1951. Since 1968 Dr. Robben Wright Fleming has been president.

MICHIGAN AGRICULTURAL COLLEGE

The state legislature of 1855, implementing a clause of the new constitution of 1850, provided for the purchase of land as a site for a state agricultural school and an experimental farm. The purpose of the school was to encourage the promotion of intellectual, scientific, and agricultural knowledge of the state and improve the practice of agriculture by the farmers.

A plot of 700 acres situated three miles east of the village of Lansing, facing on a plank road to the City of Detroit, was purchased. The first buildings constructed were College Hall, a dormitory called Saint's Rest, some farm buildings and four brick residences for the faculty. The plan of the college buildings complex had a central building facing the north with east and west wings. The west wing, 50 by 100 feet on the ground and three stories high, and a three-story boarding house were erected to enable the school to open on the first Wednesday in April of 1857. The first appropriation for financing the school was 22 sections of salt spring land.

Professor L. R. Fisk of the Ypsilanti Normal School was appointed head of the chemistry department and J. C. Holmes, secretary of the State Agricultural Society, was made head of the horticultural department.

The course of study included English and a scientific course with natural philosophy, chemistry, botany, animal and vegetable anatomy and physiology, geology, minerology, etomology, veternary art, mensuration, leveling, and political economy, as well as bookkeeping and the mechanic arts directly connected with agriculture! The school was first placed under the supervision of the state Board of Education. The law establishing the school stated: "Tuition shall forever be free and any number of pupils may be admitted who may apply from any part of the state."

Some of the first buildings were erected by money received from the sale of salt spring land. In 1857, the legislature appropriated $40,000 to pay for buildings under construction and other needed buildings, to buy furniture, apparatus, farm implements, library books, and to pay the salaries of professors and meet other necessary expenses to carry on the farm and school.

The school was dedicated on May 13, 1857. For a complete report of this dedication, see the report of the superintendent of public instruction for 1856-57, which devoted 35 pages to these exercises! The same report noted that to do the work on the farm two pairs of horses and six pairs of oxen were purchased together with the necessary plows, harrows, wagons, carts, sleds, axes, shovels and horticultural implements, as well as such labor-saving devices as Willis's stump extractor, Hedges "Little Giant" corn and cob mill, and a wood-sawing machine.

Sixty-five students were enrolled for the fall term of 1857. The law specified that each student should work at least three hours each day on the farm. He was paid from 3 to 8 cents per hour, according to his age and the kind of work done.

Joseph Williams was the first president of the college. The faculty consisted of Calvin Tracy, professor of mathematics, L. R. Fisk, professor of chemistry, and T. C. Abbot, professor of English literature. Mr. J. M. Shearer was in charge of the "peculiar" employees, M. Hodges was the first farmer. By "peculiar" employees, President Williams must have meant students, since there was the rule that required each student to work three hours each day. The average cost per student for room, board, and laundry for a year was $30. Most of the food consumed was raised on the farm.

By an act of the legislature in 1861, the state Board of Agriculture was created. By this act the control of the Agricultural College was taken from the state Board of Education and given to this newly created board. The Board of Agriculture consisted of six members, besides the governor and the president of the College, who became members by virtue of their offices.

In 1861, Congress passed the Morrell act which gave to the several states public lands in the amount of 30,000 acres for each senator and representative in Congress, provided that such state establish an agricultural college within five years. Because Michigan had such a college which had been in successful operation for five years, the legislature passed an enabling act to allow the Michigan Agricultural College to qualify under the Morrell act. Thus our Agricultural College became the first Land Grant college in the United States.

The land received from the federal government was placed in the hands of a Land Grant Board which began at once to sell these lands and invest the money. As only interest earned by this money could be used by the College, for several years the College had a precarious existence. The state legislature, however, did appropriate small sums for its maintenance.

Because of the reputation for excellence M.A.C. soon acquired, many of its graduates and even some of its professors were lured away by other newly-established land grant colleges. Of the first 24 graduates, eight became farmers, one a teacher, one a teacher-farmer, four became instructors in other agricultural schools, one a mechanic, one a surveyor, two died in the armed forces, and five entered other colleges as instructors. No record was found of the other graduate.

Candidates for admission into the freshman class were examined in arithmetic, geography, grammar, reading, spelling, and penmanship. For several years a longer vacation occurred during the winter months so that the boys could teach school to earn the money necessary to complete their education. This schedule also made them available for work on the college farms during the summer months.

By 1882 $339,058.32 had been realized from the sale of 104,612 acres of the land granted to Michigan by the federal government. I am indebted to Mr. W. J. Cocker for these statistics. In 1885, while he was the superintendent of schools of Adrian, he wrote *The Civil Government of Michigan* in which he remarked, "When all the public lands belonging to the college are disposed of, the endowment will, in all probability, be sufficient for its support." Little did he dream that by 1968 this institution would have 39,000 students on its campus.

Military training was part of the educational program because of the requirements of the Morrell Act.

For at least two decades of the school's existence, coeducation was a moot question. As attendance increased new departments and courses were added. The course in enginering was opened in 1885 as fulfillment of a provision of the Morrell Act; by 1896 this department enrolled one-third of the students. The home economics department was opened in 1896. Soon after this, the forestry and veterinary science became separate courses. Applied science was introduced in 1921 and liberal arts in 1924. The name was changed to Michigan State College in 1925.

In 1944, the School of Business and Public Service was added. That same year Basic College, with seven major schools, was established. These are: agriculture, home economics, engineering, veterinary medicine, graduate studies, science and arts, and business and public service. The Basic College is a two-year course of general education, designed to give students training in seven core courses believed necessary before specialization in the last two years.

Under President Robert Shaw the physical facilities were greatly increased by a major building program. Eight major buildings were added to the campus, including a music building, auditorium, and Jenison field house. These buildings were financed by a self-liquidating bond issue. President John A. Hannah carried on the work thus begun. During his tenure the Union Building was modernized, the center and many apartments for married faculty and married students were built.

Under its establishing act the State Board of Agriculture was directed to conduct scientific and practical experiments to aid in the instruction of students and for the promotion of the progress of agriculture. This has always been one of the main objectives of the college.

Another department of the college is the cooperative extension service. This service is divided into four main divisions: (1) county agricultural agents; (2) boys and girls 4-H club agents; (3) home demonstration agents; and (4) specialists in the technical branches of agriculture and home economics.

In 1948 the continuing education service was organized, which offers Michigan people a program in non-agricultural fields paralleling that offered by the cooperative extension service. Included in this service are the department of adult education, business and industry, and special courses and conferences. The work of these departments is designed mainly to aid Michigan citizens and enable them to expand their cultural development, improve their ability to make a living, and increase their job efficiency.

WAYNE STATE UNIVERSITY

Wayne State University, located in Detroit, has grown from a group of independent colleges to one of the largest universities in the United States. It had its beginnings in 1868, when a group of Detroit doctors founded the Detroit Medical College. In 1885, this college was combined with the Michigan College of Medicine. It was reorganized in 1913 and in 1918 it came under the control of the Detroit board of education.

The College of Education traces its formal organization to the establishment of the Detroit Normal School in 1881. Its name was changed to Detroit Teachers College in 1921, when it became a four-year college. When the University was organized, its name was changed again to the College of Education.

The College of Liberal Arts opened its doors in 1917 as the Detroit Junior College. In 1923, it became the College of the City of Detroit and for the first time offered a complete four-year liberal arts program.

The College of Pharmacy was founded in 1923 and, together with the College of Medicine, College of Education, and College of the City of Detroit, became part of the University in 1933.

Graduate work was first offered in 1930 but the Graduate School was not established until 1933.

This same year, 1933, the Detroit board of education passed two resolutions: one established the College of Engineering and the other formally established the university—to be called the Colleges of the City of Detroit. Within the next year the name was changed to Wayne University in honor of General Anthony Wayne, the Revolutionary War hero.

Since then, four additional colleges have been added: the Law School, the School of Social Work, the College of Nursing, and the School of Business Administration.

In its short existence Wayne University, now Wayne State University, has achieved a reputation as one of the outstanding universities of the United States.

MICHIGAN COLLEGE OF MINING AND TECHNOLOGY

The Michigan College of Mining and Technology was founded in 1885, mainly through the efforts of state Senator J. A. Hubbell, by an act of the state legislature. When the school opened in the Houghton Fire Hall there were 23 students and 3 faculty members. The following years the school officials rented four additional rooms in the Odd Fellows building, a block away from the Fire Hall. That year the state appropriation provided for the construction of a new building to house the school. Senator Hubbell donated the site for the building and a major part of the land that is now the campus. The new building was named Hubbell Hall in his honor. In 1889 a class of six graduated.

In 1893, a four-year curriculum was adopted and two degrees were offered: Bachelor of Science in Mining and Engineer of Mines.

In 1897, the legislature reorganized the status of the institution by changing the name to the Michigan College of Mines. Its facilities and services were expanded until 1927, when the legislature changed the name again to the Michigan College of Mining.

The governing body of the College is the board of control of six members, appointed by the governor and approved by the state senate. The College has continued to increase its facilities and services and to expand its curricula and its mineral research programs. When the legislature empowered it to offer degrees in the major fields of engineering and science it took its name of Michigan College of Mining and Technology. It is now called the Michigan Technological University.

FERRIS STATE COLLEGE

Ferris State College, mentioned briefly in earlier chapters, is an "open door" school which admits students who might not be accepted at other colleges. It is one of the nation's few four-year colleges oriented to vocational training.

The school, founded by Woodbridge N. Ferris in 1884, began its existence as Big Rapids Industrial School. It later took the name of its founder, who became a governor of Michigan and a United States senator.

Ferris became a state college in 1950 but it wasn't until the early 60's that it boomed from a sleepy school with 500 students to its present student body of 9,000, with 1,900 employees.

The strength of Ferris, as Dr. Robert L. Ewigleben—its twelfth president—sees it after a few months in office, is "that here a career is hooked onto every single program." Ferris, he says "does not believe in turning out students who cannot get a job and hold it in the trade for which they were trained."*

Ferris State College fills an important gap by training vocational teachers for community colleges.

---

*From a report by William Grant in *The Detroit Free Press*, May 30, 1971.

CHAPTER XXV

The Michigan Education Association

The Michigan State Teachers' Association was organized in 1852 at the Teachers Institute held in Ypsilanti immediately following the dedication exercises of the Normal School. It was a voluntary organization of the teachers instituted for the promotion of education and the development of the teaching profession in the state.

For many years the work of the Association consisted mainly of one state-wide meeting during the year. These annual meetings became a clearing house where new ideas in teaching, courses of study for high schools (then in the development stage), needed legislation to promote better education, and many other subjects were discussed. For example, in 1891 the best method of teaching reading came under consideration. The methods then being used were the A, B, C; the word; the sentence; and the phonic. It was decided that none of these methods was wrong, that all were good if used correctly. At least by these old methods pupils did not graduate from the eighth grade or from high school unable to read.

Another subject discussed was the place of foreign languages in the high schools. In one of the meetings, the superintendent of schools in Monroe reported that his schools were offering six years of Latin, beginning in the seventh grade. The superintendent from Saginaw reported that they were offering six years of German.

Among the many progressive accomplishments by the Association was the establishment in 1891 of the Young Peoples Reading Circle at a meeting in Grand Rapids. The governing body was a board of three members, one chosen each year for a term of three years. Its duty was to choose fifty books each year from those submitted by the publishers of library books for schools. The chosen books were then added to the list of recommended books that could be purchased by schools with library money. I served on this board for three years beginning in 1919.

A law that had far-reaching importance to the teaching profession was a law establishing teachers retirement fund. This fund was first suggested by the legislative committee of the Association in 1910, from an idea which originated in the Grand Rapids Teachers Club. In 1911, members of the MSTA from teachers' clubs in Detroit, Battle Creek, Jackson, Lansing, and Grand Rapids met during a conference of the MSTA and formed a temporary organization through which all the teachers' clubs of the state could work for the establishment of a retirement fund.

The first bill to provide for a retirement fund was passed by the legislature in 1913. A more comprehensive act was introduced in the legislature in 1915 and passed on August 23, 1915. This bill provided for the establishment of a board of control of seven members. J. B. Edmonson, of the University of Michigan, was appointed president of this board and Fred Keeler, state superintendent of public instruction, vice-president. Before putting the law into effect, it was tested in the Supreme Court of Michigan and found to be constitutional. E. T. Cameron of Mt. Pleasant was appointed the first secretary of the board of control.

By 1921 the membership of the Association numbered 14,065. It was impossible to entertain the entire membership in any one city. For several years before 1921 the annual meetings had alternated between Detroit, Grand Rapids, and Saginaw. In 1921, the new MEA constitution was written and adopted which divided the Lower Peninsula into six districts, then later into eight, which together with the Upper Peninsula now make nine districts. The consolidation with the Upper Peninsula took place July 1, 1924.

During the next five years the Association was greatly enlarged by the addition of the Michigan Association of High School Principals, the Association of Superintendents and School Board Members, the Association of County School Commissioners, and the State Federation of Teachers Clubs.

A new headquarters building was erected in Lansing, which the Association occupied in January, 1929.

In September of 1923, the Association began the publication of the *Michigan Education Journal. Moderator Topics,* published for years by Henry R. Pattengill—Michigan's grand old educator—was bought by the Association in 1924 and became a department of the *Journal.*

During the years of the Association's greatest influence many prominent educators served as president or on the board of directors. Before 1930 at least five ex-superintendents of public instruction had served as president.

In the 1930s a serious schism developed in the ranks of the Association. It is a geometrical axiom that the whole is equal to the sum of all its parts but this does not always hold true in human affairs. Rarely does a divided society have as much influence as the original association. It seems that is is true in organizations of schoolteachers.

INTERSCHOLASTIC ATHLETICS

In 1895, a committee of the high school section of the Michigan State Teachers Association was formed to develop a plan of control and supervision of high school athletics. As far as is known, the formation of this committee is the first record in the United States of the establishment of such a body with statewide responsibility. During the following year, the Michigan Intercity High School Athletic Association was formed, with five charter members. In 1910, the Michigan Interscholastic Athletic Association was formed. This organization functioned until 1924, when the present Michigan High School Athletic Association took its place.

The superintendent of public instruction was given the supervision and control over the interscholastic athletic activities of the schools of Michigan by a law enacted in 1923. This law provided for a director of the Michigan High School Athletic Association, who is an assistant superintendent of public instruction for interscholastic athletics. The legislative branch of the Athletic Association consists of a representative council of fourteen members, thirteen of whom are elected by the school men of the state for two years. The fourteenth member is the above-mentioned director of interscholastic athletics, appointed by the representative council, subject to the approval of the state superintendent. There is an executive committee of four members of the council which considers Association matters in the interim between council meetings.

Activities of the Association include the registration and classification of athletic officials, sponsorship of rules for various sporting contests and tournaments, and making of eligibility rules. Since about 1940, the Association has operated an athletic accident benefit plan which is open to voluntary membership by junior and senior high schools of the state.

Since their inception, these interscholastic athletic programs have become an integral part of the secondary schools and have contributed much in the general field of health and physical education.

CHAPTER XXVI

Private and Denominational Colleges

Act 19 of the Michigan Public Acts of 1839 states:

> It shall be the duty of the president of the board of trustees of every organized academy or literary or collegiate institution heretofore incorporated or hereafter to be incorporated to cause to be made out by the principal instructor or other officer and forwarded to the office of the Superintendent of Public Instruction a report of the financial condition and of the different activities of the institution.

These institutions were to be subject to visitation and examination by a board of visitors consisting of three members appointed by the superintendent of public instruction. It is in the reports to the state superintendent by these visitors to the various schools that some interesting history has been preserved. Because of this inspection and reporting, these private schools in pioneer days were quasi-public. Some of the early visitors were or became prominent in early Michigan school history.

The dedicated men who organized these schools may not have been conscious of the wording of the preamble of the Ordinance of 1787 which says:

> Religion, morality, and knowledge being necessary for good government and the happiness of mankind, schools and the means of education shall forever be encouraged.

In fact, however, these three factors entered into all their thinking and plans for the schools they organized. Ten of these schools were established before the end of the nineteenth century. Their graduates went into the wilderness of Michigan to teach children of the pioneers and carry the tenents of their particular faiths to all the people of the state. They have been pre-eminent in the teaching of morality and good citizenship.

It is in these privately supported and operated colleges, with personal contacts between students and instructors, that the individual can be led to see the fallacies of the Marxian ideology now being forced upon two-thirds of the people of the world. To make this ideology succeed everyone must be forced through a matrix and made to think as a soviet or group and not as an individual. The non-recognition of the individuality of man is the one *fatal* defect in the Hegelian-Marxian plan.

KALAMAZOO COLLEGE

On the 23rd of November, 1829, the Rev. Thomas W. Merrill arrived in Ann Arbor and began a classical school. He had first come to Michigan to preach the Gospel in the wilderness as an emigrant from Maine and a recent graduate from Waterville College and Newton Theological Seminary. His school enjoyed an immediate success. The next year he circulated a petition asking the Territorial legislature to charter an institution under the name of the Michigan and Huron Institute, to be under the control of the Baptist Church. The charter was held up because of objections to the church affiliation. Thinking that the western part of the state would be more receptive to his enterprise, he journeyed through the wilderness to a settlement called Prairie Ronde, near Kalamazoo, where he built a house for a school and meetings. Here he met a kindred spirit in Caleb Eldred, a surveyor who later became a judge.

In 1831, these two pioneers began to make plans to raise money to build an institution that could be used as a "house of prayer and praise" and a school where the children could have Christian learning under the shadows of the Baptist Church. They agreed that they should seek help from benevolent Baptists of the East for the purchase of land on which to build the contemplated building. The Rev. Merrill visited the Michigan Baptist Association in Pontiac, which group sent him on to the Baptist convention in New York state with a hearty recommendation. There he received seven pledges of $10 each, which fund became the nest egg for all the gifts for Baptist educational work in Michigan.

When he returned, the legislature in April of 1833 granted a charter for the proposed institution under the name Michigan and Huron Institute, without any provision for denominational control. The first president of the board of trustees was Caleb Eldred. The charter did not name a location for the Institute. After much discussion, a site of 115 acres was purchased on the north side of the village of Kalamazoo. The purchase price was aided by a subscription of $2,500 by the residents of the village. Before any buildings were built this first site was evidently traded for the present site on the west side of Kalamazoo, where the first building was erected.

For the first twenty years the course of study was largely preparatory. Because there were no high schools in the vicinity, the school was supported by local patronage or by other corporations. For a time the University of Michigan supported it as one of its branches. When this aid was withdrawn, the Baptist convention adopted it as the literary helpmate for its theological education. The privileges of the school were alike, free to both sexes.

A Mr. Marsh was the first teacher; Walter Clark was the second. Others are mentioned but with no special emphasis except on William L. Eaton, who is said to have been a well-loved coadjutor.

In 1855, the charter was amended to change the name of the institution to Kalamazoo College and to confer full college powers. The corps of instructors was enlarged to meet the demands of a college course of study.

The raising of funds for improvements in those early days was a precarious operation. However, in 1855 the sum of $10,000 was raised to erect and furnish Kalamazoo Hall for the female department. $1,000 of this sum was given by a Mrs. Van Huson and the balance by the residents of Kalamazoo.

Dr. J. A. B. Stone was the first president after the name was changed. The College had a steady growth through the first one hundred years of its history. In 1954, Dr. Weimer Hicks became president. He has become a nationally known leader as a developer of year-around education.

The early facts given here were taken from an historical sketch of Kalamazoo College written by the Rev. S. Haskell, on request of the board of trustees, and published in the report of the superintendent of public instruction for 1863. This sketch makes only one other mention of the Rev. Thomas W. Merrill in which he is quoted as having written as follows:

> The Michigan and Huron Institute is the school on which I have had my eye since I came into this territory, the one for which I drew a petition, gave it circulation, and presented it to the legislative council two years ago, the one for which I have petitioned thrice, for which I took up a subscription in the City of New York in 1832.

His third petition was addressed to Congress modestly asking for the grant of one township of land! Nothing more is told about him, but the school was his dream. We can say that everything worthwhile in America had its origin in a dream by someone, a dream come true—and this is true of Kalamazoo College.

ALBION

On March 23, 1835, the Michigan territorial legislature passed a law granting to Michigan Methodists the right to start a school at Spring Arbor in Jackson County. The school was to be known as the Spring Arbor Seminary. A board of trustees was elected but no other action was taken because the trustees could not raise the necessary building funds. In 1838 the proprietors and other prominent residents of the village of Albion made an offer of liberal assistance to the trustees provided the location of the seminary would be moved to Albion. The offer was accepted; the legislature amended the charter as requested; and the board of trustees was reorganized in the village of Albion on April 29, 1839. The name of the institution was changed to The Wesleyan Seminary at Albion.

The credit for starting the Seminary is due mainly to Benjamin H. Packard, M.D., and two Methodist circuit riders, the Rev. Henry Colclazer and the Rev. Elijah H. Pilcher. Mr. Pilcher devoted much time and labor to the development of the school. On July 6, 1841, he helped lay the cornerstone on land donated by the Albion Company, the original platters of the village.

The first students were received in the autumn of 1843. The purpose of the school can best be explained by a quotation by Delos Fall, superintendent of public instruction from 1901 to 1905, when he wrote in his 1892-1893 catalog history:

> They saw that such a school would inevitably become the center nucleus for the production of denominational enthusiasm. Here would be gathered into focus the influence of the church (Methodist) and there would be gained the interest and power to render efficient aid in extending church enterprises.

The money for the first building was obtained by the selling of scholarships at $100 each, for which the buyer would receive a four-year course at the Seminary.

In 1850, through the influence of the president of the school, the Rev. Clark Titus Hinman, D.D., an act of the legislature continued the corporation known as The Wesleyan Seminary at Albion and authorized the trustees to establish the Albion Female Collegiate Institute, which could confer degrees upon young women but not young men. The act provided that the income of the institution could equal but not exceed $2,000. In an interesting report to the superintendent of public instruction in December of 1852 Dr. Hinman wrote, "We have a freshman class of fifteen, most of whom will be prepared to enter the University at Ann Arbor."

In 1853, Ira Mayhew became president, but had held the office only fifteen months when he was elected superintendent of public instruction in 1855. While in Albion he was professor of moral philosophy and political economy.

The Rev. Thomas Henry Sinex followed him as president. During his term, the name of the Seminary was changed by an act of the legislature to Wesleyan Seminary and Female College at Albion. On February 25, 1861, still under Dr. Sinex, the name was changed to its present name of Albion College and it became a college of liberal arts.

In 1865, because the sale of scholarships at $100 each to finance the school had proved a failure, its friends succeeded in carrying through both the Michigan and the Detroit conferences of the Methodist Church a resolution to celebrate the centennial of Methodism in America by raising an endowment of $100,000. The village of Albion was asked to raise $25,000. In subsequent campaigns, endowments totaling nearly $200,000 were raised and the future of the college was made secure.

For a detailed history of Albion College, please refer to *Albion College, 1835-1960, a History* by professor Robert Gildart, published by the college in 1961. (To me, there is an interesting mention of the Rev. Seth Reed as the assistant to the agent who secured many of the pledges for the endowment. He, with his long white beard, was a familiar figure around Flint just before and during World War I. He attended many fund-raising dinners where he was invariably asked to give the invocation. He lived to be over 100 years old.)

HILLSDALE COLLEGE

The history of Hillsdale College is a courageous story of a small college founded on a belief in the need for independent higher education even though courage was its only asset when it was founded. It all started when a group of ministers and laymen met between sessions of the June, 1844, meeting of the Michigan Free Will Baptists. A board of trustees— two thirds of whom were Free Will Baptists—was named. This board chose the name of Michigan Central College at Spring Arbor. Daniel McBride Graham, age 27, a recent graduate of Oberlin, was named president.

The college, located in an old store with two rooms, opened December 4, 1844, with five students and one faculty member, the president. The college grew rapidly; in 1848 when president Graham resigned, it had 126 students. The second president was Edmund B. Fairchild, who in 1850 succeeded in obtaining from the state legislature a charter that allowed the college to grant degrees. This was the first college in Michigan other than the University that was given this privilege. The first degree conferred by the college was a B.S. to Elizabeth D. Camp in 1851. In 1852, Livonia Benedict became the first woman in Michigan to receive a B.A. degree.

Spring Arbor proved to be too small for a growing college; Jackson, Adrian, and Marshall were considered as locations but these towns found no interest in the antislavery views of the College. Coldwater offered

$10,000, but Hillsdale offered $15,000 and persuaded Esbon Blackmar to give 25 acres of land. In spite of a suit by Spring Aroborites to keep the College there, the sum of $30,000 was soon collected and work begun on the first college building in Hillsdale.

The cornerstone of the new college was laid July 4, 1853. In his speech of dedication President Fairchild said, "May the walls reared upon this foundation stand for ages to come, sacred as well to freedom and humanity, to philanthorpy and true patriotism, as to sound science, pure morality and true religion."

A reorganization meeting was held on March 22, 1855, at which time 35 trustees were elected and new Articles of Association for Hillsdale College were approved and a new charter was issued under the new name. The articles stated that "the object of this institution is to furnish to all persons who wish, irrespective of nation, color, or sex, a literary and scientific education."

That the words of President Fairfield in his dedication address were taken to heart by the students is shown by the fact that 183 young men left Hillsdale College to join the Union Army in the Civil War, representing a larger proportion of the enrollment than any other college in the United States.

Space will not allow the telling of the further achievements of Hillsdale, which have been many.

OLIVET COLLEGE

Olivet College was founded in February, 1844, by the Reverend John J. Shipherd as part of the Congregational Church's missionary effort in higher education. Previously Mr. Shipherd had shared in the founding of Oberlin College, Oberlin, Ohio. His dream was to establish a series of such schools in the Midwest and thereby bring education to pioneer communities in which young people had neither the money nor the opportunity for study in major colleges or universities.

The early catalogs of Olivet give the purpose of the institution as follows:

> We wish to have it distinctly understood that the whole object of this institution is, has been, and we hope ever will be, the education of young men and women, especially such as are not rich

in this world's goods, but heirs of the kingdom—for the glory of God and the salvation of men. All things connected with this school in all its arrangements and departments will, as far as in us lies, be made and kept subservient to this end.

The early catalogs also state that "Poverty is our endowment." The ensuing years proved this to be true, for they were years of unending struggle, with illness, a succession of fires, the Civil War, which left only girls on the campus for four commencements, and a perennial lack of money. Notwithstanding, a buoyant, resurgent spirit kept the college open and growing.

From the first, the Rev. Mr. Shipherd and his associates from Oberlin called the school Olivet College. However, efforts to secure a charter from the state met repeated refusals. At this time legislators and others involved in Michigan education did not encourage the establishment of private colleges, thinking that all resources should go to the University of Michigan. Until 1859, when a college charter was finally granted, Olivet operated under a state charter as Olivet Institute. Part of the problem in convincing educational leaders of the propriety of granting a charter for a degree-granting college was the founding principles of Olivet which are now held in high regard: equality of opportunity for all races and creeds and for both sexes.

The teacher of the first class at Olivet was the Reverend Oramel Hosford, who taught until 1890—aside from eight years as superintendent of public instruction of Michigan—and served on the board of trustees until his death.

The first Olivet class of nine has now grown to an enrollment of about 800 students and there is a modern plant of well-equipped buildings. The 65 men and women of the faculty are well qualified.

Although Olivet has always been close to the Congregational and United Church of Christ denominations, today it is an independent institution whose students come from across the nation and from foreign lands as well.

HOPE COLLEGE

When a group of Dutch immigrants, led by the Rev. Albertus Christian Van Raalte, founded Holland, Michigan, in 1847, one of their first concerns was providing education for the youth of the colony. Their efforts led in 1862 to the founding of Hope College, which received its charter from the state in May of 1866.

Hope College has always been under the auspices of the General Synod of the Reformed Church in America. In its early years it was largely dependent on churches in the East for financial support. Its purpose was to preserve and promulgate the religious faith; the dominant motif of the Dutch emigration of America was religious; they sought freedom to worship as they chose.

The predecessor of Hope College was the Pioneer School, founded in 1851, which evolved into the Holland Academy.

The college's name, seal and motto are taken from a statement by the founder of Holland, the Rev. Van Raalte, who said, "This is my anchor of *hope* for this people in the future." Those early years were years of inadequate facilities, of individual sacrifice and gallant optimism in the face of seemingly unsurmountable difficulties.

The Rev. Philip Phelps, D.D., was the first president of Hope College, from 1862 to 1878. The first commencement exercises were held on July 17, 1866, with eight graduates, all male, granted bachelor of arts degrees and an honorary M.A. degree to Dr. Arend VanderVean, an alumnus of Holland Academy.

Women were admitted to the college in 1878, but Hope was still very much a man's college until the erection of Voorhees Hall in 1907, with money donated by Mr. and Mrs. Ralph Voorhees of Clinton, New Jersey.

When the presidents of five small colleges in Michigan met in Lansing on August 18, 1948, for the purpose of incorporating the Michigan College Foundation, President Lubbers of Hope was the prime mover in organizing the foundation. The foundation now has sixteen private colleges in the group, with fifty or more industries and business firms contributing annually to it.

Although the development of Hope College has been slower than most colleges, dedicated men have guided it beyond its frail beginning, through two world wars and the depression. Today it is one of the best liberal arts colleges in the United States, widely recognized for its excellence.

ADRIAN COLLEGE

Adrian College, a coeducational college, was incorporated March 2, 1859, by the Methodist Protestant Association. At the time of this incorporation, they were looking forward in this project to a union with the Wesley Methodist Church, a union which was soon after effected. The annual report of the Michigan superintendent of public instruction for 1867 shows the college was then under the control of the Methodist Church.

The school opened with three departments, a preparatory and elective course of two years, a four-year classical and a four-year scientific course, and a four-year theological course. Older people were admitted to a shorter theological course if they were accepted as fitted to the work of the ministry.

The above-mentioned report also stated:

> The degree of Bachelor of Arts shall be given to students who complete the classical course, Bachelor of Science to those who complete the scientific course, and the Master's degree shall be conferred on graduates of three years standing who have sustained a good moral character and who shall have engaged in professional and literary studies.

The first degrees were given in 1863. Anyone interested in the complete course of study in all departments in Adrian's early days will find it in the 1867 report.

Adrian College has always enjoyed, since its incorporation, a distinguished place in the history of Michigan education. The plan for a much greater part in this participation began unfolding in 1956. Its recent growth has received both state and national attention. Twenty major facilities have been erected in the past decade. Enrollment has increased 500% and the faculty has quarupled in size. The college is traditionally dedicated to a program of student experience in Christian and higher education and is responsible for providing quality training for each young man or woman in the area of professional, social, cultural, and spiritual nurture.

SPRING ARBOR COLLEGE

The name "Spring Arbor" seems to have had a romantic attraction to the men who planned the denominational schools of early Michigan. In 1835 the Territorial legislature granted the Methodists of Michigan the right to establish a school at Spring Arbor under the name of Spring Arbor Seminary. This school was moved to Albion in 1839 and became the present Albion College. Hillsdale College was founded in Spring Arbor in 1844 and moved to Hillsdale in 1853.

The present Spring Arbor College, located in the same historic spot, will be 100 years old in 1973. Since its beginning, it has been co-educational. Founded in 1873 by Bishop Edward P. Hart of the Free Methodist Church of North America, who was instrumental in buying the site and bringing about the organization of the school, it was known at first as Spring Arbor Seminary. The first commencement was held in June of 1881 with two graduates.

In 1928, the school became a junior college and in October, 1963, it became a four-year liberal arts college.

Believing that religion, morality, and knowledge are essential to good government and the social happiness of mankind, the school has always been committed to the purpose of educating young people within the above framework to discharge properly their duties as good citizens and to exert their influence as they assume roles of leadership in education, business, science, and the professions.

At present Spring Arbor College does not have a graduate school but plans are being considered to initiate a graduate program in Philosophy-Religion which would enable students to prepare for the ministry or Christian education.

ANDREWS UNIVERSITY

Andrews University had its beginnings as Battle Creek College in Battle Creek, Michigan. The owner of Battle Creek or Emmanuel Missionary College was a corporation of Seventh-Day Adventists who organized the Seventh-Day Adventist Educational Society, incorporated by the state of Michigan on March 16, 1874. The leaders in this Society were James White, Ellen G. White, George Ide Butler, Stephen N. Haskell,

Uriah Smith, and Goodloe Harper Bell. These good people were members of the Seventh-Day Adventist Church who had a vision of what education could do for their church.

The College was moved to Berrien Springs, Michigan, in 1901, because the town of Battle Creek had grown up around the College and there was no room for expansion. Also, the president of that time was much interested in agriculture and wanted to get the school out in a country atmosphere where agriculture could be carried on and taught to the students. The school is now on a 700-acre tract near Berrien Springs.

The original purpose of the institution was printed in the Battle Creek College Bulletin of 1874-75 as follows:

> The founders of Battle Creek College have deemed it necessary, for the better protection of our sons and daughters, to establish this school in which moral and religious influences are made of first importance. This is here done by shielding them from the base influences that undermine the character in many of our institutions of learning without urging upon any person special religious views.
>
> In our times, when serious and solid studies are becoming distasteful, when all kinds of inducements to waste and worse than idle away their time, are forced upon our youth, and when morals are so lax, it is necessary that the character and general deportment of the student should be assiduously watched. The comfort and personal habits of the students will receive the same attention which they should have in their own families . . . In short, the Board of Trustees are determined that first-class school privileges, under favorable circumstances, shall be furnished by Battle Creek College to all worthy patrons.

The first degrees were given in 1879. Andrews University has a School of Graduate Studies as well as a Theological Seminary on campus. Their first graduate degrees were conferred in 1958.

The institution is financed through student tuition and by the Seventh-Day Adventist Church and the Michigan College Foundation, Inc.

CALVIN COLLEGE

Calvin College was founded in 1876 in Grand Rapids, Michigan, by the Christian Reformed Church. It had its beginnings as a theological school to provide a trained ministry, with one professor, the Rev. G. E. Boer, and seven students. In 1881, a Literary Department was established, which continued until 1906, when there was a division into a preparatory school and junior college. In 1919, there was a further division, when a Christian high school emerged, and the junior college became a full-fledged liberal arts college.

The school became coeducational during the 1910-1920 period and granted its first degrees in 1922.

Two of the early outstanding leaders in the college community were professors J. G. Vanden Bosch and Johannes Broene.

A wide diversity of study programs is now offered at Calvin, with some 400 courses listed. Besides the General College A.B., the baccalaureate degree can be procured in education, preseminary, premedical, predental, prelaw, pre-engineering, prebusiness administration, and premedical technology. Courses are also offered for students choosing careers in nursing, library, agriculture, forestry, home economics, and occupational therapy.

Calvin, however, does not neglect the physical and social aspects of a well-rounded education. It is able to provide the Christian students with an accredited higher education in which no facet is overlooked.

THE UNIVERSITY OF DETROIT

From a report to the superintendent of public instruction dated Nov. 1, 1881, by the Rev. James Walsh, the college president, we learn that the college, incorporated under the title Detroit College, was founded by the Jesuit Order of the Catholic Church in 1877. It was chartered under the general laws of Michigan as a literary and scientific institution. The full course of instruction lasted seven years. There were four departments: the collegiate, the academic, the commerical, and the scientific. The academic department was intended to prepare students to pursue the college courses and consisted of three departments, the first, second, and third with studies the same as those in regular high schools. Another department was a class in the rudiments of education to prepare boys who were not sufficiently advanced to enter any of the three academic departments.

The commercial course could be covered in four years and embraced all branches of a good general education.

The collegiate and academic courses of four years were comparable to those of other colleges of the time.

In 1881, there were 143 boys in regular attendance and the faculty had ten members. By 1889 there were 255 students. In 1893, a state visitor or inspector reported that the study of Latin was pursued by using the language itself in conducting recitations.

By 1894 the enrollment had reached a point where more room was needed and plans were made to build an addition. $30,000 was raised from subscriptions. For the next two decades the College maintained a steady growth. It was reorganized in 1911 under the title of University of Detroit. That year the College of Engineering was added and the following year, the College of Law. In 1916, the Evening College of Commerce and Finance was started and it was followed by the opening of the College of Commerce and Finance in 1922.

Although graduate degrees were conferred initially in 1885, the fuller organization of graduate studies was not effected until 1927 when the Graduate Division was established; in 1950 this became recognized as the Graduate School.

The School of Dentistry was established in 1932 and evening classes in Arts and Sciences and in Engineering were inaugurated in 1938.

An affiliation with St. John's Hospital in Detroit enabled the University to offer the degree of B.S. in Medical Technology in 1954. Providence Hospital in Detroit became affiliated with the program in 1959. Colombiere College, a division of the College of Arts and Sciences, was founded in 1959 and offers four years of ascetical and academic training to members of the Jesuit Order. The School of Architecture was established in 1964, and the same year a Division of Teacher Education was instituted as a separate administrative unit of the University.

The University of Detroit, which is coeducational, is one of a group of twenty-eight Jesuit colleges and universities in the United States. From the Jesuit Order the University receives a rich heritage of four centuries of educational experience. Because it is a Catholic university, it seeks to generate a clearly ecumenical, intellectual, moral, social and liturgical witness to the life and teachings of Christ and a climate that creates desire among students of all creeds to lead lives centered in a high sense of values.

This institution receives no funds from the Michigan Colleges Foundation, Inc.

ALMA COLLEGE

Alma College, a coeducational, residential college, was originated at Westminster Presbyterian Church in Grand Rapids on October 14, 1886, when the Synod of Michigan of the United Presbyterian Church in the U.S.A. adopted a resolution stating that "in view of all the facts brought before us, we will, with God's help, establish and endow a college within our bounds.".

Two years earlier, at the annual Synod meeting, a committee had been appointed to investigate the possibility of establishing a college in Michigan. A pledge of $50,000 by Mr. Alexander Folsum of Bay City inspired the committee to look for a favorable location. Saginaw, Ionia, Ithaca, St. Louis and Alma were considered. The final choice of Alma came as a result of a gift of two buildings and grounds for a campus from Ammi W. Wright, lumberman and businessman of Alma.

With these gifts of funds, buildings and property, plus additional pledges of money, the committee reported to the Synod meeting in October 1886. The reaction was not enthusiastic and had it not been for the name of Ammi W. Wright the whole idea might have been dropped. Mr. Wright had a reputation of making a success of his every undertaking.

The Alma College Board of Trustees held its first meeting at the home of Mr. Wright, at which time Alma was officially selected as the location of the college, and Wright's gifts of land and buildings were accepted. A charter was granted by the state of Michigan on April 15, 1887, and the doors of the college opened in September of that year with thirty-four students registering. Total attendance the first year was ninety-five. There were nine on the faculty.

Dr. August F. Bruske, president of Alma from 1887 to 1912, stated in his *History of Alma College,* Chapter X:

> The college ideal at Alma has always been a healthy body, a strong mind and a tender conscience . . . Above all ideals in Alma is the moral and religious one. The reason for the existence of Alma is religious.

The Synod of Michigan of the Presbyterian Church provides annual budgetary support for the college.

The enrollment in 1969-70 reached a new high of 1,315. The college has developed an attractive and well-equipped physical plant, appropriately dominated by the chapel and a new library, symbolic of the founders' commitment to engage young men and women in the adventure of higher learning, informed by Christian faith.

AQUINAS COLLEGE

Aquinas College of Grand Rapids, Michigan, had its beginnings in a novitiate normal school founded by Mother Mary Aquinata of the Dominican Sisters of Grand Rapids in 1887. Its first purpose was to train sisters as teachers and nurses for service in Michigan.

In 1923, it changed into a college for laywomen, operating as a two-year preparatory college until 1931 when it was made coeducational and renamed Catholic Junior College.

Further development of the college saw it become a four-year college in 1940 with the name Aquinas College. The first degrees were awarded in 1942. It is fully accredited and is licensed by the State of Michigan as a teacher training institution.

The goal of Aquinas is to provide the highest quality liberal arts education in the context of the Christian traditions and ethical systems.

The graduate program is in religious education; the first master of religious education degrees were awarded in 1956.

Aquinas has pioneered in degree completion programs for adults with special evening degree programs in business administration for people holding full-time jobs. There is a separate daytime program for the housewife, with schedules arranged to fit the schedule of a homemaker. The college also offers noncredit adult education evening courses for the people of western Michigan who wish to be better informed but are not interested in a degree program.

Msgr. Arthur F. Bukowski was the college's first president; Dr. Norbert J. Hruby is its present president.

SIENA HEIGHTS COLLEGE

In 1893, three Sisters of St. Dominic left their convent home in New York to undertake a new educational venture in Adrian, Michigan. Siena Heights College is an outgrowth of St. Joseph Academy, founded in these early years by the Sisters of St. Dominic under the leadership of Mother Mary Camilla Madden.

The Order of St. Dominic is primarily a teaching order and the best traditions of the order were incorporated in the course of study for the academy which from the beginning grew and flourished. Encouraged by the success of the academy and urged on by the need of a Catholic college of arts and sciences for women in southern Michigan, Mother Camilla began the erection of a building suitable for this purpose. St. Joseph College was incorporated in 1919 under the laws of Michigan and recognized as an institution for the higher education of women.

In 1924, through the efforts of Mother Mary Augustine Walsh, the approval of the State Department of Public Instruction was granted for the issuing of state teaching certificates to the students. The first degrees were conferred in 1924.

Mother Mary Gerald Barry became president in 1933. She was the champion of continued liberal learning and to this end she directed her strength of mind and body. With the completion of two new buldings in 1938, the Board of Trustees deemed it wise to separate the academy and college in name. A new charter was obtained and the college was incorporated under the name of Siena Heights, with St. Catherine as its special patron.

The second president of the college, Sister Benedicta Maria Ledwidge, was appointed in 1957. Under her leadership the college kept abreast of the great issues of the times. New policies were established. Programs of study were extended to include coeducational graduate work in fine arts, secondary and elementary administration, supervision, and curriculum, teaching and guidance, as well as in the areas of English, history, science, philosophy, and modern mathematics. The first degrees from the graduate school were given in July 1961.

In 1965, the Board of Trustees appointed Sister Mary Petronilla Francouer as the third president of Siena Heights College.

The institution became coeducational for undergraduates in 1969. In January of 1970, Mr. Richard Reaume was appointed its acting president.

The sociology department not only trains treachers, but also those who wish to do social work.

A four-year degree in business administration has been added. Besides this, an associate degree is awarded for a two-year secretarial course.

At the present time, the college is in the process of studying and evaluating its entire program. Soon there will have evolved something entirely different from what has existed up to this time. Curriculum and requirements will be updated or changed.

MARYGROVE COLLEGE

Marygrove College, founded in 1910 and located in Detroit, is a Catholic college for women. Each year the college admits women of all races and religions. Approximately one thousand young women from twenty states and thirteen foreign countries follow Marygrove's program of liberal studies.

Completely independent, the college is church-oriented rather than church-related. Tuition, fees, and the contributed services of its religious faculty are its principal financial assets.

Like other Michigan colleges, it is expanding. A proposed $3,000,000 science-clinic facility will contain science laboratories, a programmed learning center, and a closed circuit television studio. It will also include three clinics: reading, psychological, speech and hearing—which will provide clinical experience for special aducation majors and a needed service to the Detriot area.

Extracurricular activities are taking new directions, also. The Social Action organization of the college lists 75% of the students as volunteers serving fourteen Detroit agencies. Marygrove's tutorial program sends

107 students into center-city public schools each week to work with disadvantaged children.

NAZARETH COLLEGE

Nazareth College, a college for women, was founded by the Rev. Francis A. O'Brien and the Sisters of St. Joseph at Kalamazoo, Michigan, in 1924. The primary goal of its administration and faculty is the intellectual development of its students as women, founded on and rooted in Christian principles. When Nazareth was founded, its purpose was given as follows:

> To establish and maintain departments of higher education under the classification of a standard college . . . and to confer upon duly qualified students degrees and honors in the Arts and Sciences; to maintain a teachers' training unit; a college preparatory school or schools and an elementary school or schools.

The charter further stated:

> The curricula of such college shall be in the Arts and Sciences, with departments of Religion, Philosophy, Fine and School Arts, Education, English, History, Classical and Modern Languages, Mathematics, Music, Library Sciences, Physical Sciences, Social Sciences, Nursing Science, Home Economics, and Business Administration; such college to maintain a proper faculty for each of said departments.

Inaugurated to fit the needs of the young women of today, the curriculum offers standard four-year programs in the liberal arts and sciences. Teacher training is one of the most popular departments and an excellent teaching program has been arranged with the public and parochial schools of Kalamazoo. Also offered are courses leading to internship in social work and medical technology, as well as courses in dietetics, economics, political science, physics, speech and drama.

It is through these means that Nazareth College hopes to achieve its purpose—that of assisting her students attain in their lives that which cultivates a dedicated commitment to principles; that which contributes to the student's dignity as a woman and fits her for her distinctive role of service in whatever career she embraces, and for her responsible position in American society.

MADONNA COLLEGE

Madonna College, a Catholic college for women, at Livonia, is conducted by the Felician Sisters. It is an outgrowth of Presentation Junior College, which was founded in 1937 for members of the Felician order. In 1947, the junior college amended its articles of incorporation and became a four-year liberal arts college for women. Its first president was Sister Mary Paula.

The college is fully accredited and is authorized by the Department of Public Instruction to recommend its graduates for teachers' certificates on the elementary and secondary levels. It is also recognized by Registry for Medical Technologists of the American Association of Clinical Pathologists. In 1962, a nursing program leading to a bachelor's degree was initiated.

Madonna College offers a standard liberal arts program leading to the Bachelor of Arts and Bachelor of Science degrees. Instructors employ various methods of instruction. Lecture is used to motivate students; also coordinating seminars are conducted in English and the science-mathematics fields.

Due to increased enrollment, the College began the building of new facilities in November, 1962. The faculty residence, girls' dormitories, dining rooms and a guest house have been completed. The multipurpose building to be used for classrooms, laboratories, library, chapel, administration offices, gymnasium and auditorium is nearing completion. The new building will enable the college to provide a fine integrated liberal arts education and to train and prepare women to meet the needs of our society through teaching social work and related fields.

MERCY COLLEGE

Mercy College of Detroit, located at 8200 West Outer Drive, was established in 1941 by the Religious Sisters of Mercy. To one woman in particular goes the credit for the vision that gave a new college to Detroit —Sister Mary Carmelita Mannin, R.S.M.

The purpose of the college is to provide for the moral, intellectual, physical, and social development of its students. The first degrees were granted in 1942 to two students who transferred to Mercy College when it opened in 1941.

In the light of Detroit's changing ecological pattern, of national trends, and of the need for greater enrollment the College became coeducational in 1963. Sister Mary Lucille Middleton, R.S.M. was president of the College for fifteen years and it was she who guided the transition of Mercy College from a leading college for women to a four-year coeducational institution.

Curricula at Mercy are organized into four divisions: Arts and Sciences, Medical Associates, Nursing, and Teacher Education. The student earns the B.A. or the B.S. degree. Areas of concentration are: Art, Biology, Chemistry, Classical and Modern Languages, English, History, Home Economcis, Dietetics, Mathematics, Medical Record Library Sciences, Medical Technology, Music, Nursing, Physiology, Sociology, Speech and Drama. It is the only Michigan college offering a program in Medical Record Library Science.

Expansion plans include a building program which will more than double the number of buildings on the campus and enable Mercy College to provide even greater service as an educational institution.

Agencies in cooperation with Mercy College in its various programs are Mt. Carmel Mercy Hospital, Children's Hospital, Rehabilitation Center, Northville Hospital, various public health agencies and local social service centers and the Detroit and suburban public and parochial schools.

PRIVATE BUSINESS COLLEGES

Nearly every one of the larger cities of Michigan has or has had a business college. The earliest one of which there is a record was Gregory's Commercial College, opened in Detroit in 1850. Its stated purpose was to prepare students to enter the business world. Evidently it had a life of only one or two years. These business schools were our first vocational schools.

Cleary Business College was organized in Ypsilanti in 1892. Still in operation, it has done an outstanding service for the people of southeastern Michigan.

Eldon E. Baker came to Flint in 1911 and founded Baker Business University, still a most successful institution meeting local needs. In connection with the business school, it had for many years the Baker Conservatory of Music, now discontinued.

At first these schools taught English grammar, letter writing with special emphasis on spelling and penmanship, and commercial arithmetic. When the typewriter was invented, typing and shorthand were added to the curriculum. Before the turn of the century only a few public high schools offered such courses. It wasn't until the second and third decades of the twentieth century that many high schools began adding such courses, now common subjects in nearly every high school in Michigan.

Michigan Military Academy and Orchard Lake Schools

Before high schools became common a number of private academies and seminaries were established—an important facet of our educational system during the experimental period. One of these was the Michigan Military Academy, located at Orchard Lake. The school had its beginnings in 1877 when Colonel Joseph Summer Rogers took over a residence built by Civil War General Joseph T. Copeland in 1862. In 1872 this house had become a part of a resort hotel known as the Orchard Lake Hotel. The building and facilities remain today as a monument to tradition and education theories of days long past.

The Military Academy had a slow beginning, but by the school year of 1890-91 it had 27 boys in the preparatory class, 58 in the academic, 7 in the classical, and 6 in the Latin course. In 1891, it became an accredited high school. The tuition was $100 per year. Expenditures for room, board, washing and mending underclothes, fuel, lights, and use of arms and equipment totaled $450 annually. The school flourished for several decades, drawing students from any states. When high schools became numerous, it was forced to close its doors.

In 1885, Father Joseph Dabrowski established a Polish seminary on the east side of Detroit, known as St. Mary's Seminary. In 1909, this seminary purchased the property of the failing Michigan Military Academy. Over the years the seminary has branched out to become the complex known today as the Orchard Lake Schools. The 120-acre campus now houses six inter-related institutions: St. Cyril and Methodius Seminary, St. Mary's College, St. Mary's Preparatory School, Center for Polish Studies and Culture, Center for Pastoral Studies, and the Polish-American Liturgical Center.

The purpose of these schools is to bridge the ethnic gap that exists among the many races that make up metropolitan Detroit, and also to preserve the heritages of these different peoples, both black and white.

CONCLUSION

Many books could be written describing the trials and errors and successes of the men and women who spent their lives in building our Michigan school system. My studies show that the successes have been far more numerous than the failures. However, because of a few of these errors, our schools are now in a precarious condition. It is my hope that we will have the courage and foresight to correct these errors so that "government of the people, for the people, and by the people" shall be preserved. This can be done if we always keep in mind the words of the men who incorporated in the preamble of the Charter for the government of the Northwest Territory:

Religion, morality, and knowledge being necessary for good government and the happiness of mankind, schools and the means of education shall forever be encouraged.

Index